Social Work Practice with the Mentally Retarded

Social Work Practice with the Mentally Retarded

Martha Ufford Dickerson

THE FREE PRESS
A Division of Macmillan Publishing Co., Inc.
NEW YORK

Collier Macmillan Publishers
LONDON

THE FREE PRESS
A Division of Macmillan Publishing Co., Inc.
866 Third Avenue, New York, N. Y. 10022

Collier Macmillan Canada, Ltd.

Library of Congress Catalog Card Number: 80-2316

Printed in the United States of America

printing number

1   2   3   4   5   6   7   8   9   10

Library of Congress Cataloging in Publication Data

Dickerson, Martha Ufford.
    Social work practice with the mentally retarded.

    (Fields of practice series)
    Bibliography: p.
    Includes index.
    1. Social work with the mentally handicapped.
I. Title. II. Series.
HV3004.D53 1981   362.3'8   80-2316
ISBN 0-02-907430-4

To the students who have taught me
and to
Phyllis Manson, ACSW,
whose practice provides a beacon

Contents

vii

Foreword

IN 1978 THE FREE PRESS PUBLISHED the first of a series of books each of which addresses a particular theoretical approach of significance in the helping professions. Once this series was well underway it became evident that a second series was needed, one that differentially examines practice from the dimension of specific fields of practice.

Every profession has to face the complex question of specialization versus generalization. In this regard it has to come to terms with issues related to training and practice, and to make decisions about the relative emphasis given to those matters that are common to all areas of the profession's various fields of practice and those that are specific to each area.

There are of course dangers in emphasizing either extreme. If the generic is overemphasized there is a risk that important aspects of practice will be dealt with at a level of abstraction that bears little immediate relevance to what the worker actually does. If the emphasis is on the particular there is the danger of fragmentation and neglect of the need to search for commonalities and interconnections. Obviously, a balance between these two extremes is desirable.

Many of the human services, and social work in particular, have tended to overemphasize the generic to the detriment of the specific needs of clients with highly specialized needs. The majority of social work literature over the past three decades has focused either on modalities of practice as a single entity or on a specific theoretical basis of practice. This is not to say that there are not practitioners who are highly skilled in working effectively with specialized groups of clients. What is lacking is an organized compilation of the particular practice components of each of these specialized areas of practice in a way that is readily accessible to other practitioners in these areas.

Certainly within the periodical literature of social work there is a rich array of individual articles addressing specific components of practice involving work with particular client target groups. But such articles are scattered and not written from a common perspective and thus are of varying utility to practitioners.

It is the purpose of this new series to move in the direction of tapping this rich wealth of practice wisdom in a way that makes it readily available on a broad basis. To this end a series of specific fields of practice has been identified and known experts in each field have been asked to write about practice in their specialty from a common framework.

The goal of each book is to address not only the therapeutic aspects of practice in these fields but also the range of sociological, policy, administration, and research areas so as to present the reader with an overview of the specific field of practice as well as the specifics about therapy. In addition to helping the individual worker to learn more about a specific field of practice, the series as a whole, it is hoped, will provide an opportunity to make comparisons among fields of practice and thus facilitate the ongoing expansion of general knowledge.

Certainly there is growing awareness of the need for addressing the specific training and practice needs of each field of practice. Many schools of social work now arrange their curricula along the line of fields of practice. The NASW has utilized the notion of fields of practice to relate systematically to how some social workers are employed and to prescribe the roles most appropriate for them.

The fields selected for coverage in this series may or may not represent clearly defined areas of specialization in social work. Rather they are identifiable human needs or problem populations or even settings for which a discrete and identifiable cluster of attitudes, skills, and knowledge is thought to be needed in order to intervene effectively.

We are pleased that the first text in this series is Martha Dickerson's *Social Work Practice with the Mentally Retarded*. It is a humane treatment of the mentally retarded client and consistently focuses on how the social work practitioner can be of professional help to the client and his or her significant others. The distinctive contribution of the social work profession to the psychosocial enhancement of the mentally retarded client is well documented. The range of skills and clinical modalities that are pertinent to this field of practice is ably covered.

In this book Mrs. Dickerson and her colleagues have provided us with a special focus. They are very much wedded to the idea that the mentally retarded person should be helped to lead as normal a life as is possible. Consequently, much of the material in this volume relates to how the social worker can enhance the mentally retarded client's interpersonal, economic, social, psychological, and sexual life.

The many vignettes in this volume, drawn from Mrs. Dickerson's extensive practice, and the attitudes, philosophy, and clinical skills that are pinpointed will no doubt help to raise work with the mentally retarded client in any setting to a higher level.

FRANCIS J. TURNER
HERBERT S. STREAN

Preface

DURING THE PAST TEN YEARS, it has been my privilege to work with many graduate social work students from the University of Michigan and Wayne State University, as well as students from other disciplines who have been in practicums at the Institute for the Study of Mental Retardation and Related Disabilities. Over the years, the students and the clients we served have been a never-ending source of learning about social work practice with the mentally retarded.

Ten years ago, when I took a position in a public agency serving the mentally retarded, I brought with me a maturity based upon having lived a long time through a variety of experiences. I had raised a family, completed graduate school, and practiced social work in other settings with other client populations. I had been taught well, and I believed I was ready to assume responsibility as a field instructor for students who wanted to practice with mentally retarded individuals.

I remember discovering for myself what others have learned, that I was involved in self-education as I helped students with their learning. It was an awesome experience—testing our thoughts, ideas, interventions, and designs. We shared anger, joy, and frustration. We sharpened our minds and polished our practice. I have been taught by students who cared about their own growth and—what's more—about the growth of our mentally retarded clients. The students and I shared countless experiences with retarded individuals, their parents, and their families. We worked in urban, suburban, and rural areas—in institutions, group homes, nursing homes, family homes, schools, and training centers. We worked in small rooms, gyms, offices, and elevators. We practiced as group workers, as caseworkers, and as community workers. We listened, clarified, interpreted, supported, confronted, and listened some more. We advocated, modeled, taught, and trained.

We soon learned that the clients were teaching *us*. As social workers, we had knowledge about the etiology and symptomatology of retardation. We had an awareness of community resources. From the clients, we learned about the *experience* of retardation. They helped us understand how retardation causes social dysfunction and how that dysfunction causes alienation and rejection. Parents and family members helped us to understand the enormous impact the retardation of one family member has upon the entire family.

Through it all, we began to experience a common awareness. There was a continuity in what we were learning, practicing, and advocating. We came to know that social work practice with the mentally retarded can be a hopeful, positive experience for practitioners and clients alike. The secret was to acknowledge the fact that each person is in a process of becoming human throughout his or her entire life span. The process is slower for some, but the process of "becoming" is constant, hopeful, and productive.

The students with whom I have worked and learned practice social work all over the nation. When I receive a letter or phone call from a distant place—Denver, Providence, Atlanta, Miami—I am nurtured by the experiences they share with me. I am grateful to be a part of their growth and to have them be a part of mine. The practice examples included in this book reflect those years of mutual sharing.

This book is further enriched by a practical experience I have shared with my husband, Wade, during the past seven years. As foster parents of four retarded adolescent boys, we have been forced to keep our feet on the ground. The boys keep me honest and practical. My colleagues and students at ISMRRD provide my inspiration.

This book was prepared to teach practice with a special population to social workers who have already developed generic skills in social work. In order to achieve this purpose, the following learning objectives are identified for the reader:

1. To develop awareness about mental retardation: definition, etiology, frequency, classification, etc.
2. To become sensitive to the impact of retardation upon the individual and the family.
3. To identify the basic survival needs of an individual, and how these needs may be affected by the presence of mental retardation.
4. To identify those systems, institutions, and agencies that are resources to the individual with retardation.
5. To become familiar with the contributions that can be made by diverse disciplines in an interdisciplinary approach to the helping process.

6. To become familiar with the language special to the field of mental retardation.

7. To recognize the unique roles and responsibilities of the social worker in relation to the individual with mental retardation, the family of the individual, and the community where the individual and family must live.

As a way of achieving these objectives, the book will present information supported by disguised case material and descriptions of actual practice concerns and resolutions.

The scope of the book has been expanded by the inclusion of Chapter 8, "The Social Worker as Part of an Interdisciplinary Team," by Eleanor Whiteside Lynch, Program Director for Special Education at the Institute for the Study of Mental Retardation and Related Disabilities, and Chapter 9, "Issues of Social Policy," by Gerald Provencal, Director of Macomb-Oakland Regional Center.

Mary Phillippo provided valued assistance in the review of the literature. Several colleagues and former students have critiqued the materials included here: Michael J. Eastman, Jerry Garfield, Carl Hartman, Michael Herley, Dr. Hsi-Yen Liu, Phyllis Manson, John Miller, Dr. Maria Paluszny, Phyllis Santo, and Janice Stevens. A special thanks is due to Judy Biskner, who prepared the final manuscript. The manuscript has been improved by the helpful comments provided for me by the series editors and the skillful editing of Gladys Topkis of The Free Press.

I also wish to acknowledge the influences of certain individuals on my professional life and on the philosophy of practice expressed in this book. They are William Cruickshank, Mary Lee Nicholson, and John Younger.

MARTHA UFFORD DICKERSON
Ann Arbor

CHAPTER 1

Social Work with the Mentally Retarded: An Overview

At THE PRESENT TIME, social workers in diverse settings are expected to provide service to mentally retarded clients (Kirman and Bicknell, 1975). No longer are mentally retarded children and adults invariably removed from the community; rather, they are staying in or returning to the community or are seeking service from traditional agencies. This text has been prepared for the social worker who wishes to enhance his or her professional skill and personal artistry in working with clients who are mentally retarded.

For purposes of this book, the following definition is presented. *Mental retardation refers to significantly sub-average general intellectual functioning existing concurrently with deficits in adaptive behaviors and manifested during the developmental period.* Chapter 3 discusses the definition in detail.

Perhaps no other client population is so vulnerable to stereotyping by the general public and the uninformed professional. Until recent times, parents of a mentally retarded child were typically advised to place the child in an institution as soon as possible and try to "return to normal life." As recently as 1960, social workers were participants in the referral process that resulted in the placement of thousands of young children and adolescents in institutions because of mental retardation. Most social workers focused their energies on helping parents deal with the guilt, frustration, anger, despair, and loss they experienced as a result of permitting their children to be removed from their homes. The practice emphasis was on healing the family and protecting the child.

1

Times have changed. Professionals of all disciplines have come to a broader understanding of mental retardation. It is time to consider mental retardation as one of many descriptors that may be applied to an individual. As an individual, the person is entitled to acceptance and service based on his or her personhood. Social workers must continuously remind themselves that there is as wide a range of individuality in the mentally retarded segment of the population as in the population as a whole. It follows that there is as much diversity among the families of the mentally retarded as among families in general. Mental retardation can occur in any sociocultural situation. It has no respect for wealth, power, or position. It comes to the mighty and the humble, the rich and the poor, and each individual with mental retardation must be considered as a unique person in a unique situation.

As more and more retarded men, women, and children strive for a normal life within the community, they and their families will require increased service from private and public agencies. No longer will the mentally retarded receive service exclusively from some remote custodial institution located far from the community where the family resides. Schools, clinics, hospitals, recreational facilities, churches, and guidance clinics as well as family-service agencies will be called upon to include the mentally retarded in their client roster. Social workers, as well as other professionals, must be prepared to respond to this request for service. Of all the professions, social work, by its own definition, is the best prepared to deal with the lifetime of concerns and issues that confront the individual who must deal with mental retardation, either in his or her own life experience or as a support person to someone else who has the disability.

The practice of social work is based on the optimistic assumption that every individual can be helped to grow and change so as to achieve his greatest potential as a human being. Social work is concerned with helping the individual learn to contribute to, utilize, and grow through his interactions and interdependencies with other human beings in the society. Additionally, social work is committed to helping the society as a whole learn to meet the needs of each of its members.

Social workers agree on two primary values: "the dignity of each individual human being and the responsibility of human beings for each other" (Konopka, 1963). The *dignity* of the individual demands that he be treated fairly, be provided with protection from harm, and be given opportunities to grow and learn. Every individual has a right to basic respect for his human dignity and thus acceptance as an individual regardless of any differentiating characteristics such as race, sex, age, religion, prowess, or handicap. The responsibility of human beings for each other is based on our need for other human beings in order to survive, mature, and prosper. To assume responsibility for others is to acknowledge this interdependency and to recognize that other human beings have needs and rights comparable to our own. "Man's need for food and shelter, for love and tenderness, for accomplishment, and for fulfillment of his thirst for knowledge, are all dependent on the interaction of man with man" (Konopka, 1963). These needs are no less valid for the individual who has mental retardation.

The mentally retarded person needs the same things from society as any other citizen. However, when parents or other relatives seek service *on behalf of* a mentally retarded family member, their concerns usually have to do with maintaining health, providing supervision, and/or ensuring educational opportunities. When the mentally retarded person becomes involved on his or her *own* behalf, the concerns expressed are apt to be interpersonal in nature. Frequently, when seeking help, the client or client's family has definite ideas as to what service is desired, but these may be very different from what is *needed*. The client or family may seek brief, crisis-oriented service without any awareness of the scope or duration of the problems of retardation.

The individual and his situation are the factors to be considered as the social worker determines the mode of practice that is most useful at a given point in time. As with other populations, the social worker will provide some services directly to clients through the use of social casework and social group work. Other services, on behalf of the client, will be extended into the community or other large systems. Persons with mental retardation, their parents, and their families may be seen individually, as a family unit, or as participants in a small group with others who share their concerns.

The person who has mental retardation is viewed as the primary client needing service, and his or her family system is viewed as the secondary client. The age of the individual as well as the severity of the condition will determine priorities among the various services provided. Usually physicians, parents, family members, care-givers, or educators are the initiators of service at a point in a child's life when there is question about his or her growth and development patterns. Frequently, on behalf of a family, the social worker will be expected to serve as team leader, coordinator, or liaison in relation to the many different services available. Therefore, it is of paramount importance that the social worker have a thorough understanding of such professional disciplines as education, medicine, occupational therapy, physical therapy, psychiatry, and psychology in order to represent to parents their particular contributions, competencies, and methods of working.

During the early stages of service, the focus is on assessing the extent of the retardation, identifying the cause, evaluating the child's potential for cognitive and skill achievement, and then designing a schedule of interventions that will maximize the child's growth and development. The family is provided with guidance and support as they attempt to integrate these individualized interventions into the family life and routine. Additionally, the family is referred to resources within the community, such as the school, and is helped to gain access to its services. Gradually, the family will come to realize that they will need to utilize generic community services for the lifetime of the family member who has retardation. As the child matures, his specific service needs will shift and change, and the family will need to have access to continuous consultation, guidance, and support. As the individual with retardation develops cognitive abilities and acquires a repertoire of functional behaviors, he may become the primary negotiator for his own life planning and decision making. This is certainly to be expected for the individual who is classified as moderately or mildly retarded. The individual who has been classified as severely or profoundly retarded will undoubtedly require the active involvement of his family (or an advocate or agent) in all decisions related to his life plan.

Like all other members of society, mentally retarded adults have concerns about income, health, housing, education, vocation, recreation and leisure time, interpersonal relationships, and the management of life crises. In recent years, parents and professionals have focused their attention upon securing lifetime financial support and educational opportunities for the mentally retarded. During the 1970s increased attention has been given to the development of alternate living arrangements for the mentally retarded who are ready to leave their parents' homes or the residential institutions where they were placed for training. To date, less attention has been paid to other concerns, especially as they relate to the adult, aging, or aged mentally retarded. Health services and vocational opportunities are minimal. Recreation and leisure-time experiences are more apt to be sporadic attempts to entertain rather than efforts to promote creativity, participation, and self-fulfillment. It is rare that the mentally retarded adult has the opportunity to initiate, develop, and maintain relationships based upon mutual selection, caring, commitment, sexual attraction, and love. Mentally retarded individuals have been given little guidance, support, or opportunity to learn how to select friends, establish relationships, enjoy sexual expression, and otherwise experience human fulfillment, which is an intrinsic part of a normal life. Too frequently, the mentally retarded adult has no opportunity to be other than an informed, obedient, quiescent participant in any crisis that involves him.

Social workers must introduce interventions to enable the mentally retarded adolescent or adult to assume his rightful place in the community. Such interventions must involve the client as a participant on his own behalf. Social workers must model for the community the need to treat adults as adults, and thus diminish the infantilization and patronization of retarded adults that is so common.

Professionals must use the latest methods to assess the needs of the mentally retarded. The results of such evaluations may be used in a positive manner to obtain the most appropriate service for an individual. However, professionals must struggle vigilantly to resist limiting the individual because of the descriptors or labels that result from evaluation. Basic to the role of modeling for the community is the social worker's responsibility to individualize the client. We must learn to use the diagnostic descriptors or labels to open the doors of service systems. (Chapter 4 describes this process). Beyond that, we must learn and teach others that a person is an individual first of all.

It is past time for social workers and others to learn to discuss mental retardation openly with the individual who is retarded. Practitioners must overcome their own feelings of fear, distaste, or alienation to dare to address the feelings of the retarded client. As practitioners, we must deal with the anger, fear, distrust, alienation, and depression that the individual experiences because of the handicapping condition that separates him from others. Only by bringing these feelings into the open will workers be able to assist the individual in establishing his personhood and achieving his potential. To do less is to deny a part of an individual's personhood about which he is painfully aware. To do less is an act of nonacceptance on the part of the professional.

Sexuality is a central concern for the mentally retarded individual as it is for all other people. Unfortunately, because of retardation, the individual is hampered in the establishment of a self-image, and in the development of social-sexual awareness and appropriate behaviors. As though it were not difficult enough for any individual to establish himself as a social-sexual person, the mentally retarded must accomplish this while coping with the confusions and distortions caused by his disability. Added to this is the tendency for the community at large to expect asexuality from those citizens who are identified as mentally retarded. Chapters 5, 6, and 7 provide examples.

Social work practitioners function on behalf of the mentally retarded and their families as they establish and develop relationships with the community and tap existing resources. Schools, residential institutions, voluntary agencies, churches, and parent groups are a few of the resources in the community that need to be mobilized to meet the unique needs of the mentally retarded. Further, practitioners should be involved in planning and implementing new programs within the community to further expand the available resources. Social workers should serve as knowledgeable, outspoken advocates on behalf of the mentally retarded at every jurisdictional level. Within the local school system, social workers should be active in helping educators involve parents in planning for the pupils. Within the larger community, social workers should be informed participants—for example, at public hearings that are considering the location of group homes. At the state level, social workers should be able to provide statistical information and case examples to support request for improved legislation. Furthermore, social workers need to be active participants in any systems intervention that will result in the prevention of mental retardation or in early detection and remediation. All social work strategies and intervention should have as their major goals the prevention of mental retardation for those children yet unborn and the insurance of a fulfilled life for children and adults who already have mental retardation.

Social workers must be prepared to modify their practice techniques so as to work creatively and innovatively with the mentally retarded population. They can do this because their knowledge, training, and experience are eclectic, rooted in many different psychosocial theories and practice modalities. The challenge to social work practitioners is to acquire the special knowledge and skills necessary to meet the unique needs of the mentally retarded. This challenge is complicated by the difficulty most practitioners have in establishing an empathetic relationship with an individual who is mentally retarded. In generic practice, most social workers are able to establish meaningful relationships with clients partly because they can identify intellectually with their clients and their concerns. I believe that social workers must develop unusual sensitivity for mentally retarded clients. By so doing, they may avoid perpetuating the patronization and infantilization that have characterized the treatment of retarded clients in the past. This personal bias is reflected throughout the following chapters.

CHAPTER 2

Historical Overview

IN THIS CHAPTER WE VIEW in historical perspective the attitudinal and behavioral changes that have occurred in the understanding and acceptance of mental retardation. We briefly describe the unique contributions of certain pioneers and the positive and negative impacts of the development of instruments to measure intelligence. The formation and influence of parents' groups are recorded, as well as certain administrative, legislative and judicial actions which have brought positive change to the lives of the mentally retarded. The philosophical concepts of mainstreaming, normalization, and deinstitutionalization are introduced. The chapter concludes with a recognition of the need for comprehensive services.

Attitudes

Down through the centuries there have been members of every population who were unable to adapt fully to the demands of the larger society because of limited intelligence. As civilization became more highly industrial and complex, the individual with limited intelligence became more conspicuous because of his deficiencies, and the community in which he lived assumed greater responsibility for the care and maintenance of the person we now call mentally retarded.

For centuries, in some societies, the individual of limited intelligence was ignored, ridiculed, avoided, shunned, ostracized, neglected, or persecuted; in other societies he was tolerated; in a few he was honored or revered. The early Spartans considered such individuals to be subhuman and permitted them to die of exposure. However, during the fourth century A.D., the bishop of Myra provided food and shelter for the unfortunates known as idiots and imbeciles. For his kindness and consideration he was eventually canonized as St. Nicholas, and he is known today as Santa Claus.

In the Middle Ages, the mentally retarded were frequently attached to the court of the nobility, where they earned dubious favor as fools or jesters. In France they were called *les enfants du Bon Dieu*, "children of God" and were perceived by many as sacred and as having a special connection with God and the mysteries. On the other hand, John Calvin, the French Protestant reformer, and Martin Luther, the German theologian, were of the opinion that the mentally retarded were "full of Satan." The American Indians allowed the mentally retarded to live unharmed as children of the Great Spirit. Depending upon the ignorance or superstition of the times, the mentally retarded were treated respectfully or cruelly, but always differently.

Some attempts were made to care for the mentally retarded, or to protect them by removing them from society. The first colony for the mentally retarded was established in Belgium during the thirteenth century. In 1325 King Edward II of England provided a guide to protect the rights and properties of the "idiots" as well as to ensure their daily care. In the statute *De Praerogitiva Regis* he distinguished in practical terms between a permanent mental handicap and a temporary mental illness (Kirman and Bicknell, 1975). The Elizabethan Poor Law provided for relief to all English citizens who were poor, abandoned, ill, or handicapped. As a way of meeting the needs of the mentally ill, orphaned, aged, and mentally impaired, workhouses were established in various communities throughout Great Britain. These forerunners of our modern institutions offered little in the way of differentiated services to the inmates. The most humane situations gave them food and shelter, minimal restraint, and menial work experiences. There was no provision for education or training.

Contributions of the Early Pioneers

During the eighteenth century, the first attempt to base the training of the handicapped on the development of the senses was made by the French physician Jacob R. Pereire, who had a sister who was a deaf mute. Pereire noted that a baby born deaf often understood and even used speech as long as it was held on the mother's vibrating chest while she spoke. Once the child began to crawl and walk and lose this frequent touching with the parent, he became mute. Pereire concluded that a person could learn speech from sight and touch. He proceeded to demonstrate this thesis by having a child watch a teacher's facial movements while grasping the teacher's throat, thus feeling the vibrations of the teacher's speech. Pereire was so successful in teaching speech to his deaf pupils that they even acquired his accent (Levinson, 1965).

Influenced by Pereire's work, Jean Itard, a physician, tried in 1798 to educate a boy who was found living in a wild condition in the woods of France. This boy, who appeared to be about eleven years old when found, became widely known as the Wild Boy of Aveyron as a result of a book Itard wrote using that title. Although the boy learned many new behaviors and ultimately was able to live with some degree of acceptance in a rural situation, he never achieved the skills that Itard had hoped to teach him. Itard viewed his work with the Wild Boy of Aveyron as a failure, although he did succeed in demonstrating that children are able to develop preferred habits even when there are limits to their capabilities.

Edward Seguin, a physician and educator who was a student of Itard, continued to develop Itard's methods and opened the first school for the mentally retarded in Paris in 1837. Seguin believed in approaching the mind through the body and the senses. He regarded touch as the basic sense, and all other senses as modifications of touch. He placed great importance on muscle training (especially of the hands), sensory training designed to develop discrimination in auditon and vision, speech training, writing, and reading (Hutt and Gibby, 1976). Seguin wrote extensively about his belief that children should be taught in an atmosphere of happiness and acceptance where the emphasis was on teaching "the nearest thing to that which the child knows or can know" (Levinson, 1965).

Maria Montessori, an Italian educator and student of Seguin, developed a system of training young children which emphasized training of the senses and guidance rather than control of the child's activity. Montessori's work has been so widely acclaimed and popularized by middle-class parents of normal children that today it is seldom connected with its original target groups, the disadvantaged and mentally retarded children of Rome.

In 1848 Seguin came to the United States, where he continued to teach and espouse his philosophy that education was a universal right and that all members of society, including the mentally retarded, were entitled to an improved life situation (Crissey, 1975). He assisted in the founding of institutions for the mentally retarded in Massachusetts, New York, and Pennsylvania.

In the United States in the latter half of the nineteenth century, large, isolated state institutions were founded to provide lifelong service to and segregation of the mentally retarded. Efforts were made to develop facilities in rural areas that were considered healthful so that the residents could enjoy the benefits of country living: fresh air, good food, and ample space for outdoor play, walks, and other health-maintaining activities. Some attempts were made to provide educational and vocational experiences. Plans were developed for smaller facilities with staff trained to respond to the individual needs of residents, but because of the problems of financing, only a few pilot programs were implemented and these focused on helping the retarded to acquire basic self-care skills (Crissey, 1975). Under the best of circumstances, the learning experiences were limited to the brightest of the residents, and only a few graduated into the community. The waiting lists for the institutions lengthened as increasing numbers of individuals were identified as retarded and were referred for care and training.

Research

During the late nineteenth century attempts were made to discover the causes of mental retardation and to determine preventive measures. Some of the efforts had negative effects upon community attitudes. In 1875 Richard Dugdale published a report about the Jukes, a five-generation family whose members exhibited extensive antisocial behavior. He concluded that the tendency to commit criminal acts was passed down through families. Although Dugdale found only one subject of the 709 he studied to be mentally deficient, a frightened public began to regard retardation as an inherited disease that was strongly linked to crime (Hutt and Gibby, 1976).

In 1910 a poorly researched book by the psychologist Henry Goddard—*The Kallikak Family: A Study in the Heredity of Feeblemindedness*—appeared. Goddard's study traced the descendants of two different liaisons initiated by a colonial soldier. In one instance, the soldier had a relationship with a feebleminded barmaid that supposedly resulted in several hundred retarded individuals in the subsequent six generations. By contrast, the soldier's marriage to a colonial maid resulted in fewer descendants, and many of them were persons of eminence. The study persuaded many individuals that the condition of mental retardation was not only hereditary but incurable, and further, that it led to poverty, degeneracy, and crime. "Such matters as health, nutrition, education, child care, community status, and all the indicators of early stimulation were interpreted as products of the genetic differences, rather than the *producers* of the difference in life success" (Crissey, 1975). Increasing numbers of the general population accepted the "evidence" that the mentally retarded were dangerous, oversexed perverts with criminal inclinations. Frightened people formed committees to lobby for governmental regulations and actions designed to stamp out the mentally retarded, using a range of interventions such as sterilization and segregation of the sexes.

The Need for Training and Assessment

During the late nineteenth century and the early twentieth century, the public developed increased awareness of the need to provide educational and training programs for the mentally retarded, and organized scientific efforts were conducted in their behalf. During this period, most state institutions were providing custodial care in residential facilities isolated by distance and program from the general community. Some institutions came to recognize the need for special classes and learning experiences for the residents, and these evolved into training schools, where educational experiences were added to the traditional services of providing a safe, secure, healthful place to live.

In 1904 Alfred Binet, a French psychologist, was appointed by the French minister of public instruction to head a commission to bring the benefits of education to the mentally retarded. Starting from the premise that mental retardation could be judged by physical signs, classroom successes and failures, and direct observation, Binet determined to develop a method of assessing an individual's capabilities in terms of comprehension, judgment, reasoning, and invention (Levinson, 1965). By 1904, Binet and Théodore Simon had developed the Binet-Simon test for the identification of mental retardation. The test, developed in France, was subsequently translated for use in many other countries. The intelligence test increased the accuracy of measurement of intellectual potential and deficiency. However, during World War I its mass use revealed flaws in the instrument. Group intelligence tests administered to members of the armed forces resulted in the finding that more than half of those tested had a mental age of twelve years or less. These results led to the theory that the intelligence quotient (IQ) was not the only criterion in the determination of mental retardation, but that social, cultural, and educational experiences needed to be considered as well. It became evident that the test was biased in terms of racial and ethnic factors and was heavily based on middle-class cultural values (Hutt and Gibby, 1976). As a result testing procedures were modified to control for these biases.

In 1914 Charles Scott Berry began to train a few teachers of the mentally retarded at Lapeer State Home and Training School in Michigan, and Charles M. Elliot organized the first college program for such teachers at what is now Eastern Michigan University. Special classes for the retarded were introduced into the public schools in the early twentieth century. The use of IQ tests had increased the accuracy of screening some candidates for the special classes. Teachers of these classes began to emphasize the educational use of objects and materials instead of the more traditional emphasis upon the three R's: "reading, 'riting, 'rithmetic" (Levinson, 1965).

The Great Depression of the 1930s brought a halt to the development and support of these classrooms, and the number of people enrolled declined. After World War II special classes were once again promoted, with much greater success, partly owing to the increased involvement of parents and their insistence on improved educational opportunities for their children.

Medical Advances

Prior to World War II the life expectancy for the mentally retarded individual was lower than for the rest of the population. This was partly because of such an individual's susceptibility to complications resulting from upper-respiratory infections. The so-called miracle drugs developed during World War II proved to be successful in the treatment of infectious conditions for the entire population and served to extend the life expectancy of the mentally retarded.

Great strides were made during the 1960s and 1970s in the areas of genetics, medicine, and nutrition. Chromosomal studies resulted in precise information as to the cause of Down's Syndrome (the most common form of mental retardation); recognition of the negative impact rubella (German measles) could have during the early months of pregnancy led to the development of interventions to prevent the tragedy of birth defects; screening techniques used at birth yielded immediate diet recommendations that could halt brain damage to infants born with PKU (phenylketonuria). As the standard of living improved across the nation, prenatal care and improved diet reduced infant mortality. Early detection of mental retardation made early intervention possible, thus maximizing the child's chance to develop by enhancing the skills of the parents and other care-givers (Robinson and Robinson, 1976).

Emergence of Parents' Groups

In 1950 the National Association of Retarded Children (NARC) was founded in Minneapolis, Minnesota. This association, made up of parents and other interested individuals, has been active in the initiation and support of diverse programs such as clinics, workshops, activity centers, residential alternatives, and legislative reforms. In 1979 the association changed its name to the National Association of Retarded Citizens, to reflect its expanded focus, since it now includes retarded adults.

NARC is a voluntary organization, and its membership tends to reflect the middle class. It is not surprising that the greatest impact NARC has made in terms of improved services reflects the needs of middle-class parents. In cooperation with school systems, NARC chapters have been instrumental in establishing resource rooms and day-care centers, employing special educators, and improving educational procedures. NARC chapters have consistently supported the idea of maintaining the mentally retarded within the community in as normal a life-style as possible. The parents and professionals have supported the American Association on Mental Deficiency (AAMD) and the Council for Exceptional Children (CEC) as programs have been expanded to encourage seminars, conferences, research, and publications.

Executive, Legislative, and Judicial Action

In the twentieth century parents and other persons have been involved in many processes in behalf of the mentally retarded citizens.

President Theodore Roosevelt focused attention on the unmet needs of children when he convened the First White House Conference on the Care of Dependent Children in 1909. Subsequent presidents have convened such conferences every ten years since. During Herbert Hoover's presidency the conference was entitled "Child Health and Protection," and it produced the Bill of Rights for Children. This charter entitled each handicapped child to:

1. The right to as vigorous a body as human skill can provide.
2. The right to an education so adapted to his handicap that he can be economically independent and have a complete life.
3. The right to be brought up by those who understand him and consider it a privilege to help him.
4. The right to be brought up in a world that does not set him apart.
5. The right to a "life in which his handicap casts no shadow."

In 1950 President Harry S. Truman convened the Mid-Century Conference on Children, which made a major recommendation that a long-range plan be designed for the provision of improved services to the mentally retarded. The late 1950s and the 1960s saw the passage of several significant laws that served to improve services to the mentally retarded by training professionals to work in the area of mental retardation (P.L. 85-926, 1958), funding demonstration projects and research (P.L. 88-164, 1963), providing federal funds to support state schools (P.L. 89-313, 1965), allocating funds for educational purposes from pre-school through high school (P.L. 89-750, 1966), and developing university-affiliated facilities to train teachers, conduct research, and prepare educational materials (P.L. 91-230, 1969).

During the 1970s two important pieces of legislation were enacted. Section 504 of the Rehabilitation Act of 1973 barred discrimination against handicapped persons in all public and private agencies that received federal funds. The regulation ensured that all publicly funded facilities constructed after 1977 were to be "barrier free," or readily accessible and usable by handicapped individuals. It further required that older facilities make the necessary structural changes in order to adhere to the regulations. The Education for All Handicapped Children Act (P.L. 94-142, 1975), which became fully effective in September 1978, assured the availability of special education to handicapped persons who required it, regardless of the severity of their handicap; impartial and objective educational decision making; appropriate educational programming; accountability at all levels of government; federal financial assistance to state and local school districts; and individualized educational programming.

The 1960s and 1970s were not only a period of executive decision and legislative action resulting in increased funds for service to the mentally retarded; the same period also fostered much judicial activity. In *Brown* v. *Board of Education*, the Supreme Court established a precedent for subsequent court actions when it denounced "separate but equal" education. This famous decision, which had to do with the right of black children to attend school with white children, was destined to have an impact upon the retarded as well, for parents demanded that such children should also have the opportunity to be "mainstreamed" in the public school experience, thus bringing about the elimination of the dual system which long had been the pattern.

In 1968 the U.S. Court of Appeals for the District of Columbia upheld a decision made a year earlier, in Washington, D.C. *(Hobson* v. *Hanson)* declaring that the tracking systems utilized in Washington schools were illegal since they were in violation of the equal-protection clause of the U.S. Constitution. As in the *Brown* case, the presenting issue was racial discrimination, but the decision led to subsequent suits against schools for placing and keeping some students in special classes for the mentally retarded. The plaintiffs contended that nine Mexican-American students had been given intelligence tests that were culturally biased since they were standardized on the scores of native-born, English-speaking Americans. As a result of this case, it was mandated that all children should be tested in their native language. Furthermore, all Mexican-American and Chinese-American children in classes for the mentally retarded were to be retested to redetermine their placement needs, and those who had been misassigned were to be given special tutoring to help them catch up. It became evident that more appropriate tests needed to be developed to ensure all children the opportunity to be tested under optimal conditions regardless of sociocultural background.

In 1972 the decision in a case in Pennsylvania *(Pennsylvania Association for Retarded Children, Nancy Beth Bowman, et al.* v. *Commonwealth of Pennsylvania, David H. Kutzman, et al.)* mandated that all children requiring special education were to be identified and provided with services unique to their requirements.

In 1977, U.S. District Judge Raymond Broderick ruled that keeping mentally retarded individuals in institutions, isolated from the rest of society, was a violation of their constitutional rights. This ruling was the result of a class-action suit filed in May 1974 by parents of clients at the Pennhurst School for the Mentally Retarded in Pennsylvania. The opinion pronounced by Judge Broderick ruled that segregation of retarded persons in an isolated institution violated their guarantee of equal-protection rights under the Fourteenth Amendment to the Constitution.

Thus, in addition to the legislative action of the 1960s and 1970s, court decisions served to provide new and effective means for bringing individuals with mental retardation into the mainstream of twentieth-century American society.

Mainstreaming, Normalization, and Deinstitutionalization

Educational philosophies regarding mentally retarded children have shifted throughout the twentieth century. In the early part of the century, the mentally retarded child was removed from the regular classroom to relieve the teacher and other students of the stress caused by his presence. Subsequently, educators adopted the notion that mentally retarded students would be safer and happier in a classroom that minimized competition. Attempts were frequently made to teach them a simplified version of traditional academic subjects. Today these attempts have been replaced by the philosophy that encourages individual educational planning to help the person with mental retardation to achieve realistic goals. Great emphasis is placed upon the individual's inherent dignity and his right to receive training that enhances his strengths and minimizes his deficiencies (Hungerford, DeProspo, and Rosenzweig, 1952).

During the 1970s the concepts of mainstreaming, normalization, and deinstitutionalization became guides for parents and professionals as they attempted to plan meaningful interventions with and on behalf of mentally retarded citizens.

Mainstreaming is based on the assumption that all children will be accepted into the school system because they are people. It assumes that *all* children will be included in *all* the plans designed by school personnel. The inclusion of all students in all plans is accomplished by identifying each child's capacity, style, and rate of learning and by preparing all children to accept all other children because of their shared humanness.

Many different approaches or strategies have been used to achieve mainstreaming. Team teaching by professionals and peer teaching by classmates, including mentally retarded classmates, are techniques that have proved successful. Some mentally retarded students spend a part of each school day in a resource room, or with a classroom aide, as a way of having an individualized learning experience. Special classrooms, adjacent to a regular classroom, have been designed to give the retarded child an opportunity to learn in a self-contained classroom even as he is motivated by the modeling of the other students whom he observes in the adjacent room. The goal is always to help the retarded child join the regular classroom as soon as possible for as long as possible (Hutt and Gibby, 1976).

The intent of mainstreaming is to desegregate education for mentally retarded children. There has been much research to demonstrate that such children "learn less in a special classroom than they do in a regular classroom, even if they are a few grades behind!" (Menolascino, 1977).

To mainstream a mentally retarded child is only one part of the larger principle of *normalization*. According to Bengt Nirje (1969), "The normalization principle means making available to all mentally retarded people patterns of life and conditions of everyday living which are as close as possible to the regular circumstances and ways of life of society." Normalization means participation in the normal activities of a household, a neighborhood, and a community, with all of the usual customs that are maintained and celebrated. Normalization means the opportunity to engage in age-appropriate experiences that prepare the child for adolescence, the adolescent for adulthood, and the adult for maturity and aging. Normalization implies self-determination and self-fulfillment in developing and maintaining social-sexual relationships. For those retarded persons who cannot live with their families, provision must be made for living arrangements that are neither unusually large nor more isolated than the situation from which the person must move.

Normalization ensures that retarded adults have a life experience separate from that of retarded children. This runs counter to the institutional model of the early twentieth century, when retarded adults were frequently trained to assist in the care of retarded children. The principle of normalization holds that such a practice creates a damaging perception for the adult and limited, if not negative, modeling for the child. Strict adherence to normalization makes certain that a retarded person goes to school, training or work at a location different from where he lives. It is hoped that the retarded person may attend school, work, and live in situations where he is in daily contact with nonretarded peers. He then can be guided, trained, taught, and parented by several different adults (Menolascino, 1977).

The 1970s witnessed increased commitment on the part of the general public to ensure normalization for mentally retarded citizens by working to integrate them into every aspect of the usual life of the community. In addition to the efforts of the school programs described earlier, integration has been accomplished through the provision of service by agencies that do not focus primarily on mental retardation. Organizations like the Girl Scouts, the Boy Scouts, and the YMCA, demonstrate leadership in providing recreation and leisure-time activities. Many religious denominations have successfully included the mentally retarded in the rituals of the church. Families of nonretarded children have provided guest and respite time to the mentally retarded. These experiences have helped the handicapped person learn behaviors that are perceived as normative. Of equal importance, they have helped nonretarded individuals to develop more positive attitudes toward mental retardation; thus perceptions of difference, alienation, distrust, and deviancy are being altered. According to David Braddock, "Normalization is not a cure for mental retardation, but rather it is an orientation offering the 'relative independence' of the individual as the highest goal" (Braddock, 1977).

Deinstitutionalization is a concept that dramatically affected the state institutions as they existed in the early twentieth century. It reduced the population by returning those residents who could be rehabilitated to the community and discouraging the admission of new clients. The deinstitutional movement established and maintained smaller residential settings within the community for those residents incapable of rehabilitation. These smaller settings (nursing homes, group homes, foster homes, and apartment hotels) were intended to protect the human and civil rights of the mentally retarded individual as he or she strove to return to a normalized life-style within the community (Braddock, 1977).

For some mentally retarded individuals who were profoundly disabled, competitive employment was impossible, attendance in a "mainstreamed" school was inappropriate, and residential options were limited. Nevertheless, small nursing facilities and special-purpose mini-institutions appeared to provide individualized programs that were improvements over the huge institutions of the early part of the century.

Critics of normalization charged that the mentally retarded were inappropriately placed into communities that were not attitudinally prepared for the introduction of so many strange and inept individuals. Some parents and professionals protested that community services were not available to support and monitor the life experiences of the socially inadequate mentally retarded. Others believed that support services would not come into existence until the demand had been created. Some argued that it was less of a burden to the taxpayer to maintain the mentally retarded in remote institutions. Many professionals in the human service delivery systems held a paternalistic view toward clients in their charge and were guilty of infantilizing and patronizing them.

In the 1960s President John F. Kennedy stated, "We must provide for the retarded the same opportunity for full social development that is the birthright of every American." Fifteen years later the General Accounting Office, an independent investigative arm of the U.S. Congress, conducted an eighteen month survey (1975–1976) to assess the impact of federal deinstitutionalization programs on facilities serving the mentally retarded and the mentally ill in Maryland, Massachusetts, Michigan, Nebraska, and Oregon. The results of the study were discouraging. There was indeed a noticeable trend toward facility depopulation, but too frequently the clients were moved to other settings that were less than adequate. Because of the lack of alternate living arrangements and educational or employment opportunities, many individuals who would have benefited from leaving the institution were unable to be placed (Braddock, 1977).

Many communities blocked the deinstitutionalization process by exclusionary zoning laws which effectively discouraged the establishment of group homes in other than slum sections. Unfavorable attitudes reflecting ignorance, fear, and apprehension about mental retardation were common among property owners in middle-class neighborhoods. As recently as 1978 homeowners in Michigan were bringing legal action to stop the establishment of family-style homes designed to accommodate adults with retardation (Magnusson, 1978). Yet during the same year the citizens of Michigan were shocked by the revelation of child neglect and child abuse in state institutions (Magnusson and Watson, 1978). Such attitudes were not unique to Michigan residents, for many other communities across the nation refused to support the rights of the mentally retarded to live out of the institution and at the same time expressed dismay over the way retarded were treated within the institution.

The Need for Comprehensive Services

Publicity about such issues served to confront the citizenry with the prevalence of mental retardation. Additionally, communities came to realize that retardation could occur in all types of families, regardless of socioeconomic factors or educational background. Parent groups and professionals joined forces to educate the community about mental retardation and thus allay the fears and anxieties that were impeding the deinstitutionalization and normalization processes. Federal, state, and private money was used to conduct surveys of programs and their effectiveness; coordinate the services of diverse agencies; and train and develop manpower to work in all types of settings (schools, residences, sheltered workshops). All fifty states as well as the District of Columbia and the Virgin Islands have developed plans for comprehensive service to the mentally retarded and their families.

Some parents and educators began to consider the needs of the aging and aged developmentally disabled person. Beginning steps were taken to identify, anticipate, and meet the unusual needs of the individual who found himself in the double jeopardy of being old and mentally retarded (Dickerson et al., 1974). Other parents and professionals began to realize that intrinsic to the normalization process was the right to be expressive and fulfilled in relationships, both socially and sexually (Kempton et al., 1973). In some states legislation was passed permitting sex education in the public schools for all children, which, as a result of mainstreaming, included those children who had mental retardation.

By the late 1970s parents, professionals and affected individuals were becoming militant in their demands for full rights of American citizenship for the mentally retarded. As these groups developed skills as advocates, they addressed such issues as guardianship, health insurance, and sterilization. Increasing numbers of people agreed that in order for the individual with mental retardation to enjoy a "normal" life, he needed to have the opportunity to be educated or trained, receive medical and/or psychiatric treatment, live in a situation of his choice with people he had selected, experience privacy, and enjoy social/sexual fulfillment. Additionally, the individual with mental retardation who wished to refuse being sterilized or being the subject of medical experiments within an institution needed support in this position.

CHAPTER 3

Definitions, Etiology, Classification

FOR MANY YEARS MUCH ENERGY AND EFFORT has been spent in developing an acceptable definition of the condition we have come to know as mental retardation. As we have noted, at one time the mentally retarded were considered to be throwbacks to primitive man or "changelings" possessed of the devil. Until modern times little practical differentiation was made between mental retardation and mental illness, even though as early as the fourteenth century differences had been noted and recorded. Until modern times, profound and severe degrees of mental retardation were noted almost exclusively in the families of the wealthy, for infants with gross retardation born to families of the poor rarely survived beyond an early age.

In the United States, mild retardation was not a great issue in the years preceding the industrial revolution, for the majority of the nation's citizens were illiterate or semiliterate and many of them lived in poverty, with inadequate or insufficient food, clothing, shelter, and medical attention. Education for the masses was still in the future. Children worked beside their parents in mines, on the land, and in the early factories. Under such circumstances a child who was slow to develop, had difficulty expressing himself, or otherwise gave signs of retardation was hardly noticed. "In an almost wholly illiterate population, functioning at the simplest vocational level, the group we now label "educable retarded" no doubt was indistinguishable" (Crissey, 1975).

As industrialization swept across the nation, Americans experienced great socioeconomic changes. Population patterns shifted. By the middle of the twentieth century most Americans lived in urban or suburban areas that were interconnected by complex communication and transportation networks. The standard of living for many persons improved dramatically. The middle class became larger, while the poverty of the lower class became more visible. Educational opportunities became recognized as the right of every citizen. With greater opportunities for learning, a higher level of sophistication was demanded of all persons as they dealt with a complex world of interrelationships and interdependencies. Within such a complex system, some individuals were unable or slow to learn the adaptive behaviors needed to survive and were identified as retarded.

There was great variation among those so identified. Some individuals were so incapacitated physically and mentally that they were totally dependent and needed help with all their needs. Others were not so easily identified by the casual observer; they gave no physical signs of their disability and behaved in socially acceptable ways; yet their ability to function intellectually was impaired. Physicians, psychologists, educators, social workers, and others came to recognize that there was a wide range of differences in the condition of retardation. "Not only are there degrees of retardation, there are degrees of ability within the various areas of intellectual functioning" (Attwell and Clabby, 1971). There evolved as many definitions of mental retardation as there were professional disciplines dealing with the population. Some definitions emphasized etiological factors and others emphasized symptoms and behaviors. The American Association on Mental Deficiency brought some order to the chaos by developing a definition that has gained wide acceptance. This is the definition presented in this book, since it is viewed as the most meaningful for social workers and teachers: *Mental retardation refers to significantly sub-average general intellectual functioning existing concurrently with deficits in adaptive behaviors, and manifested during the developmental period.*

There are three important concepts in the AAMD definition that require amplification. *Sub-average general intellectual functioning* means that the individual's score on an intelligence test was two or more standard deviations below the average scores of individuals of the same age. *Adaptive behaviors* refers to a range of diverse behaviors needed by an individual in order to cope with his or her natural or social environment—sensory-motor skills, communication skills, and self-help, socialization, academic, and vocational skills. *Developmental period* is the term used to describe the years of a person's life between birth and age nineteen (Grossman, 1977).

It should be noted that even though this definition of mental retardation includes the phrase "existing concurrently with deficits in adaptive behaviors," an individual usually is classified as retarded solely on the basis of an intelligence test score. In instances where deficiencies in adaptive functioning are identified, such deficiencies are perceived as support for the classification. It is not uncommon for a person who has been classified as mentally retarded during his school years to acquire such a high degree of adaptive behavior skills that he functions in a normal fashion in his adult years. In 1965 Nancy and Halbert Robinson reported "an increasing emphasis on the problems and education of children whose intellectual handicaps are relatively mild and who may under propitious circumstances achieve at least limited social independence." Every community has citizens who did poorly in school but in later years developed vocational skills that permitted them to support themselves and become contributing members of that community. It was with this segment of the mentally retarded population that the educational/vocational systems had their greatest success during the mid-twentieth century (Robinson and Robinson, 1976).

Identification and Classification

With mandatory school attendance, educators became aware of the term "six-hour" retarded child. The term refers to the "concept of a child who comes from an impoverished environment within which he is seen as normal, but who then attends school [for six hours a day], where he is academically retarded" (Tymchuk, 1973). Many parents and professionals challenge such labeling of the disadvantaged child. They contend that intelligence tests under the best of circumstances do not fairly assess functional intelligence, defined as "primarily the ability to cope with the interaction of social and personal focus; intelligent behavior can be defined as successful coping" (Leland and Smith, 1974).

The assessment of intelligence usually involves one or more tests, usually administered by a psychologist. The tests most frequently used are:

Cattell Infant Intelligence Scale: intended for use with children between three and thirty months of age; assesses imitative behavior, motor skills, language, and perceptual development.

Stanford-Binet Intelligence Scale: intended for use with persons aged two years through adulthood; assesses both verbal and performance skills.

Wechsler Intelligence Scale for Children (WISC): designed to test children between the ages of five and fifteen years; assesses verbal and performance skills.

When any of these intelligence tests are completed, a protocol, or score sheet, is prepared and is tabulated by the evaluator. The intelligence quotient (IQ) is then determined by comparing these raw scores along with the chronological age of the client to the standard norms suggested for each test. The number of standard deviation units from the mean of this continuum determines the category of retardation in which an individual is placed.

Adaptive behavior is more elusive and difficult to assess objectively. The following tests may be completed by a parent or another person who is familiar with the behavior of the person being tested:

Adaptive Behavior Scale: developed under the auspices of the American Association on Mental Deficiency (AAMD) and designed to gather information about a retarded individual in the areas of independent functioning, physical development, use of language, comprehension, use of numbers and time, and social skills.

Vineland Social Maturity Scale: designed to gather information about an infant or young child's social, motor, and cognitive skills.

Using a *behavioral* classification system for studying mental retardation, there are four categories, based on intelligence and adaptive behavior:

Mild (frequently referred to as "educable"): IQ 70–51; slow development; usually can achieve independent life-style.

Moderate (frequently referred to as "trainable"): IQ 51–36; delayed development; with training can achieve semi-independent life-style.

Severe: IQ 35–20; motor, speech, and language much delayed; may acquire self-care skills and other independent behaviors, but requires a supervised, protected environment.

Profound: IQ less than 20; gross impairment in coordination and sensory development; totally dependent upon others for survival.

The mentally retarded population in the United States is classified as follows:

Mild	(IQ 70–51)	89	percent
Moderate	(IQ 50–36)	6	percent
Severe	(IQ 35–20)	3.5	percent
Profound	(IQ less than 20)	1.5	percent

Earlier systems of behavioral classification included the category of "borderline." The recent trend is for educators and practitioners to refer to borderline intelligence when a particular individual has scored in the IQ range above 70 but may at any given time be reclassified as retarded because of dysfunctional behavior and defective reasoning. This deliberate avoidance of rigidity of classification may be due to the recognition that there is no absolute score below which an individual can be regarded as retarded and above which he is normal. It is frequently recognized that one person could easily be perceived as less retarded because of a higher IQ, but another person with a lower score could surpass the first because of a high level of adaptive ability (Attwell and Clabby, 1971).

For purposes of social work practice, the behavioral classification system described above is preferred to the medical classification system. However, it is important for social workers to recognize that medical specialists must attend to a medical classification and thus focus on organic causes and physical abnormalities. The system of categories designed for medical use in hospitals, clinics, and medically oriented residential facilities is as follows (Grossman, 1977):

1. Retardation caused by infection.
2. Retardation associated with disease or intoxication.
3. Retardation associated with trauma or a physical agent.
4. Retardation associated with disorders of metabolism.
5. Retardation associated with new growth.
6. Retardation associated with prenatal conditions.
7. Retardation associated with unknown disease but with structural reaction manifested.
8. Retardation associated with only functional reaction manifested.

The organic causes of mental retardation may be introduced in the prenatal, perinatal, or post-natal stages of development. *Infectious diseases* of the mother such as syphilis and German measles may have a negative influence upon the fetus she is carrying. *Drugs* such as alcohol, certain prescribed medications, and the infamous thalidomide may adversely affect the infant in utero. *Infectious childhood diseases* such as encephalitis, meningitis, whooping cough, and measles may cause retardation in the infant or young child who suffers the illness.

Metabolic disorders account for some cases of retardation. In recent years, the general public has become familiar with PKU (phenylketonuria), a metabolic disorder transmitted by a recessive gene, which results in an excessive amount of phenylpyruvic acid in the urine. There are marked symptoms of this disorder early in the infant's life that can be detected early and partially remedied by diet modifications. The results can be dramatic. If treatment is initiated within the first two years of the child's life, the severity of retardation can be lessened. About one of every 10,000 live births in the United States results in a PKU disorder.

Hypothyroidism (cretinism) results from insufficient secretion of the thyroid hormone, which leads to arrested physical development and mental retardation. A person with this condition has unusual characteristics that are obvious: a large head, thick, coarse hair, a round face, a low forehead, eyes set far apart, a flat, broad nose, a thick, protruding tongue, a short neck, a squat body, and short limbs.

Biochemical and nutritional disorders are becoming increasingly recognized as causes of mental retardation. Certain abnormalities have been associated with pathology in the metabolism of carbohydrates, lipids (fatty substances), or proteins. Maternal malnutrition impairs the development of the human fetus in that fewer brain cells are developed.

Rh incompatibility between the mother and the fetus can be a cause of retardation. If a mother with Rh-negative blood carries a baby with Rh-positive blood, during the pregnancy the mother's body may produce anti-Rh antibodies, causing increased destruction of the baby's red blood cells with release of a pigment, bilirubin, into the baby's bloodstream. Excessive bilirubin accumulation can be damaging to the brain of the newborn infant. This condition is easily diagnosed, and the infant can receive transfusions upon birth (Sarason, 1949).

Chromosomal abnormalities of specific types always result in birth defects and mental retardation. Simply stated, chromosomes are microscopic intracellular bodies which transmit hereditary characteristics through the genes they carry. Any disorder of the chromosome which results in an imbalance of genes being transmitted will cause an abnormal condition for the human organism. Down's syndrome (mongolism) is the most frequent and recognizable chromosomal abnormality in that it involves certain facial characteristics: round face, vertical fold beside the nose (epicanthal fold), slanting eyes with no fold in the eyelid, low-bridged nose, protruding lower lip, small square ears, and a sallow complexion. Cri du Chat syndrome is a chromosomal anomaly that is recognizable by the presence of a catlike cry, severe mental retardation, a small head, and an abnormally small jaw. Turner's syndrome is manifested in short stature, a webbed or short neck, a broad nose, low-set ears, and the absence of secondary sexual traits.

Occasionally, *unknown prenatal influences* or accidents cause cerebral and cranial malformations such as microcephalus (small head) and hydrocephalus (enlarged head). Microcephalus is characterized by the premature or early closure of the sutures in the skull, resulting in an unusually small head. Hydrocephalus is produced by increased fluid accumulation within the ventricular system of the brain, causing separation of the skull bones, enlargement of the head, and atrophy of the brain. This condition may be corrected or temporarily remediated by the introduction of a shunt to carry the fluid out of the ventricles, but the condition may be reactivated at a later time. Hydrocephalic children tend to be passive and quiet. Blindness, deafness, and disorders involving seizures may also be present.

Some instances of mental retardation are caused by *physical or traumatic damage* such as the mother's unsuccessful attempt to abort the fetus, deprivation of oxygen (anoxia), overuse of X-rays, prolonged birth process, misuse of instruments to assist birth, and severe stress or pressure. Such traumas occurring during the prenatal or perinatal stages may cause asphyxia (lack of oxygen), skeletal fractures, or injuries to the cerebrum, vital organs, or nerves. Abusive and neglectful treatment of an infant or young child is a suspected cause of mental retardation.

Prenatal brain damage may be hereditary, as in the case of Down's syndrome, or it may be caused by conditions that are congenital (existent in utero or at birth), such as metabolic disorders like PKU. Perinatal and postnatal brain damage are more apt to occur if the birth is premature, postmature, or accompanied by extended labor or anoxia. The risk of brain injury increases when the mother is having her first child.

According to Henry Leland, brain damage sustained during birth (perinatal) is likely to result in the milder forms of retardation. Brain damage sustained immediately after birth (neonatal) will result in severe neurological problems even though the retardation as such may range from profound to nonexistent. Brain damage occurring later in the child's life is most likely to be manifested in subsequent emotional problems or learning disabilities (Leland and Smith, 1974).

It should be emphasized that not all brain injuries result in retardation. The terms "minimally brain-injured" and "minimally neurologically handicapped" are used interchangeably to imply damage that is not easily identified because of the minor degree of severity. Behaviors often perceived as resulting from brain injuries include hyperactivity, hypersensitivity, distractibility, short attention span, poor memory, poor muscle control, explosive reactions, and perceptual difficulties (tendency to see part of a problem rather than the total problem). Any of these behaviors may cause learning problems for the individual who has them, but in and of themselves they do not constitute mental retardation.

Certain terms are used to describe a child's participation in school and his use of the learning process. Occasionally a school report or record will describe a child as having "minimal brain dysfunction." This alludes to brain damage so slight that no neurological handicaps can be identified, but there is evidence that the child has great difficulty learning. Often such a child may be perceived inaccurately as having mental retardation. Recently the term "learning-disabled" has gained common usage. It refers to the inability to read, write, and use speech and arithmetic adequately in the school situation (Kirk, 1972). While not necessarily connected with mental retardation, certain sensory defects impede a child's maximum use of an academic situation by interfering with learning and thus the development of cognition. (Cognition refers to a range of behaviors such as hindsight, foresight, insight, awareness, memory, reasoning, generalization, judgment, recognition, abstraction and thought.) Sometimes tics, grimaces, and unusual postures develop as a result of sensory defects and further complicate the child's school experience.

Some researchers and diagnosticians differentiate between mental deficiency and mental retardation. They contend that *mental deficiency* describes a condition of intellectual deficit that is a result of organic causes such as heredity, disease, or injury. On the other hand, *mental retardation* describes the condition of defective intellectual functioning due to nonor-

ganic causes when the individual fails to develop his native aptitudes or po-
tentials or does not function within the normal range of either intelligence
or adaptive behavior (Sarason and Gladwin, 1958).

Nonorganic causes of mental retardation may include social or psychological damage produced by lack of adequate medical attention for mother
and child, poor housing, underemployment, minimal education, inadequate parenting techniques, ghetto living, and other sociocultural factors. A
negative relationship is evident in the high incidence of mental retardation
in children born into racial-minority and/or low-income groups.

People who live in noisy, overcrowded housing in the ghettos of America's cities do not share in the good life as portrayed in the American dream.
The urban poor have a harsh life, with insufficient money for obtaining
shelter, warmth, clothing, and food. Pregnancies are frequent and often unwanted. Medical attention for any reason is not readily available, and prenatal care an unusual luxury. Malnutrition is a common occurrence that
does not spare pregnant women and nursing mothers (Hutt and Gibby,
1976).

A baby born into such a situation may be lovingly treated but ineffec-
tively parented by adults who themselves are listless, discouraged, unhealthy, malnourished, and unfulfilled. Frequently, the adults in the household find surcease from their hopeless lives in the excessive use of drugs,
alcohol, and tobacco. Such a situation of discouragement, despair, low
motivation, and minimal reward for intellectual superiority does not bode
well for the human infant, who relies upon his family to prepare him for his
later years. Often a ghetto child is indulged as an infant. He is passed from
lap to lap for cuddling and knows a series of attending adults—until a new
child arrives to displace him. Then he is abruptly thrust away from the indulgent nurturing process and required to learn quickly to fend for himself,
to survive in the world the best way he can. In spite of erratic meals, shared
beds, and inadequate medical attention, such a child grows up, even though
he has experienced casual parenting and few models to encourage him to
achieve a different, improved life-style. By the time he comes to the attention of the school, he has little sense of respect for self or others. He has little
readiness or motivation to attend and learn in school. He has little sense of
the value of planning for himself, and earning delayed rewards, or otherwise becoming a good user of the educational process. Such a child may not
have been retarded at birth, but the absence of wholesome interactions in
his early years has left him dull and lacking in curiosity, invention, enthusiasm, and excitement. Unless steps are taken to reverse the process of the
ghetto life, such a child will become another marginal person in the community.

Head Start and other early detection and intervention programs have
served to reverse this process for some youngsters, but far too many pass
through school having disassociated themselves from the educational en-

deavor. Leland speaks of "learning turn-off" as the condition, caused by socioeconomic factors, that affects achievement in school, even though its roots precede the school experience (Leland and Smith, 1974).

Many authors suspect a high incidence of mental retardation as a result of psychosocial-environmental influences. Some researchers believe that such influences cause 80 to 90 percent of all instances of mental retardation (Kauffman and Payne, 1975). Consider that statement in relationship to the fact that less than 6 percent of all cases of mental retardation have known etiologies; the remaining cases are unclassified or unknown (Jordan, 1976).

Certain psychosocial factors must be considered as contributory to mental retardation: insecurity of the family in terms of income and home maintenance; minimal attention to health maintenance (i.e., nutrition, cleanliness, preventive care); low level of motivation of parents, household, and subculture; inadequate and poor communication patterns; inadequacy of parenting (i.e., absenteeism, rejection, neglect, abuse, inappropriate role and behavior modeling); presence of dangerous influences (i.e., alcohol, drugs, prostitution); negative perceptions of the ghetto member by the society as a whole; and lack of reinforcement by society as a whole for any movement away from the life-style of the impoverished. A sobering thought to contemplate is the effect that continued and continuing impoverishment may have upon generations of children yet to be conceived.

Those socioeconomic factors that would respond to modification most quickly and easily (malnutrition, poor disease control and social ecology) are exactly those causing high risk (Leland and Smith, 1974). There are ways of reducing the incidence of mental retardation: improved prenatal care; quick treatment for lead poisoning; careful monitoring of births to allow for immediate diagnosis and treatment of PKU or blood transfusions for the infant with Rh-factor incompatibility; and corrective surgery for malformations of the skull.

There are difficulties in distinguishing mental retardation from other conditions that may be present in early infancy because of complexity of cause and individual variation. Usually a person who will subsequently be classified as severely or profoundly retarded according to the *behavioral* system is recognized and classified at a very early age according to the *medical* system. Conversely, many of the children who will subsequently be classified as mildly or moderately retarded according to the behavioral system may not be identified by the medical system and will remain unrecognized until they are part of an educational system. In other words, children who may appear normal at an early age may in fact be mentally retarded.

Most children who are classified by the behavioral system as mentally retarded show signs of possessing other handicapping conditions. For example, there is a high incidence of speech and hearing problems in the retarded population. It should be noted that when other handicapping conditions or physical anomalies accompany mental retardation, retardation is always given as the primary diagnosis. Problems of speech, hearing, vision, perception, and gait are all perceived as secondary to retardation. The condition known as epilepsy is a result of brain damage and may or may not be related to mental retardation. However, if retardation is present, the epilepsy or seizure disorder is perceived as the secondary diagnosis. Mental retardation is frequently complicated by the presence of emotional problems and other psychiatric disorders. In such instances also the primary diagnosis is mental retardation.

The condition known as cerebral palsy presents a unique situation in terms of classification. Cerebral palsy refers to any abnormality of motor functioning as a result of a brain disorder. Contrary to popular belief, individuals who have cerebral palsy represent the entire range of intelligence. In situations where mental retardation accompanies the cerebral palsy, the primary diagnosis is always cerebral palsy.

The determination of primary and secondary diagnosis is of critical importance to the individual with the disability because educational treatment and training programs traditionally have focused upon the primary diagnosis—sometimes to the neglect of secondary handicapping conditions such as speech.

Whatever clasification system is used, it is important for social workers and educators to recognize that every human organism is a product of biomedical and social influences. If there is either a biomedical impairment or a social impediment present, the individual's level of intellectual functioning will be adversely affected, perhaps to the extreme of mental retardation. There are hundreds of causes of mental retardation, both organic and nonorganic in origin. In most instances of retardation, the causes cannot be specifically identified.

During the twentieth century research projects have attempted to bring clarity to the historical confusion around mental retardation. Successful efforts have resulted in educating professionals, parents, and the general public to recognize the differences between mental retardation and such other conditions as mental illness, physical deformity, epilepsy, and dwarfism. In spite of the great improvements in the diagnosis of retardation, the treatment and training of the individuals so diagnosed still remain a major challenge for the parents and professionals who live and work with them (Leland and Smith, 1974).

Incidence and Prevalence

The *incidence* of mental retardation has to do with the rate of frequency with which it occurs in terms of a certain number of births. For example, Down's syndrome occurs in one out of 600 live births. By contrast, Turner's syndrome occurs in one out of 2,500 live births.

The *prevalence* of mental retardation is more important to service providers, for it has to do with the *total* number of mentally retarded individuals living at any one time in relation to the general population (Kirman and Bicknell, 1975). Approximately 6.5 million of the 214 million persons living in the United States in 1970 were identified as retarded. As many as 25 million people live in a family in which there is a mentally retarded person.

Factors of age, sex, race, and sociocultural milieu are determinants to be considered in any discussion of prevalence. For example, an individual could be classified as mentally retarded during his school years, but at the point when he successfully joined the work force such a classification would be outgrown and removed. It has been stated that at any point in time, 3 percent of the general population would achieve an IQ score of less than 70 and thus might be classified as mentally retarded. However, when the multidimensional definition developed by AAMD (see page 21) is applied, the number of individuals identified as mentally retarded is greatly reduced, so that scarcely 1 percent of the population is considered retarded (Neisworth and Smith, 1978).

At the present time, it is almost impossible to gather information about the national prevalence of retardation because of the difficulties of judging adaptive behaviors as well as intelligence (Harris and Roberts, 1972; Scanlon, 1973). As indicated earlier, the assignment of the label "mental retardation" varies as a result of changing conditions of age, school attendance, and vocational involvement. It is perhaps more appropriate to consider the issue of prevalence in terms of what needs to be done and where it should be done. For example, a local school board needs to be familiar with the prevalence of mental retardation in a certain school jurisdiction in order to provide appropriate special educational opportunities. The vocational rehabilitation department serving a large number of underemployed inner-city inhabitants may require information about the prevalence of retardation in order to plan for sheltered workshops (Robinson and Robinson, 1976).

Certain factors affect the estimated prevalence of mental retardation. In highly developed, industrialized nations an individual must cope with many complexities of living—whether he lives in an urban or rural setting. The trend toward the consolidation of schools provides the rural student with an educational process, complete with evaluation procedures, not unlike that of his urban counterpart. No longer is it possible for the mildly retarded individual to be unidentified during the school years. Compulsory education and entrance and promotional examinations serve to make the mildly retarded student visible to educators. Once such a person leaves the school setting, it is very usual for him to gain anonymity in the community by becoming a part of the society that is perceived as marginal and semi-dependent upon the community for support services. Ultimately, as a marginal person, he may receive financial and medical support from generic agencies but without being identified as mentally retarded.

Whereas mildly retarded individuals may go unnoticed or unrecognized until school age or even adolescence, those classified as moderate, severe, or profound cases are usually detected during infancy and early childhood, generally by medical personnel who either attend the birth or monitor the child's early growth and development. It is very unlikely that once classified as moderately, severely, or profoundly retarded a child will outgrow this classification; rather, the classification or "label" will determine which agencies, institutions, and bureaucracies will provide him with the necessary services.

As indicated earlier, many authors believe that more than 80 percent of all cases of mental retardation are a result of psychosocial-environmental influences. Therefore, it is not surprising that depressed areas of the nation, whether urban or rural, have a relatively high prevalence of retardation. Since a preponderance of racial and ethnic minorities live in such areas, retardation is prevalent in these unique groupings—not because of racial or ethnic characteristics per se, but because of the influences of poverty.

Medical evaluations and psychological assessments determine the extent of an individual's mental retardation. From these assessments, treatment plans are made that will have lifelong impact upon the client. As indicated earlier, the diagnosis of mental retardation is perceived as primary and is the focus of all interventions, with one notable exception: when both cerebral palsy and mental retardation are present, cerebral palsy becomes the primary diagnosis. The tendency to focus upon mental retardation results in overlooking the many other dynamics and factors present in the person's life. The retarded individual is apt to be stereotyped or labeled. As with all stereotypes, negative perceptions are attached to the label. Parents and professionals begin to perceive and relate to the disabled individual as though he were a second-class citizen, to be patronized and infantilized. Patronization and infantilization are often manifested in the denial (or withholding) of necessary, appropriate services.

Although the classification process may be clinically objective, thorough, and necessary in order for the retarded person to gain access to appropriate resources, it has serious social and political implications. A disproportionate number of children from minority groups and poverty settings are labeled mildly retarded. Many parents and professionals argue that the label tends to add to the child's burden of retardation, for the child perceives himself as less than desirable and therefore unwanted and unaccepted by his peer group. The child's low self-esteem tends to stifle his desire to achieve as much as he is able. Some parents and professionals believe that labeling which emphasizes the negative aspects of the individual distorts his expectations for performance and/or achievement. Uninformed members of the community tend to be afraid to offer employment, housing, recreation, or leisure-time opportunities to individuals who are labeled mentally retarded. A few citizens equate mental retardation with inappropriate sexual expression and thus are restrictive in their interactions with individuals so labeled (MacMillan et al., 1974).

In spite of the negative results of labeling, it appears that identification and classification are necessary to establish the frequency of mental retardation. The frequency must be determined in order to marshal resources and services to meet the needs of the individuals who have the condition. The social worker must learn to use the identification and classification given to a particular client in order to obtain all the services that are uniquely available because of the classification. However, the social worker has the responsibility of considering the many variables present in the client's personal life and family situation. He must become an advocate for his client and gain for the client access to service systems and treatment programs that speak to his total experience, rather than the limited options available to the so-called retarded.

Summary of Classifications and Case Examples

MILD RETARDATION

"Mild retardation" is the classification given to 89 percent of the mentally retarded citizens in the United States. Sometimes mild retardation is organic in origin. However, a disproportionally large number of mildly retarded children are born to families who live in abject poverty. The deprivation of the households, the climate of hopelessness and alienation in the homes, and the absence of stimulating early childhood experiences serve to negatively affect the growth and development of millions of children.

The mildly retarded individual is frequently unidentified until he enters school, where he is perceived as an underachiever. He is often described as being "impulsive" or "inattentive," or manifesting "poor judgment" or a "short attention span." Psychological testing will result in an IQ score between 70 and 51, and it will be determined that the child is "educable," or capable of learning basic academic skills that can be applied to the activities of daily living. Most children who have mild retardation are able to achieve an education equal to fifth to eighth grade by their late teens. The challenging curriculum of high school is beyond their capabilities, but vocational training is appropriate and usually makes an independent life-style possible.

Although it may take a mildly retarded individual longer to master his environment, the expectancy is that most mildly retarded persons will be able to develop the ability to reason and make decisions and to acquire the skills necessary to experience an independent life, complete with social-sexual relationships and responsibilities. Since the mildly retarded individual appears quite normal in his physical presentation and behavioral style, he blends into the community once he completes his education and finds employment. For example:

Joseph, age nineteen, was born into a large, poor family who lived in the city. There were many other families who lived in the crowded tenement house, and during his preschool years no one noticed if Joseph spoke. As his mother was to report later, Joseph was a strong boy who "seemed to make his way." His mother recalled that she was surprised when someone came from the school to talk to her about Joseph. The school reported that Joseph was disobedient and inattentive, and refused to speak. After four years in the school program, Joseph had grown large for his age and was constantly fighting and acting the bully in school. He rarely spoke and was making little academic progress. His mother was relieved when Joseph was sent to a residential training school for the retarded. Joseph did not see any member of his family for the next several years. While in the institution, he acquired language skills and many other socially acceptable behaviors. He became known as a physically strong, stubborn, and taciturn teenager. The psychologist determined that he had an IQ of 58 and thus he was considered educable. Joseph learned to manage money and to recognize and read survival words. At sixteen he went to live in a group home not far from his parents' home. He began to attend an activities center and a pre-vocational-training program. He stated that he wanted to make new friends. With the assistance of the group home operator, Joseph located his mother and visited her. He appeared interested in reestablishing a relationship with her, but his mother did not encourage him.

It appeared that Joseph had suffered from a lack of stimulation and other learning experiences as a small child, and this had caused insurmountable difficulties when he entered the school system. His classroom was overcrowded and there was little opportunity for him to receive the individual attention he must have needed. He handled the situation in the only way he knew—by fighting. It would appear that the years in the institution had helped Joseph develop his potential. However, during these years he had developed a style of behavior, manner, speech, and dress acceptable in the group home but strange and alienating in his former neighborhood. In the group home, humble as it was, Joseph lived with more comfort and security than his family had ever known. In an interview with a social worker, initiated on Joseph's behalf, the mother expressed her disinterest in her son: "I hope he does all right, but I can't be busy with him; I'm too tired, too old, too poor."

The trend, in recent years, for professionals to establish a strong causal relationship between poverty and mild retardation has provoked consternation among parents who are *not* impoverished and who yet have a child identified as mildly retarded or educable. Frequently middle-class parents have difficulty accepting the child who is a poor student. Sometimes this lack of acceptance is expressed in the form of overprotection.

Sara Beth, age thirty-one, is a mildly retarded woman who has spent her entire life as an active member of her family, neighborhood, and community. She was the first daughter and third child born to a professional couple. Sara Beth was considered slow to develop and had great difficulty learning to walk and to use her hands. She attended regular classrooms in school until she reached junior high, when her parents reluctantly accepted the advice of the educators and permitted her to attend special classes. Sara Beth eventually earned a special education high school certificate. The parents were reluctant to recognize that Sara Beth was experiencing rejection from her peers in the Girl Scout troop, church group, and community house teen group.

Sara Beth matured into an attractive, well-groomed woman who has learned to use braces to support one leg and one hand. She is self-supporting, as she works as a classroom aide for severely impaired children. She lives at home and uses public transportation. Sara Beth is able to read, write, take care of her own money (including her checkbook), prepare simple meals, and assist her mother with the housework. She enjoys latch hooking, television, and the movies. Her social life is limited to occasional invitations from the staff of the school where she works and outings with her parents and their friends. She does not date and has no friends of her own age.

Sara Beth's parents have consistently refused the offer of social services. They are resentful that Sara Beth has been labeled "retarded" and forced to work with "those poor children." Her mother hopes that Sara Beth will meet a suitable man in the church who will marry her and protect her. Sara Beth is more realistic and says her parents do not understand how it is with her. She appears to accept her life stoically. Sara Beth is apprehensive about continued contact with the social worker, for her parents do not approve.

Sara Beth's parents are still struggling with their negative feelings about the label that describes their daughter's disability. Their adamant denial of the reality of Sara Beth's life, coupled with their attempts to keep her involved with their preferred circle of friends, only serves to intensify Sara Beth's stressful situation.

MODERATE RETARDATION

Approximately 6 percent of all mentally retarded people are classified as moderately retarded, or "trainable," with an IQ score between 50 and 36. Such an individual may appear "normal" or may have other disabilities such as impaired speech or vision or epilepsy, not noticeable to the casual observer. During infancy and early childhood he will be slow to achieve such developmental milestones as walking, speech, and toileting. Frequently these delays are not so extreme as to cause alarm for the family, and the condition may go undetected until the child enters school, where his limited capacity for academic learning is detected. Moderately retarded children whose condition is undetected until school years usually appear quite normal as small children and frequently are from families who lack awareness and knowledge about parenting and the normal growth and development of children. Those moderately retarded children who have seizure disorders or some other obvious conditions are more likely to be detected early in childhood.

Moderately retarded individuals can learn concrete, routinized tasks and are able to achieve total independence in personal care. They are able to assume responsibility for home-maintenance chores and can achieve full employment in a sheltered workshop or comparable highly supervised work situation. They are able to initiate, develop, and maintain relationships. Usually they are able to move around local neighborhoods or small communities in a responsible manner. Because of their cognitive deficiencies, the moderately retarded may not understand such concepts as delayed gratification, cause and effect, time, and the necessity for choices and decision making. They will require active supervision and guidance for their entire lives in order to shield them from their own inappropriate decisions and actions.

Marie, age sixteen, was the sixth and last child born to a middle-aged couple. Her father owned a business in a suburb of a large city. Early in Marie's childhood it became apparent that she was backward in her development, slow to achieve all the various skills that her older siblings had accomplished at an early age. Marie was very blonde (almost to the point of being an albino), with poor eyesight. She had difficulty managing her mouth and had a continuous drool.

Marie never entered public school but was enrolled in a private residential school for children with disabilities. Psychological testing placed her in the "trainable" range and this determined her educational program at the school. At age sixteen, Marie had outgrown her eligibility for the private school, and was transferred to a family-care setting a few miles from her parents' home. The family-care setting was operated by a religious order, and the other five residents were elderly nuns.

At age sixteen Marie had developed several competencies. She recognized several printed words, played cards, and could count money up to $2.00. She wore very thick glasses and was prone to drool. She was capable of maintaining her personal grooming, but always wore clothes that were too large and out of fashion. She was a well-mannered girl who was affectionate and overtly demonstrative with her friends. She was distant with strangers and earned the nickname "Full Steam Ahead" as a description of the way she walked into an unfamiliar situation. She learned to use the city bus to commute to the training center where she was enrolled, as well as to make a regular Thursday visit home to see her mother.

In this case, Marie's parents had recognized her disability early in her life. In the following case, Frank's disability was undetected for several years.

Frank, age fourteen, was the second child born to a young couple in a rural southern community. Frank's father, a miner, was killed when the boy was four. Soon afterward his mother took her two children to a northern city, where she looked for work. She had little success and finally applied for welfare. At the recommendation of a welfare worker, Frank's mother took him to a clinic to request help with his seizures. Since she herself had seizures, she was not alarmed that Frank did also. Subsequently Frank was diagnosed as having epilepsy and moderate retardation. The mother was perceived as an inadequate parent owing to "epilepsy and borderline intelligence," and the medical authorities did not believe she could provide Frank with the supervision he required. The mother relinquished guardianship of Frank and he was placed in a rural foster home. He was enrolled in a public school program for "trainables."

At age fourteen, Frank had learned to take good care of himself and his belongings. He was helpful to his foster parents and enjoyed the many tasks on the farm. He had become a bully and frequently solved disagreements with the other children in the family by fighting. He had frequent seizures, but it was suspected that he faked many of them as a way of manipulating the situation and controlling other family members.

SEVERE RETARDATION

Severe retardation is the classification given to approximately 3.5 percent of the individuals who are classified as retarded. Usually severe retardation is organically caused and the condition is evident in the early stages of the child's life. Severe mental retardation is usually complicated by impaired sensory-motor development, which becomes apparent as the individual experiences extremely slow progress in achieving such developmental milestones as sitting up, holding a toy, repeating words, or walking. The obstetrician and pediatrician may identify severe retardation and seek corroboration from a psychologist. In any event, early intervention should be introduced in order to maximize the child's strengths and to prevent the retardation from worsening as a result of lack of adequate stimulation.

The severely retarded individual need not remain *totally* dependent for his entire life. He is capable of achieving most of the self-maintenance skills—i.e., toileting, feeding himself, and dressing. He is able to learn to do simple chores to contribute to the maintenance of the household. He enjoys recreational activities and peer interaction. He may become proficient at some routinized chore that will permit him to work in a supervised setting, but he will need to live and work in a protected environment for his entire life, for his level of functioning does not permit him to make thoughtful choices and decisions for himself and others.

Tom, age eleven, was the second-born of a set of twins; their young mother already had a daughter a year older. The father was away from home on military service. Birth records are sketchy, but there was evidence of brain damage at early infancy. At age two Tom and his siblings were left alone in an apartment for several days. Subsequently the children were removed from the mother and custody was given to the absent father. The children were placed in separate foster homes. Because of Tom's delayed development and uncontrollable behavior, he was removed from the foster home and placed in a state institution, where he remained until age eleven, when he was again placed in a foster home. At the time of the placement Tom had speech and some self-care skills, although he was not completely toilet-trained. He had numerous fears and was destructive, self-abusive, hostile, distrustful, and angry. His body was in constant motion and he was constantly talking. He had tantrums, smeared feces, soiled, overtly masturbated, and used obscene and profane language. He was unable to read, write, or recognize colors. He had no friends, although he obviously wanted to have them. The only family member he ever mentioned was his grandmother.

A second example of a severely retarded person is a "good" baby, whose condition was not recognized for several months.

Grayce, age ten, was the third child born to a suburban mother. The father was a real estate broker. The family home was well equipped and the mother had household help three days each week. From early infancy, Grayce was described by her parents as "the best baby—she never cries." Later they were to describe her as "the laziest baby." Grayce had a sunny disposition; however, she did not walk or feed herself until she was two years old. She did not say "ma-ma" or "da-da" until she was eighteen months old. Grayce enjoyed eating and was frequently given things to munch. At age four, Grayce was considerably overweight and inactive. The parents arranged for a temporary placement for Grayce, partly because of the mother's fourth pregnancy. During the "temporary" placement, which lasted six years, Grayce continued to be a pleasant child, although she developed a streak of stubbornness. She slimmed down considerably because of a monitored diet and increased activity. She learned to dress herself and toilet independently during the day, but frequently had night accidents. She developed a speaking vocabulary of about thirty words that were clearly understood. She continued to be awkward in her walk and clumsy as she handled objects, frequently breaking things. Grayce had a real sense of her family and was always glad to see them when they visited her. She had never appeared homesick—in fact, no one had ever observed her being sad—so the family and residential staff were surprised by her overwhelming joy upon rejoining her family at age ten.

PROFOUND RETARDATION

Of all the persons classified as mentally retarded, fewer than 2 percent are so disabled as to be labeled "profoundly retarded." Profound retardation is usually organic in origin in that it is the result of genetic factors, physical trauma, or disease. A profoundly retarded child may be born to a family from any walk of life.

Medical advances are such that in the future some types of birth defects may be prevented, and this should positively affect the incidence of profound retardation. However, increased medical knowledge has already made it possible to prolong the lives of infants born prematurely. Infants born before the gestation period is completed have a low birth weight and are generally underdeveloped and considered to be "high risks." Since the lives of high-risk infants can be prolonged, it may be that the incidence and prevalence of profound retardation will remain constant in the foreseeable future.

The profoundly retarded infant or child is usually identified at birth or within a few weeks of birth, for marked handicaps will be apparent. Usually he will have experienced damage to the central nervous system, with considerable residual disability. He may be orthopedically impaired, blind, or deaf. He may give evidence of any of the following symptoms: spasticity, physical or emotional lethargy, convulsions, poor muscle tone, difficulty swallowing and feeding, aimless movements, and lack of alertness. As the weeks pass he will be slow to demonstrate developmental progress—slow to smile, sit up, crawl, stand, walk, and talk. He may be unable to feed himself or gain bladder control. When he is tested for his intelligence, he will score less than 20 on the Stanford-Binet Intelligence Test. Because of his profound retardation, the child will be dependent upon others for his care and survival for the rest of his life.

It should be noted that the sequence of growth and development is usually the same for all children, but the rate of development is highly individual. In the case of a child with retardation, the more profound the retardation, the slower the rate of development. Since each developmental learning is the basis upon which the next one takes place, the achievement of any one developmental milestone is important far beyond the singular accomplishment. Every child needs to develop sensory-motor skills, speech and language, self-care skills, and social skills. Frequently parents become aware of their child's retardation gradually over a period of weeks or months as they observe unusual slowness in skill achievement.

Usually the infant or child is identified and diagnosed as profoundly retarded by a medical person, and this diagnosis will be subsequently corroborated by psychological testing. At what point the diagnosis of retardation is shared with the family varies from situation to situation. It is important, however, to share the diagnosis immediately if preventive, remediative, or other interventions must be initiated. Sometimes the physical deformities are obvious to the parents, who seek confirmation from a doctor. Sometimes the physician decides, for any one of several reasons, to withhold the information from the parents until a more propitious time. Some professionals argue that a delay in sharing the diagnosis gives the parents time to establish a positive, loving attachment to the newborn child which will be very helpful to them when they subsequently must accept the reality of the child's retardation. If delay does not impede treatment, the time of announcement of a diagnosis is irrelevant. Certainly a delay will allow observational time to determine what progress the infant makes in his growth and development.

Professional experience equips the clinician to generalize about the needs of the profoundly retarded; therefore, he is prepared to communicate those needs, on behalf of the individual, to the parents and family. First, the client needs to be recognized and his limitations identified. The implications of these limitations should be assessed in terms of future growth and development, and developmental supports should be provided immediately in order to prevent any additional handicapping conditions from arising. Thus, the client begins to undergo a process of evaluation and reevaluation that will continue for many years, for it is imperative that his progress be monitored. Down through the years the client will need health care, training, education, behavior modeling, family stability, and social peer experiences. As an adult, he will need financial support, assistance in living in a situation separate from his family, and continued opportunities for learning and socialization.

In some instances, the client may need to be institutionalized for a period of time in order to have some of his needs met, or to avoid negative influences from the home and community. There are some problems that come from the social milieu itself which cause too many complications for the profoundly retarded person, who has a limited repertoire of adaptive behaviors. Sometimes the problems within the family setting serve as impediments to the client's growth and development and in effect worsen the retardation.

Donald and David were identical twins who were evaluated together at age five. The parents had known from the time of birth that their sons were profoundly retarded. They had been able to care for the children at home but sought an evaluation for their sons in order to plan for their future. The physical examination brought to light two ways in which the otherwise identical boys could be told apart. Donald had a single hair whorl which ran counterclockwise and David had a double hair whorl in which the major components were counterclockwise. Donald's head circumference was twenty and one-quarter inches, with less facial fullness on the right, while David's head circumference was twenty inches, with less facial fullness on the left. Both children were small and thin. Their oddly shaped heads had protuberant posterior parietal and occipital areas, and the sloped foreheads of their small, triangular faces—in which there were close-set eyes with dark circles under them—created a pinhead effect. Although the children could walk, they were unusually awkward in their gait and seemed to have little sense of direction.

The unusual physical characteristics were undoubtedly the result of a deviant pattern of growth and development that originated as early as the first trimester of the mother's pregnancy. However, the characteristics did not appear to fit any syndrome.

The evaluators believed the boys to be visually and auditorially handicapped. Behaviorally, the twins had acquired no self-help skills and were dependent on others for total care. They had no recognizable language but did respond to other peoples' voices and touch. Both boys engaged in bizarre self-stimulating behaviors such as head banging, eye blinking, eye rolling, kicking, screaming, and hand biting. The boys were erratic in their schedules—frequently staying awake for the entire night, usually keeping the family awake by their screaming. It was common for the two boys to be engaged in identical behavior at the same time.

In summary, it is important for the social worker to understand the effects that nonorganic or organic causes may have upon mentally retarded individuals, for their disabilities may range from conditions amenable to modification (as in the case of Sara Beth) to irreversible handicaps (as in the case of the twins). However, the social worker must avoid the entrapment of stereotypic thinking when considering diagnostic impressions of individual clients. Each client should be considered as a unique individual with strengths and weaknesses, and interventions that focus upon a disability, to the exclusion of the individual's totality as a human being, should be avoided.

CHAPTER 4

The Evaluation Process

THE PURPOSE OF INITIATING AND MAINTAINING an evaluation process for the client who presents symptoms of retardation is to determine whether he is in fact retarded, and if so, to what degree. Assessing the client's assets and liabilities will provide clarification in terms of the diagnosis, thus legitimating the client's access to the resources available to individuals identified and classified as retarded. Furthermore, it will serve to provide a sense of the child's potential to achieve diverse behaviors and develop certain abilities and skills.

At the present time, such evaluations are provided by diagnostic clinics, residential institutions, and university-affiliated programs such as the Interdisciplinary Appraisal Service (IAS) of the Institute for the Study of Mental Retardation and Related Disabilities (ISMRRD) in Ann Arbor, Michigan. The IAS Clinic is described here as an example of how an interdisciplinary evaluation process can work on behalf of a profoundly retarded client and his family.

The parents as well as representatives from public or private agencies can request an evaluation from ISMRRD. The intake worker responds to the request by sending the parents or agency representative a client information form designed to elicit pertinent facts about the client, his family, his medical background, and his developmental, educational, and behavioral history. Finally, the parents are asked to complete a records-release form for each doctor, hospital, agency, school, or professional that has worked with the child. The intake worker reviews the information provided by the parents as well as the records and case material obtained from the professionals who have seen the child before and prelares a preadmittance summary to be used by the clinic admitting committee.

The clinic admitting committee includes representatives from several disciplines who together decide on the appropriateness of the clinic's services for the client's needs. They determine whether adequate background information has been provided, identify any additional material required, assign a case coordinator, and recommend the evaluation procedures to be followed and the consultations to be sought.

An evaluation schedule is prepared (usually covering two or three days), and parents and evaluators are notified. The case coordinator may call a preappraisal meeting of the evaluators to determine the best strategy for providing an effective evaluation.

The case coordinator and intake worker meet with the family upon their arrival for the first day of evaluations. The parents are introduced to the evaluation procedure and are asked to consider themselves as active participants in the process. They are encouraged to ask questions and to volunteer any information that seems relevant. The case coordinator explains his or her role as the person who is responsible for managing the process so that it will be as thorough, productive, and comfortable as possible. A comprehensive appraisal could include evaluations or consultations from any or all of the following disciplines (depending on the nature and severity of retardation and the age of the child): audiology, dentistry, medicine, nursing, nutrition, occupational therapy, opthalmology, pediatrics, physical therapy, psychiatry, psychology, special education, social work, speech and language and vocational rehabilitation.

The medically oriented members of an interdisciplinary team provide information about the client's general well-being, physical assets and liabilities, and achievement potential in terms of sensory-motor development. Those members of the team whose primary concern is education and training determine the client's potential in terms of learning and acquiring skills. Finally, members of the interdisciplinary team who are primarily concerned with psychosocial factors add information pertaining to the dynamics surrounding the child in his primary environment and relationships.

As in any thorough medical examination, the team is interested in the general appearance of the client-patient: his mood, level of awareness, and interaction with his environment. Special attention is paid to the condition of the skull, for certain skull lesions may indicate corresponding brain lesions. The head is checked for size and shape, since conditions such as microcephaly or hydrocephaly may be suspected. Abnormalities of the eyes, ears, nose, mouth, and teeth are carefully noted, since they may provide clues to the etiology of the retardation as well as a basis for predicting the developmental limits of the individual. A consultation with a dentist or dental hygienist may be indicated to check unusual dental concerns. An audiologist and opthalmologist may be asked to provide information as to hearing or visual impairments. Anatomical defects of the trunk, arms, hands, fingers, legs, feet, and toes are noted, as well as the enlargement of any organ such as the heart, liver, or spleen, since unusual findings may indicate metabolic, endocrinological, or genetic causes for the condition. Any unusual development of the genitalia may be associated with genetic or endocrinological causation as well. Special attention is paid to reports of erratic body movements, head jerks, eye blinking, or seizure activity. X-rays or electroencephalograms (EEGs) may be required to assist the team in determining the presence of epilepsy, lesions, tumors, or brain damage associated with cerebral palsy. Laboratory procedures permit the team to check for any indication of lead poisoning. Reflex patterns are checked to determine the existence of neurological abnormalities. The presence or absence of certain reflexes at certain stages in an infant's development serves as an indicator of possible abnormalities such as cerebral palsy.

The occupational therapist on the team assesses the client's adaptive skills and abilities to cope with tasks of survival and daily living. The client's use of his arms and hands is tested, and his perceptual motor development is appraised. From these tests and observations the occupational therapist is able to make a judgment about the individual's accomplishments in sensory integration, body concept, perception of spatial relationships, and language development. The physical therapist on the team uses a variety of tests and exercises to measure the client's ability to manage his body—to walk, stoop, sit, climb stairs, maintain his balance, and otherwise use the body to accomplish the activities of daily living. He checks for various types of paralysis, muscle weaknesses, fractures, or other orthopedic abnormalities.

A family medical history is obtained and a record is developed of past illnesses of each family member, as well as the client-patient. Data are gathered about the client-patient's infancy and early childhood, with notations of the ages at which he received immunizations and achieved certain developmental milestones such as raising the head or sitting up and holding a spoon. The eating habits and food preferences of the client-patient and his family are recorded. Finally, the child is observed both alone and with family members in many of his daily activities—i.e., eating, dressing, walking, and playing. Preferably this information is obtained from observing the child in his own home or another similar setting.

The medically focused data described above may be gathered by an interdisciplinary team. Some of the necessary information can be obtained only by a highly trained specialist such as an audiologist. However, much of the important data about the child's behavior and early growth and development, as well as the family diet, may be obtained by a social worker if a nurse, nutritionist, or occupational therapist is not available.

The speech pathologist works with the audiologist in the evaluation process. Audiometric tests determine the client's hearing ability and the type of remediation, if any, that may be needed. The speech pathologist, in consultation with the dentist, checks the client's mouth for any abnormalities that would impede the production of speech. Tests are administered to determine receptive and expressive language competencies, and speech distortions such as lisping or stuttering are identified. The speech pathologist will learn from the parents the communication patterns present in the household, paying special attention to their observations about the child's awareness and response to stimuli in his natural environment.

Although some retarded clients are incapable of educational programming in the traditional sense, the educator is a critical participant in the interdisciplinary evaluation. Since he has expertise in the patterns of normal growth and development, he is uniquely prepared to identify areas of limitation in the child's performance. He will use a variety of materials and techniques to determine the client's reaction to sensory stimulation, level of responsiveness, learning style, and patterns of interaction with family, peers, and environment as a whole. The educator is able to recognize the client's potential for learning and developing skills based upon former and current accomplishments. He will work in collaboration with the occupational therapist, physical therapist, psychologist, and speech pathologist to prepare an individualized, minutely detailed and specific educational profile that permits the interdisciplinary team to determine a plan to maintain existing behaviors and skills and to identify the tasks to be focused upon for maximum growth and development.

The psychologist is a key participant in the interdisciplinary evaluation, for he has the responsibility of analyzing the client's behavior in qualitative and quantitative ways through the use of a variety of tests. As a result of this process, he will determine an IQ score. Although the present trend is toward a general description of a client's abilities, the IQ score still is an integral part of that general description. The psychologist has several tests from which to select the most appropriate for use with an individual client. Factors of age and predetermined limitations are considered in the selection of the tests. Tests have been developed for use with the client who is autistic, blind, cerebral-palsied, deaf, nonverbal, or otherwise limited. The tests most frequently used are:

Cattell Infant Intelligence Scale: for ages three months to thirty months.

Columbia Mental Maturity Scale: for ages three years to ten years; a nonverbal test used with deaf, cerebral-palsied, nonverbal children as well as retarded ones.

Gesell Developmental Schedules: for pre-school-age children.

Goodenough-Harris Drawing Test: for age three years or older.

Hayes-Binet: used with the blind or partially sighted.

Illinois Test of Psycholinguistic Abilities (ITPA): for ages two and a half years to nine years; especially useful with retarded children who have language and speech difficulties.

Nebraska Test of Learning Aptitude: for ages three years through sixteen years; appropriate for testing a deaf child.

Peabody Picture Vocabulary Test (PPVT): for school-age children; permits maximum use of the child's own vocabulary.

Pre-School Attainment Record (PAR): designed to measure children up to age seven years.

Stanford-Binet Intelligence Scale: for all ages from two years upward; the most commonly used test for the moderately (trainable) retarded.

Vineland Social Maturity Scale: designed to assess the infant or young child's social, motor, and cognitive skills; may be administered by a parent.

Wechsler Intelligence Scale for Children (WISC): for children between ages five years and fifteen years; widely used in the testing of the mildly (educable) retarded.

Wechsler Adult Intelligence Scale (WAIS): similar to the WISC but for use with individuals sixteen years or older.

In addition to administering the selected tests, the psychologist will talk with the client's parents and other family members in order to assess the family's interactions. Special attention is focused upon the client's pattern of initiating and responding to behavioral situations, as well as upon the way in which these patterns are affected by his abilities or disabilities. The psychologist is interested in learning about the kind of stimuli introduced in the home—i.e., toys, music, language, playtime, or cuddling. He gathers information about the extent to which the client is included and involved in the family routine and special activities. Finally, family dynamics unrelated to the client but intrinsic to the family life-style are assessed.

A psychiatric evaluation or consultation is requested if there is indication of current or potential emotional disorders in addition to the mental retardation. The psychiatrist is prepared to assess these emotional problems to determine whether they are organically based or a response to the psychosocial environment in which the client lives.

Sometimes the social worker functions as the case coordinator on the interdisciplinary team. In that role he or she will work with the client, family, and evaluators to ensure a beneficial experience for everyone. Often the social worker will accompany an evaluator from another discipline to make a site visit to a training program, school, or home. Depending upon the purpose of the visit, the social worker may be asked to obtain specific information—e.g., data regarding the nutritional intake of the client-patient. However, whether or not these tasks are assumed by the social worker, the interdisciplinary team always looks to the social work evaluation to contribute understanding and interpretation of factors pertinent to the client's family, home, neighborhood, and community.

The Social Work Interview

The social work interview is conducted with both parents, if possible. When indicated, additional interviews are conducted with other members of the household as well. The social worker must be prepared to deal with resistance, shock, denial, anger, frustration, ambivalence, and anxiety on the part of the parents as the evaluative process changes focus from the client to the client's family. The objective of the interview is to gather information in the following areas:

1. Family composition; ages; pertinent descriptors.
2. Family history and relationship patterns before the client's birth.
3. Parents' recall of their earliest recognition of the child as having a disability.
4. Impact of the client upon the family as a unit; each individual member's perception of and accommodation to the impact.
5. Evidence of the parents' ability to realistically assess *each* family member's strengths and weaknesses.
6. Parental expectations and plans for each family member including the client.
7. Evidence of parenting style: family routines, schedules, provision of growth-producing experiences and opportunities, behavior-management techniques; response to crises.
8. Recognition of support systems and concrete resources available to the parents within the immediate or extended family.
9. Evidence of coping and problem-solving skills.
10. Parents' expectations from the evaluations and from the agency.

The following excerpts from a social work evaluation demonstrate the breadth of information that may be obtained in one interview. The information provides unique and valuable impressions for the consideration of the interdisciplinary team as they strive to develop an accurate, complete assessment of the client and his family system.

Mark T., son of Bob and Cathy Mason, was referred for a complete diagnostic evaluation to help school personnel determine the most appropriate educational programming for him.

> Bob, age thirty, completed twelfth grade (not in home)
> Cathy, age twenty-three, completed eighth grade
> Mark, age 3

The following family-background data was reported by Cathy, who attended the evaluation sessions without her husband. They have recently separated and she does not know his whereabouts.

Cathy is one of four children. She described her childhood as a happy one and expressed close feelings for her father. However, she did not regard her parents as a source of support for her because "they have enough problems of their own." "The less they know, the better," she commented. She would turn to them only as a last resort. At age sixteen, Cathy married her first husband, Jerry; she described this union as a good marriage. Three and a half years later Jerry was killed in an automobile accident, and shortly thereafter Cathy married Bob, who had been Jerry's best friend. Cathy commented that the marriage was "a mistake in the first place" because of her expectations that Bob would be just like her first husband and because she attempted to remake Bob in his image. According to Cathy, their separation was precipitated by the fact that she came home from work one evening an hour early and found her husband in bed with her girlfriend. "When I came home, they got up. I was very calm. I told them to go back to bed, which they did, and I slept on the floor. The next morning I made breakfast for everyone. I suggested to Bob that we go away someplace together, and he said no. That's when I decided to leave him. I went to work early that day and then I remembered I had left Mark at home with Bob. I called him and told him to bring Mark to the restaurant. One of his friends brought him to me and said that I could have him if I gave Bob the checkbook. Since there wasn't much money in the checkbook, I said, OK."

During the five months after the incident, Cathy moved six times and changed jobs twice. She was doubtful that marriage counseling would be helpful because "there has been so much hurt."

Cathy was employed as a waitress from 9:00 P.M. until 6:00 A.M. Fridays, Saturdays, and Sundays, and occasionally one day during the week. Mark was cared for during those times by the fourteen-year-old daughter of one of her friends. She was very satisfied with this child-care arrangement and felt that the baby-sitter had exercised mature judgment in the care of Mark with "one exception." The sitter and her three older siblings were using dope. Cathy expressed her displeasure with their actions to the sitter and stated that it was no longer a problem. Mark was treated as a member of the sitter's family, a factor Cathy appreciated.

Cathy was dating a man named Pete, who accompanied her and Mark to the evaluation sessions. Pete had attended trade school, where he learned to be a cook. He had been working at this trade but was unemployed. Pete was on parole for a year after having served a prison sentence for involvement in drugs. Cathy stated that he was different from any man she had ever dated because he had been raised in a city. Cathy met him when she picked him up while he was hitchhiking. She reported that he and Mark got along and that he was firmer with Mark than she was able to be at times. Cathy was wary of considering marriage with Pete because he was a "free spirit" and she was afraid that he would decide at any moment to leave her. She said she was beginning to enjoy "paying my own way" and the independence she was experiencing. She wanted to learn to assume responsibilities for herself before considering remarrying or living with Pete. She concluded this statement with the comment, "Maybe we'll move in together in December," thus implying that she could learn these skills in three months.

Cathy indicated that she had suspected her husband of cheating on her long before she was faced with the reality of the situation. As their marital relationship began to deteriorate, she began drinking heavily as an escape and was arrested twice for driving while under the influence of liquor. As a result, she was ordered by the court to attend traffic school and to attend three counseling sessions at the Substance Abuse Center near her home. She found the group "share" sessions very helpful and voluntarily returned to them after termination of the required sessions. She described her drinking habits as sharply reduced in the six weeks prior to the evaluation. She no longer went "bumming" at bars and confined her drinking to a beer or two on the weekends at home.

Cathy stated that she perceived Mark as a cute little boy whose temper tantrums were the behaviors she had the most difficulty managing. She used spankings to discipline Mark, but admitted that on many occasions she had been so mad at him that she had been afraid to spank him because she would have harmed him. Instead she had chosen to remove herself from Mark until she had her emotions under control. Cathy also recognized the fact that she took her anger out on Mark and gave him inconsistent messages which were contingent on her moods.

Diagnostic Impressions

Cathy impressed the worker as a young woman of "fifteen going on forty-five." In other words, she was "streetwise" but had had little opportunity to observe or develop capabilities and responsibilities of mature adulthood. She was a very appealing, open woman who seemed starved for a relationship with someone she could rely on for emotional support, perhaps even mothering and nurturing for herself. She lacked well-developed coping mechanisms and could become very stubborn, explosive, and impulsive when frustrated or anxious. It appeared from her description of her relationship with her husband and peers that she was casual in all aspects of her life-style, including her sexual relationships, and was accustomed to a high degree of instability in her life. It appeared to the worker, based on her submissive, passive acceptance of her husband's unfaithfulness, that her self-image was poor and that she felt a need to punish herself. This may relate to her ambivalent feelings toward her husband and guilt for perceiving Mark as an unwanted responsibility who "gets on my nerves," a "big chore." Cathy's perception of her mothering role with Mark was characterized by many expressions of "I should" rather than "I do," indicating her lack of readiness to fully assume a parenting role. Cathy denied the severity of Mark's retardation, preferring to believe that the evaluation would show he had the potential for higher functioning, and she wept whenever the discussion focused on the possibility of Mark's limitations being unremediable.

Cathy was very receptive to insights offered her regarding her own or her husband's behavior and reflected intently on them during the interview. This was perceived as an indication that she may be ready to invest herself in a therapeutic relationship.

Cathy lacked awareness of the fact that her child-care arrangements for Mark could potentially be discrediting to her as a "fit parent" in a custody issue. She was in a legally vulnerable position because: (1) three days out of seven Mark was cared for by a sitter; (2) the sitter was a minor, and there was no adult present during much of the time that she was with Mark; (3) there was a possibility that the sitter or other members of her family had had some illegal drug involvement when Mark was present in the home.

Recommendations

1. In view of Cathy's need to learn appropriate adult behaviors and her need for an in-depth emotional and supportive relationship, she should be encouraged to obtain therapeutic counseling in addition to the group therapy she engages in at the Substance Abuse Center.

   Counseling should focus on her denial of, and guilt surrounding, her son's condition and her ambivalence regarding her marital relationship.
2. Cathy should continue her involvement in the Substance Abuse Center's group therapy program and request a detoxification treatment plan if her drinking habits get out of control.
3. Cathy needs training to become a parent so that she can effectively manage a child with special needs. She needs to learn to manage temper tantrums. She needs to involve other care-givers and baby-sitters who work with Mark in this process.

Results of an Evaluation

Upon the completion of the evaluation process, each clinician prepares a written report that reflects his findings. These reports are circulated in advance of a staffing, where the evaluators meet to discuss their perceptions, impressions, and recommendations. From this staffing a consensus evolves regarding recommendations, plans for informing the family, and follow-up. The case coordinator prepares a written summary that includes findings and recommendations under three major headings: (1) health concerns, (2) educational-vocational concerns, and (3) psychosocial concerns. The case coordinator is expected to have a thorough understanding of the diagnosis, etiology, prognosis, and treatment program as agreed upon by the interdisciplinary team.

The case coordinator schedules time for the family informing and invites representatives from the community and/or the evaluation team if a need for their contributions seems indicated. Every attempt is made to conduct the family informing in an organized, unhurried, thoughtful manner. Several sessions may be scheduled for the informing process if required.

Family Informing

The purpose of a parent/family informing is to provide the persons concerned with a diagnostic picture of the child and to project a treatment program for him. It becomes the primary responsibility of the social worker to help the parents accept the diagnosis and to follow through on the recommendations for a program. A second responsibility for the social worker is to function as a liaison to the resources in the community on behalf of the client and his family, and this includes an interpretation of their unique needs.

There are no standard procedures to follow for informing parents about the developmental disabilities of their child. This must be a highly individualized experience that is managed by a person who is sensitive to the parents and their unique strengths and weaknesses. In the case of the profoundly retarded infant it is common for anomalies and disfigurements to be obvious to the most untutored observer. This situation demands an immediate informing by the attending physician. In those instances where retardation does not become apparent until later in the child's life, the informing may take place much later, with professionals other than the obstetrician or pediatrician sharing the diagnosis with the parents.

Parents' attitudes toward their child and their ultimate acceptance of the conditions of his life are dependent to a large degree upon the way they are treated when they first hear a professional assessment of the child's condition—his potential and his limitations. Therefore, careful consideration should be given to the time, place, and tone of informing. Parents told for the first time that "there is something wrong with your child" should hear this in a private place where they can manage the initial shock without intrusion. They should be given ample time. The parents need to be given such painful information in a sympathetic and truthful way, with an emphasis upon any positive factors that are present. They should have ample opportunity to ask questions, discuss the answers, and ask the same questions again and again. They need to receive ongoing, consistent support over an extended period of time from an empathic, informed person. Frequently other parents in similar situations help themselves as well when they reach out to provide support and comfort to the parents who are hearing distressing diagnostic statements for the first time.

Usually parents who participate in a comprehensive evaluation process with their child have some sense of the child's problem beforehand. These parents require the same kind of sensitive, honest exchange with any professional who is discussing the child's future growth and development. Parents have a right to expect professionals to know what they are talking about and to be able to express this information in understandable language. Professionals must avoid the use of jargon and acknowledge their own inadequacies and frustration about the lack of scientific knowledge and guaranteed remediation plans.

Parents are not to be viewed as "like all *other* parents of mentally retarded children." They resent professionals who do not honor their individuality and the individuality of their child. They wish to discuss the nature of their unique problem because they have a child who has his own individuality. Parents want to understand, accept, and act in the most loving, caring way for their child. They look to professionals to provide the resources that will enable this to happen without their developing defensiveness or guilt as a result of messages implied or stated by the professionals. Parents need to be helped to accept the fact that the condition is real and permanent.

Parents need to hear and discuss the diagnosis and prognosis of their child's condition in a situation where empathy is the style and professional jealousies are absent. Parents do not need to hear accusations and recriminations about other professionals who may have served them in the past.

Professionals involved in the parent informing need to be aware that the security and happiness of the client are at stake. Parents' strengths must be cultivated and the family members supported so that they can develop and maintain a meaningful life for themselves and the child who is retarded. In essence, if a professional really wishes to help the child, he will offer support to the family—and that support should start at the first family contact. Generally the informing session will emphasize the immediate concerns and needs of the client. Particular attention should be placed upon the impact that immediate training and stimulation can have upon the child's growth and development. The parents must be encouraged to accept the findings as baseline information to which future growth and development may be compared, thus setting the stage for reevaluation and revision of goals and plans for achieving them. During the informing session(s) the parents have the opportunity to read and discuss the case summary and other written reports. They learn how to use the reports in their demand for services from the community resources.

Impact upon Parents

Under optimal conditions, the family informing will result in the parents' taking the beginning steps to accept the problem and to move toward understanding the potential growth and development of their child. They become actively involved in learning new skills and techniques of child management that may prevent or eliminate conditions that could worsen the situation. They will reach out to use the available resources in the community. The social worker's role in such instances is to provide support to the family as they work to improve parenting; consider the rights and responsibilities of each family member in terms of the needs of the retarded child; modify home management to take into consideration unusual demands of the child with special needs; develop and maintain rest and recreation for each family member; utilize community resources; monitor and evaluate progress; and manage the inevitable crisis.

Under less than optimal conditions the parents will find it difficult or impossible to accept the statement that their child is retarded and will resent the professionals who dare to give them such unpleasant information. It is not uncommon for parents to seek other opinions, for it is difficult to accept the finality of retardation and its implications.

People have certain conscious and unconscious needs from the parenting process. A child is a unique, personal object of an adult's loving and caring. When a child is a biological descendant, he is an extension of the parent—a link to the future, to immortality. The child is an opportunity for the parent to realize his dreams of success, achievement, goodness, godliness and perfection, albeit vicariously. To parent a child is an opportunity for the adult to ensure his own importance, to satisfy his own need to be needed. Usually parenthood is anticipated as a joyous, fulfilling experience even though there is an awareness of increasing responsibility, problems, and stress. It is an experience that is anticipated with excitement, exhiliration, satisfaction with self, and a desire to shout from the housetops "Hey, look at me! I have a child who is better than I in every way!"

Parents experience deep shock when confronted with the pronouncement that their child is retarded. No one ever dreamed of having an imperfect baby, a less-than-improved extension of one's self. All fantasies about a joyous future with a loving and loved perfected replication of one's self are dashed against a brutal reality. The parenting process suddenly appears as a mountainous burden that must be endured in order to ensure the safety of a child who is from the beginning a disappointment, an insult to one's ego.

Feelings of shock may be accompanied by denial—the absolute refusal to accept the diagnosis as presented by the professionals. Parents may search for someone, anyone, to tell them the diagnosis of retardation is inaccurate. They may beseech the doctors and other professionals to prescribe a cure, to make it "go away." They may become very angry because of the unfairness of this occurrence in their lives and seek to place blame on someone, anyone, outside themselves—the doctor who attended at the birth or an unkind relative who criticized them. The anger may be turned toward an unjust God who treated them malevolently; it may be linked to a growing suspicion that a sinful life is the cause of their despair. Eventually the anger may become inwardly focused and manifested as depression. A certain period of depression is therapeutic, since it permits the parents to bind their wounds, become used to the situation, and begin to mobilize their psychic energies to accept the sadness and develop ways of coping with the situation that will help them regain self-reliance and self-respect. Extended depression, however, is cause for alarm—for the parent and the rest of the family.

The acceptance of the child's retardation may happen abruptly or over an extended period, the timing cannot be determined, for it is different in each case. Sometimes one parent will be able to accept the situation much sooner than the other, which may place an unusual strain on the relationship between the two. Some parents seem able to accept statements such as "Your child will learn slower than most children" or "The growth progress will be delayed for your child" without comprehending the implications of such statements. It is as though parents accept partial truths and, bit by bit, accept the totality of the awesome truth. For some parents total acceptance occurs only after several years of monitoring their child's growth and development against a baseline provided them by a professional diagnostician.

Some parents try very hard to accept the unpleasant truth and to manage the situation as they believe they are expected to by the church, relatives, neighbors, and even the other parent. Sometimes they try to maintain a personal style of "that's life" and deny their feelings of sadness and disappointment.

Parents may experience a loss of self-respect and self-confidence. They may feel vulnerable and out of control of their own lives because they are unable to reverse their child's retardation. They may be repulsed by their child, especially if the child is grossly deformed, and then feel guilty about their feelings. They may harbor concerns about their own normality. Some parents may consider the child evil. They may resent the handicap to the extent that they become bitter about the child's intrusion upon the family and the disruption of family plans and life goals. They may be envious of other families that appear intact and untroubled.

Resentment is a factor in parental feelings of guilt and shame. Parents dread the pity, ridicule, and loss of respect they anticipate will be a part of the responses their plight will elicit from the extended family, the neighbors, and others in the community. "What will *they* say?" Parents fear the isolation and stigma that may be attached to raising a retarded child. The more deeply religious the parents, the deeper their concern may be about deserved punishment for some evil, error, or sin in their personal past or in the partner's past. In either case, recriminations may be made which only exacerbate the turmoil of feelings.

Parents may have ambivalent feelings about their child and their involvement with him. They love the child as an extension of self and despise him for the manner in which he is an extension of self. Parents frequently harbor thoughts such as "Why did he have to live? Why couldn't he have died at birth? I wish he would die. I wish something would happen to us and it would all be resolved." Parents may speak of their despair over God, who gave them an imperfect child, even as they acknowledge His gift; "He sent us a special child to cherish for a very special reason."

Ambivalence may be expressed in many kinds of behavior. A parent may assume the role of the martyr: "I will live my life to make this child comfortable and happy." Other parents overtly reject the child by neglecting or abusing him. Parents who scream and yell at their children may be displacing their anger and frustration over their feelings of ambivalence and disappointment around their failure to "parent perfectly." Covert rejection may take the form of "put down" behaviors (i.e., criticism, humiliation, ridicule, and negative comparisons). Ambivalence may be expressed by expecting little or nothing from the child; thus the parents end up doing everything for him, for they are unable to see his strengths. Parents may have unrealistic expectations for their child so that he is set up to fail and thus may be "legitimately" punished or rejected. Rejection may be expressed by parents as they try to be completely separate and physically apart from the child. Frequently parents deny that they have any negative feelings because such feelings are inconsistent with their self-images as perfect parents—all loving, all accepting, all wise.

There seem to be some feelings unique to fathers. Frequently fathers express concern about the future for their children. "Who will take care of him when I die? Who will pay all the bills?" Fathers may express anger over the drastic changes they have made in terms of career goals and plans for personal achievements and rewards. They are frustrated that the problems around their children "never go away—never get resolved."

Mothers, on the other hand, may have concerns unique to their role. Sometimes women possess self-images that are based on their physicality, their good looks and stylish appearance. They believe that their relationship with their partners is contingent on how well they maintain their appearance. Such mothers find it threatening and difficult to have less time to spend taking care of themselves because of the need to nurture their children. To deny themselves this attention may result in their becoming reproachful toward themselves and frustrated with their children. It is usual in American society for mothers to assume responsibility for primary parenting—this means a never-ending impact upon those who have handicapped children, an impact that requires endurance and patience. Mothers are often dismayed by the absence of positive responses from their children. This causes them to feel even more inadequate as mothers. They may have feelings of diminished esteem for having given birth to such children in the first place. Not all women have an interest or personality style that prepares them for parenting under the best of circumstances, and children with retardation pose additional problems for such mothers. Some mothers become so engrossed in the care of their handicapped children that other family members are neglected, and this elicits negative responses.

As couples, parents must confront the issue of genetic counseling which will indicate whether or not they should have more children. Family routines and plans are disrupted, which may cause arguments and discord. The feelings and concerns of the siblings in the family add to the distress of the parents. Sometimes a parent will devote his or her life to the attention of the retarded child as a way of avoiding marital strife.

Despite all these problems, most parents do *not* continue to deny the retardation of their child, and many of them achieve a level of acceptance that ensures an optimal home and family experience.

As the years pass, the retarded child does not achieve or experience the growth steps of his age peers (i.e., participation in general education, preparation for a vocation, management of sexuality, separation from family, and establishment of an independent life-style.). Parents may experience a recurrence of pain as each plateau is approached and not achieved. They may suffer "chronic sorrow" throughout their lives. Some professionals suggest that this is non-neurotic behavior on the part of parents of profoundly retarded children (Olshandky, 1966).

As parents work through their feelings of sorrow, disappointment, despair, guilt, and anger they become increasingly aware of their child and his individuality. When they are first confronted with their child's retardation their lack of acceptance is indicated by their refusal to use the language of the condition, to even say the word "retarded"; by their need to seek magical cures; and by the wish to blame others. As parents become increasingly accepting of the reality of their child's retardation, they are able to say the word and understand all the limitations it implies. As acceptance and awareness develop, parents become more realistic about what they expect from treatment, and more receptive to guidance and support in the search for the most appropriate training and experiences for their child.

The following summary of a family experience over a six-year period will serve to document some of the reactions parents may have as they confront the unexpectedness of mental retardation.

The Coreys considered themselves a loving couple, whose five happy children between the ages of six and fifteen were bright and happy. They were surprised but not dismayed when they realized that Mrs. Corey was pregnant with a sixth child. Mrs. Corey suffered a high fever during the pregnancy but was not alarmed, for, as a deeply religious woman, she knew that "God would take care of things."

Suzie's birth was uneventful and the Coreys recall no expressed concern on the part of the staff at the hospital. After a few weeks, Mrs. Corey began to worry about Suzie, for she was not responding as the other children had, and she observed the infant's legs shaking on two occasions. Her husband comforted her with "You've just lost your touch—Suzie is O.K." However, when Suzie was several weeks old, she developed pneumonia and was hospitalized for two weeks. During this time she began to experience frequent and extended seizures, and the doctors told the parents that Suzie had a myclonic seizure disorder and was profoundly retarded. The parents were distraught. Mrs. Corey refused to discuss it and wept as the father shared the bleak news with the other children. She vowed that Suzie would not be like that forever, and "I'll never let *her* go to an institution." For several months the parents and children prayed and tried to comfort each other. Gradually, the family arrived at an uneasy acceptance of the situation.

The father recalled, six years later, how the children had reacted. Mark, six at the time, resented Suzie from the beginning—not because she was retarded, but because she received so much of Mrs. Corey's attention. As the youngest, he felt a loss of indulgence. Karen, ten when Suzie was born, initially promised to "love her anyway, for she can't help it," but over the years she resented the demands placed upon her for additional help around the house. Cynthia, two years older than Karen, was so preoccupied

with her adolescence that she had little pleasant interaction with her family about anything and frequently accused her parents of lack of understanding. When Suzie was
born, Darryl was fourteen. He was mortified that his parents had had a baby at their advanced ages (father thirty-nine and mother thirty-seven). He told his father he had not
realized people of their age still had sexual intercourse. He maintained a distant and
clumsy relationship with his parents through Suzie's early childhood. Tom, the oldest
child, was a great comfort to his father and evidenced much compassion for his
mother.

Mrs. Corey appeared to suffer the greatest impact because of Suzie's condition.
She rearranged the house and the family routine in order to spend all of her time and
energy on Suzie. A downstairs study was converted into a bedroom, which Mrs. Corey
shared with her daughter in order to meet her responsibility. Mrs. Corey rarely permitted anyone else to do anything for Suzie but expected all of the family members to do
household chores. She became sullen, withdrawn, and sloppy in her appearance, and
seldom talked with the family except to give orders about the chores. This situation persisted for six years until Mr. Corey finally convinced her to take Suzie for an appraisal.

At age seven, Suzie was becoming too heavy for her mother to lift. She was able to
walk once she was helped to a standing position, but she needed help in flexing her
knees to sit down. She was not toilet-trained, could not feed herself or dress herself. She
was able to drink from a cup. She had no language, and her only communicative response was to smile when she heard her father's voice.

During a session with the social worker, Mr. Corey and his wife talked with each
other in a way they had not experienced for years. He told her, "I know we have a problem with Suzie, but we could manage it if we only did it together." He went on to say to
her, "I am more concerned about *you*, for I love you and I miss you." His wife assured
him, "I love you, too," and then released a torrent of pent-up feelings, accompanied by
tears.

"I do absolutely everything for her, and she never even knows me. She only smiles
at him [the father]." "How could I have wished her dead? I have, many times, and I'm a
religious woman! I shall be terribly punished, as if I haven't been already." Her final
statement in the session revealed her anguish throughout the years: "You know why
God did this to us? Because I'm too sexy—I've always liked to make love with you, and
I always knew it was wrong."

Not all parents have as difficult an adjustment as the Coreys, but the
fact remains that many parents are severely tested when they face the handicapping conditions of their child's mental retardation. Fortunately for the
Coreys, they were able to meet with a social worker regularly for several
months. He was able to help them express their range of emotions about
Suzie and her condition, and also helped them to understand that their marriage was negatively affected by their habit of withholding honest feelings
from each other. The Coreys learned that nothing was to be gained by pretending to be strong and assuming a valiant posture for the partner's benefit, but that such behavior only intensified their alienation from each other.

They learned to accept the range of feelings they experienced and recognized that they could expect these feelings to last a long time. They acquired insight into the ways in which their feelings could be displaced and expressed inappropriately toward each other and all the children in the family including Suzie. The social worker helped the Coreys accept their vulnerability, anguish, and disappointment in order to help them become accepting and realistic parents to Suzie.

CHAPTER 5

Meeting the Needs of Parents

IN ORDER TO PROVIDE SUPPORT, guidance, and service to the mentally retarded the social worker frequently intervenes on *behalf* of the retarded client by working with parents and other professionals. This is always the service design when the client is profoundly retarded or very young. If the retarded individual is not classified as profoundly retarded, as he progresses through his teens into maturity he should become increasingly involved in planning for his own life, and therefore should become the recipient of *direct* social service. As the young adult assumes greater responsibility for himself the need for services to his family should be evaluated. Often the parents and family will need support in order to permit the retarded family member to achieve maximum independence and to gradually discontinue their efforts to function on his behalf, which can be counterproductive. Thus, as the mentally retarded individual assumes increasing responsibility for himself, services to the family should decrease in frequency and intensity until eventually they terminate.

Later chapters will address the issues to consider when providing direct service to the mentally retarded client. This chapter will focus on the services that parents of a mentally retarded child or young adult should expect from social work.

Necessary Competencies for Social Workers

In order to help parents and families, the social worker must be competent to provide counseling and willing to be available at times of crisis as well as for regularly scheduled contacts. The worker should have a broad knowledge of mental retardation and the service implications that are related to the condition. He should know how to gain access to and utilize specialized services as well as traditional community resources. He should have experience in direct service to the mentally retarded and be aware of the many techniques and methods used in their training and development. Finally, the social worker should have a commitment to the belief that every mentally retarded individual has a right to achieve his maximum potential in as near "normal" a situation as possible. Such a commitment assumes that the worker is free from steroptypic thinking about mental retardation and that positive attitudes about growth and development are basic to his practice. Even as the social worker negates stereotypic judgments in regard to mentally retarded individuals, so must he avoid thinking of parents in stereotypic terms.

The Goal of Social Work Intervention

The primary goal of social work intervention with parents and family of the mentally retarded is to help them face the problem and actively accept it by following through on recommendations designed to enhance their child's growth and development. In order to achieve this goal the social worker acts as the link between the family and the service system, providing feedback as to the success or failure of the recommended activities. The type of intervention that is utilized will be determined after several factors have been considered: source of referral, results of the diagnostic process (including diagnosis, prognosis, and recommendations), the particular functions of the agency to which the parents have been referred, availability of service outside of this agency, and the parents' readiness for service.

The family and the retarded child may be referred to the social worker by colleagues within the agency or system where he practices. For example, the pediatrician or family physician may refer the family to a social worker affiliated within the medical system, or the teacher may make a referral to the school social worker. Sometimes an agency social worker will be contacted by another community agency on behalf of a family. Frequently, public health nurses, recreation leaders, and vocational rehabilitation counselors will look to a family-focused agency to provide service to an identified family. Occasionally parents or other family members will request social work services for their child and themselves. The social worker must tentatively evaluate the level of the parents' understanding and acceptance of their child's retardation and determine whether they are seeking help for themselves in order to understand the situation better or require assistance in carrying out the recommendations made for their child by other professionals.

The worker must assess the service scope of his agency in terms of the needs presented by the family. He must be prepared to utilize other existing programs in the community to supplement the assistance he can offer. Finally, the worker must determine the parents' readiness to cooperate in addressing the needs of their child.

It may be decided that initial services to the family can best be provided by an interdisciplinary team because of the multiple concerns that need to be addressed, such as nursing care, physical therapy, nutrition counseling, and medication review and monitoring. In these instances the other disciplines will tend to focus their attention upon the individual who is retarded and will look to the social worker on the team to concentrate on the parents' concerns. It is generally accepted that the social worker brings the professional expertise required to relate to the impact one family member's retardation has upon the family as an entity and upon each individual family member. The social worker may decide to continue to make joint visits with the interdisciplinary team or to establish a routine of home or office visits more typical of a casework relationship. Group experiences for the parents may be indicated. The social worker may work with the parents, the siblings, and the retarded client simultaneously in some instances and separately in others. He may choose to work with the parents as a unit or as individuals. The method of intervention may shift and change over a period of time depending upon the stress in the situation at any given point. For some families it may be important to involve grandparents or other relatives.

Social work intervention does not necessarily begin with the birth of a retarded child, but is set in motion whenever the family, for whatever reason, comes to the attention of a clinician or an agency. For purposes of this chapter, the concerns of the family and possible social work interventions will be discussed in a developmental sequence.

Initial Contacts

During the initial contacts with the family the social worker must determine if there are circumstances present in the home that will complicate the family's attempts to provide a safe environment for a child who is retarded. For example, family problems such as alcohol or drug addiction, unemployment or underemployment, poor diet, inadequate housing, overcrowding, desertion, and separation are in themselves stress-producing and need attention. Such circumstances will be aggravated by the presence of a retarded child. The social worker must obtain information about each individual member of the family in order to determine whether there is a history of instability, irrationality, or psychotic behavior, for the presence of such dynamics may have a negative impact upon the family's perception of the child. Furthermore, the social worker must learn how the family has managed stressful circumstances in the past and to what extent they may have been resolved. The worker must accept the responsibility to provide support, guidance, counseling, therapy, or referral to assist the family in addressing any concern, issue, or problem existing in the home that, if left unresolved, would jeopardize the growth and development of the mentally retarded child. For example, in the case of Mark T. (described on page 46) there were many conditions present in his home before his birth (i.e., immaturity of parents, excessive drinking, unstable marriage) that, left unresolved, would have negative effects upon his chances to reach his maximum potential.

Sometimes concerns or problems in the family that were not previously apparent surface under the stressful situation of having a retarded family member. The mother of Suzie (described on page 55) had never confronted her ambivalence about her own sexuality until she experienced Suzie's retardation as punishment for her own enjoyment of sexual intercourse. The mother's concerns in this regard needed to be addressed in order to free her to provide adequate parenting for her daughter.

Once the worker has ruled out the presence of any unresolved conflict-laden dynamics or situations in the family, he should focus on the problems brought about by retardation. A worker must be sensitive to the grief and disappointment that the parents are experiencing and permit ample expression of feelings about their tragic situation. He must not lay down expectations and admonitions such as "You must accept it" or "It's time to stop crying over it," for such statements, though well intended, serve no purpose. Clients do not shut off sorrow and turn on acceptance as though it were a light switch. They must slowly and laboriously live through their pain, gradually become inured to it and perhaps, move to overcome it. Social workers should question whether it *is* an appropriate goal for family intervention to help parents "get over" grief. Perhaps the goal should be to help the parents develop coping skills and adaptive behaviors so that they begin to regain their self-esteem because they are managing a difficult situation.

To regain self-esteem and a feeling of personal worth may be a greater or lesser challenge for parents and family depending upon the neighborhood or community in which they live; the sociocultural norms that shape, modify, or otherwise influence their lives; and the family history of accomplishment and achievement. Sara Beth's parents (see page 33), successful professionals in a suburban community, appeared to have much more difficulty regaining their feelings of self-esteem than did Joseph's mother (see page 32), who had experienced a lifetime of alienation, poverty and need. Learning that Joseph had mental retardation did little to disturb her already tenuous hold on self-esteem. It could be conjectured that Sara Beth's birth had been planned and anticipated as a continuation of a family that was vigorous, healthy, bright, ambitious, and attractive. The introduction of

Sara Beth into such a family was experienced as an insult, a cruel act of fate. On the other hand, Joseph may have been "just another mouth to feed" in a family that was already too large for a crowded apartment and a limited income.

To whatever extent the parents can maintain or regain their feelings of pride and self-respect it will positively affect the attitudes they have toward their retarded child. The parents' attitudes and resulting behavior will foster similar expressions and actions from other family members. It is common for the unusual demands and needs of a retarded child to provoke parental anxieties. They should be reassured as to their ability to learn the necessary ways to cope with this new situation.

Relieving Stressful Situations

Assuming that the parents and other family members were considered healthy and stable prior to the birth of the retarded child, the social worker's interventions should be focused on relieving the stress of the situation. The worker should be prepared to support the family as they learn about the concrete, specific things they can do with and for the child and the measures they can take within the home to make it a safe, secure environment for him. The social worker should model acceptance of the child and give advice as to how to stabilize the family relationships. Some culturally deprived parents may need frequent, if not daily contacts in order to learn to manage their child in their home.

The Smiths, considered to be of borderline intelligence, lived in a rural village where Mr. Smith worked as a carpenter's helper and Mrs. Smith as a kitchen aide. They had two moderately retarded children, aged four and six. At the time the Smith children were identified as mentally retarded, a home assessment was made in addition to many client-focused clinical evaluations. It was determined that the Smiths maintained a clean home and provided simple, monotonous meals. It was apparent that the parents were loving and kind with their children and made a great effort to provide them with a safe home. The Smiths worked alternate shifts so that one of them was always home, for their one big worry was that "someone will take them away." The children were held and cuddled a great deal and often sat in a parent's lap for a meal. They were not toilet-trained because the parents did not wish to "make them." There were few toys in the home, which was sparsely furnished, although there was a large TV set which was always on.

The social worker and nutritionist initiated visits as a team in order to introduce early-intervention and stimulation strategies to the parents and to encourage an improved, balanced diet. The parents were eager, if slow, to learn. Both parents rearranged their work schedules in order to be home to meet with the professional team. Ultimately the nutritionist reduced the number of visits she made to the home, but the social worker was in touch with the family three times a week for several months during the time the children acquired some independence in self-care and were enrolled in special programs provided by the local school district.

As parents learn more about their child—his disability, his likes and dislikes, his strengths and weaknesses, his usual responses and behaviors—he becomes more of an individual for them. As parents learn to experience their child as an individual, it becomes easier to manage his behavior, to train him and to satisfy him. As they grow in their understanding of the child the parents begin to experience satisfaction and even pleasure in being *his* parents. Increased knowledge and use of preferred child-rearing techniques, stimulation, exercises, and communication serve to increase the parents' ability to manage the difficult challenges and crises that occur. As they develop knowledge and coping skills, their fear of the child in his situation begins to dissipate. As fear diminishes, the parents' self-confidence, self-worth, and self-respect are reestablished.

Parents need to learn about the numerous resources the community has to share and how to obtain services from them. Some agencies are prepared with special programs to help the family with a handicapped child. For example, some guidance clinics have established "respite" programs designed to provide the family with trained adult child-care workers to take care of the mentally retarded child for short periods of time so that parents can manage family emergencies, illnesses, or vacations. Some traditional service agencies help all kinds of families with programs such as day care, homemaker services, and health services that may be useful to the parents of the retarded child. It is not unusual for a generic agency to be hesitant to provide service, since the staff may feel unprepared to serve a family with a retarded member. This type of agency and/or staff needs consultation and training about mental retardation in order to serve the client and his family. Frequently the social worker working on behalf of the retarded client must reinforce the request for service from the agency with a willingness to provide consultation or training about mental retardation to the agency staff.

As the parents grow more comfortable with the use of services and resources outside the family, they should be supported in becoming more than recipients of service. They can learn to become participating, contributing members of a team that works together to meet the needs of a special child. The social worker may need to be an advocate for the parents' right to this role. Increasingly parents are demanding to be recognized by the professionals as knowledgeable about the retarded child in their own family. In response to being respected as the authority on the retarded child in their home, the parents are much more able to respect and utilize professional expertise based on practice with several children with similar concerns.

The Smith family needed assistance to become involved with the educational resources available to them. Although the staff was prepared to work with the two children in terms of their unique learning needs, they were not prepared for such dependent parents. The social worker was able to initiate a plan that enabled the parents and the educators to communicate by means of a very simple "log" of events.

Eventually Mrs. Smith visited the classroom once a week and proved to be an interested student of new child-rearing techniques. Mrs. Smith never did become a team member in that she rarely contributed to the planning for her children. However, she earned the respect of the entire school staff because of her desire and willingness to learn "for my babies."

The social worker assigned to the Smith family was respectful of the parents' efforts to provide a good home for their children and gave them constant reassurance and guidance to help them function more adequately in the immediate situation. The worker was successful in not imposing her own middle-class expectations upon the family, thus avoiding the feelings of confusion and alienation this would have engendered. She was able to provide the parents with the opportunity to learn and to demonstrate the new skills learned. Certainly the social worker was authoritative and appropriately so, for the parents needed direction from someone with her expertise and experience in child management and the special needs of mentally retarded children. In this particular instance the worker's knowledge replaced the usual resource for child-rearing hints: relatives. Through guidance, training, modeling, and advocacy the worker was able to reassure the Smiths that they were competent as parents in the day-to-day routine of child rearing. She was able to assure them that support services would be available to them on into time as they faced new challenges and decisions.

Ineffective child rearing is not limited to disadvantaged families. Affluent parents often need guidance too. Sometimes enlightened, educated parents work so hard to accept the mental retardation of their child that they do just that—they accept a classification, a label, without recognizing the individual who has the disability. Such "acceptance" often is reflected by statements like "He can't help it, at least he can be happy." Frequently it is the pattern in such homes to provide for the child to do "for" him and to deny him the opportunity to try, to risk, to fail, and to achieve.

Of all the self-care skills, independent toileting is the behavior that parents and teachers agree should be a goal for all individuals regardless of the level of retardation. There are many reasons for this to be a high priority. The older a child becomes, the more objectionable it is for others to provide this personal bodily attention. Learning to toilet independently and privately is a basic achievement that must precede the individual's further sexual development, such as the ability to learn to masturbate in private.

Lawrence W. came to the appraisal clinic at age sixteen. He was the oldest of several children born to a professional couple. Since the family was financially secure, the decision had been made at Lawrence's birth that he would always live at home. The parents had never had any outside appraisal service since learning that their son was profoundly retarded. Down through the years they had retained a succession of nurse-maid-companions. Recently the length of stay for each one had progressively become shorter in spite of the good wages. The teenage siblings were beginning to date and objected to Lawrence's presence.

Lawrence was five feet, five inches tall. He could ambulate and spoon-feed himself but had no language. He was not toilet-trained and wore disposable diapers. One nurse-maid-companion had some success in training Lawrence to use a pot for bowel movements, but recent workers in the home did not follow through with this. Lawrence spent a great amount of time fondling his genitals with his hand stuck inside his trousers and diapers.

The parents had passively accepted Lawrence's condition, provided for him, and attempted to ignore his bizarre behavior. They took pride in the fact that he had never been institutionalized and had always been a tolerated member of the family. They were very distressed by the way the other children treated him but did admit that his continuous and overt mastrubation was offensive to them as well. With many misgivings and much distrust, Lawrence's parents permitted him to go to a residential training center where in a relatively short time, he accomplished toilet training. With the achievement of independent private toileting Lawrence began to be less overt with his masturbation. He returned to his home, where his parents agreed to continue to encourage and reward his independent toileting skills and to ensure his continued opportunity to learn new skills at home. At the insistence of the authorities, Lawrence was enrolled in an educational program.

As incomprehensible as it seemed to Lawrence's parents, they had been guilty of child neglect. The affluent home complete with nursemaid-companion had served to infantilize him. He had been treated kindly while he was being fed, bathed, and diapered. Yet he had been neglected, for he had not been enrolled in an educational program, where he would have been urged to learn as much as possible. This type of child neglect is far too common and is difficult to detect. Relatives and neighbors heap praise on parents who wait upon the retarded child "hand and foot." Rarely do casual observers recognize the harm done to an individual who is denied the right to learn, make mistakes, to take risks. When the social worker detects infantilization he has a responsibility to the retarded family member to confront the parents and help them acquire more growth-producing behaviors.

Physical abuse and neglect are more obvious to the casual observer and the professional alike. There is no doubt as to the action to be taken. The parents need to be confronted with their actions and the governmental department responsible for protecting children must be informed. Depending upon the severity of the situation, the child may be removed from his parents' custody permanently or temporarily, or may remain in his family home with constant monitoring to prevent a recurrence. Child abuse and/or neglect occurs in a situation fraught with anxiety, frustration, anger, and unresolved conflict. The possibility of mistreatment increases when problems related to poverty are present, and frequently the most dependent child becomes a target. Therefore, a social worker must be alert to signs of abuse such as unexplained cuts and bruises and timid, even frightened behavior. A more blatant example of abuse is presented here.

Shirley, age eighteen, was the first child born to an inner-city street-walker. During her infancy Shirley lived with her mother and several of her mother's friends. When Shirley was three and a half years old, her mother was jailed for a period of time and Shirley was placed in an institution with the diagnosis "severe retardation due to undetermined causes." Shirley lived in the institution until age fifteen. During that time she acquired good self-care skills and was perceived as attractive, well-groomed, and interested in her appearance. She was a well-mannered, docile, obedient girl who rarely asserted herself or demonstrated any negative feelings. Her speech was unintelligible, although she understood approximately two-hundred words. "Put the dish on the table" was a task she could complete; "Fill the dish with cookies and put it on the table" was a bewildering request for her. During the years Shirley lived in the institution her mother maintained contact with her, and at age fifteen Shirley returned to the inner city to live with her mother and the mother's boyfriend/pimp.

Shirley was provided a daily training program by a local developmental center. Very quickly she learned to use the city bus (several stops) to get to the daily program. However, this accomplishment in addition to her excellent grooming seemed to exhaust her abilities. She was unable to recognize her name, write, count, identify colors, or perform the simplest pre-vocational task (such as sorting objects by shape and color). However, she thoroughly enjoyed washing dishes and ironing (both tasks she had learned in the institution).

At the developmental center Shirley reestablished friendship with Louis, a man a few years older than she, whom she had known in the institution. He had more streetwise skills than Shirley, and he began to accompany her to many activities in the community, including visits to his sister's apartment. Eventually they became involved sexually. Shirley seemed to have a loving relationship with her mother but appeared frightened of the mother's male companion.

The following excerpts from the case log describe the relationship between mother and daughter.

Shirley continues to come to the program dressed exceedingly well in the latest style. She is very proud of her appearance and likes her clothes. Her mother is cooperative about the few demands for money the center places upon them. She is not displeased about Shirley's relationship with Louis, but rather sees her need for sexual expression as normal, and she has taken the initiative to have Shirley use birth-control pills. Shirley seems to be making a good adjustment.

[Six months later] Shirley's behavior has worsened. She is frequently moody, sullen, and uncooperative, and on one occasion had an unexplained outburst of violence. She is not as regular in attendance. When a contact was made with Shirley's mother, she said Shirley had not been feeling well and she had kept her at home. There had been no medical attention.

[A few weeks later] Shirley arrived at the center badly bruised, as though she had been beaten about her face. Her mother was called and came in immediately. She explained that Shirley had been punished by the pimp. The mother reported that Shirley had been working the streets with her and that everything had been ok until the pimp had pushed Shirley to have sex with him and she had refused. The mother was at a loss as to what to do. The man had been living in the apartment and protecting them for a lengthy period of time. The mother indicated that she had no other way to earn her living and that Shirley needed to "help out."

Attempts on the part of the social worker and other staff members to help Shirley and her mother consider other alternatives such as a group home placement were unsuccessful. The mother took the position that *her* mother had been a prostitute, she was a prostitute, and Shirley could do the same. She declared that the girl's retardation did not interfere with her earning money, and that as her mother she would make sure that Shirley did not become pregnant, for she did not want the risk of another retarded child. At the time, Shirley had reached adulthood and there was no indication from her that she wanted any change in the situation as long as the pimp left her alone. The mother agreed to protect Shirley from the man. Gradually Shirley's attendance at the center decreased and then it stopped altogether; the family moved and contact with Shirley and her mother was cut off. Attempts to locate Shirley were futile.

This is not an unusual situation. Clients who are returned to the inner city from an institution are frequently lost in the process. Shirley's level of functioning as a severely impaired woman made her especially vulnerable to exploitation. Since she was attractive she would not lack for companionship, and her docile well-mannered, obedient pattern of responding made her an easy target. The exploitation was no less cruel because it was imposed upon her by a mother who herself knew few other choices for survival. In fact, the irony was that the mother believed herself to be a responsible parent in that she was helping her daughter to support herself and monitoring her so that she would bring no more children with retardation into the world.

Admittedly, the social worker and other staff members of the center reflected a middle-class orientation and may have been ill-prepared to serve Shirley and her mother in the reality of their life experience.

Sometimes stressful conditions etiological to neglect and abuse are eased in the home by providing training, as with the Smith family (see page 62). In other instances a stressful condition can be relieved for the family by confronting the parents and advocating for service, as in the case of Lawrence. The most extreme action taken to resolve stress in the family is to remove a child from the home. Such was the intervention implemented in the case of the twins Donald and David (see page 39).

Donald and David's parents were at wit's end by the time the boys were five years old. They reported that they had been devastated when the boys were born but not completely surprised. Although the pregnancy and birth had been uneventful, the parents were aware of other family members who had mental retardation or emotional disorders. The parents had decided to take the children home and keep them there as long as possible. They reported that they had used the services of the visiting nurse, pediatrician, and helpful relatives during the five years.

The parents had a son, Jason, four years older than the twins. During the twins' early infancy Jason had learned to be cautious and caring around his brothers, but as the years passed he began to be resentful of them. He was having trouble in school and was unable to maintain relationships with his school or neighborhood acquaintances. The family described a life-style and home routine that were chaotic, noisy, and stressful for everybody. However, the mother carried the greatest burden of responsibility for the twins and had little opportunity to be away from them and their demands.

It was the consensus of the evaluators who worked with the twins that the family would benefit as much as the twins from an institutional placement of unspecified duration. Such an experience could provide objective training/treatment for Donald and David not available in their home. The evaluators conjectured that the parents' marriage, as well as Jason's school experience, was endangered by the stressful situation.

The social work interventions were focused upon maintaining and supporting the twins' family even as the necessary procedures were followed to gain their admittance to an institutional program. The social worker consulted with the parents about scheduling and routinizing the family activities in order to ensure each of the twins stimulation activities from each of the parents; to provide Jason with time for sharing with his parents individually and together, but separate from the twins; to provide the mother with time away from the home to develop some interests of her own; and to provide the parents, as a couple, with time out of the home by themselves and, on occasion, with Jason. The parents were given the opportunity to join other parents with similar concerns in a counseling group, where they were encouraged to work through their feelings of anger and frustration about the twins and to begin to develop the positive aspects of their relationship.

In the process of implementing an institutional placement for the twins the social worker encouraged Jason's participation in the family's decision making. As a family they visited the institution and participated in each step of the admitting procedure. After the placement was accomplished, a social worker functioned as a liaison between the institution and the family to ensure continuing family involvement. The following excerpts are from log entries made thirteen months and eighteen months, respectively, after the twins' commitment.

Unfortunately, they were both in quarantine at the time of my visit so that I could only observe them through the window. I was surprised that they both came to the window showing interest in my presence. They watched me carefully, establishing eye contact. Their hair had grown to a fashionable length and they both appeared less apprehensive than they had on earlier visits. The staff reported that they relate fairly well with each other and with others. David is apparently trying to talk and will follow directions. The parents visit frequently and apparently hope to have the twins back in their home. Meanwhile they are enjoying the time with each other and their son Jason.

[5 months later] Plans are pending to transfer David to a multiply handicapped diagnostic classroom in the school district near his home. He will be placed in a foster home. The foster mother is also an aide in the diagnostic classroom. Similar plans have been implemented for Donald, and he now is enrolled in a special program and lives in a foster home a few blocks from his family home.

Some parents realize that their child has a limited life expectancy. They may need to be supported as they accept the prospect of their child's ultimate death. The parents may be confused about their feelings at such a time, for they may simultaneously experience relief and genuine sorrow.

Parents must be helped to attend to the medical and ego needs of the child even though his death is imminent. All patterns of communication (i.e., holding, stroking, lulling, rocking, and talking) should be maintained even though responses are minimal. Parents should be encouraged to explore their feelings and reactions about the death of their child for themselves as individuals and as a couple. They should be encouraged to discuss the child's death with other family members.

Frequently professionals providing early intervention services to profoundly retarded children become involved with the family as they experience the ending of the child's life.

Mrs. Carpenter brought her profoundly retarded daughter, Sara, to weekly sessions for parents and infants. Sara was ten months old at the first session they attended, and she accompanied her mother until her death at eighteen months of age.

Initially Mrs. Carpenter was skeptical about the contributions professionals could make to alleviate her situation. She was filled with anger toward the medical staff who had attended Sara's birth and believed that Sara's difficulties were the result of poor medical attention. Mrs. Carpenter had become a martyr in her attempts to meet Sara's needs and had become neglectful of her four-year-old son, Sammy. Sammy accompanied his mother to the sessions and soon became a favorite of the other parents and staff. Mrs. Carpenter appreciated the exercise techniques she learned from the physical therapist and soon began to use them at home with Sara.

Sara was not an attractive child, and her body was not enhanced by the tube in her stomach that was necessary for her feeding. Nevertheless, the interdisciplinary team fondled, cuddled, rocked, and talked to Sara even as they did the other infants. Mrs. Carpenter was comforted by this acceptance of her child and began to trust the workers. She had several sessions with the social worker on the team to discuss the impact that Sara's condition had upon her, her marriage, and her interactions with Sammy. Eventually Mrs. Carpenter enrolled Sammy in a nursery program and arranged to spend more time with him.

Sara had been an unresponsive baby from the beginning and she made few gains. She had experienced several bouts with upper-respiratory infections and it became apparent that she had a short time to live. After a very difficult hospitalization that included great efforts to sustain Sara's life, Mrs. Carpenter decided that Sara would not be subjected to another similiar experience. Thus, with the support of the physician and the early intervention team, Mrs. Carpenter sustained Sara at home with her family for the last few days of her life. Mrs. Carpenter was comforted by bathing, cuddling, and soothing her dying child.

Shortly after Sara's death Mrs. Carpenter returned to the center to thank the staff for their support during a difficult time. She brought with her a sum of money that her husband's friends had gathered in honor of Sara and presented it to the center. Mrs. Carpenter told how much her husband's attitude had changed from suspicion to respect as he observed the benefits the early intervention sessions had brought to his family.

Ensuring Family Stability

Once the parents have established a daily routine that includes stimulation, language, and self-care training for the mentally retarded child, other issues should receive attention in order to ensure a stable home environment.

Throughout all of the parenting years each parent should learn to attend to himself in the ways he needs to maintain his own mental, emotional, and physical well-being. Parents should be encouraged to continue personal interests, hobbies, vacations, and educational and social activities. As a couple they must continue to provide for the "together time" they need to maintain a stable marital experience. Parents need to be supported in their efforts to maintain themselves and their marriage as a healthy, loving, interesting, comforting, and pleasurable experience, for the child nurtured within such a situation will have a greater opportunity for optimal development. The need to be nurtured by secure parenting figures is of special importance for the retarded child. As the parents learn to maintain a schedule that considers their needs and the needs and preferences of each of the other family members, the retarded child will find his place in the family. His place will ensure him respect, consideration, attention, and love, but will not put him in the position of ruling and directing a household because of unusual, unrealistic demands. Maintaining their own routines, activities, and interests is one of the acts of loving and acceptance a family can give the retarded member. To do otherwise is to contribute to the development of a tyrant who will become a target of resentment and a scapegoat for the family.

If the parents are exhausted from months or years of care for the retarded child or just want a vacation, it is helpful for the social worker to arrange for a "respite" experience. Respite services may take several forms. A child-care worker may come into the family home for a period of time to relieve the parents. A preferred arrangement is for the child to spend a few days or weeks in another home or an institution. This arrangement provides maximum rest for the parent and the opportunity for a growth-producing change for the child. If the respite service is provided by an agency or institution that also conducts an appraisal service, the benefits to the family can be twofold. Often a respite experience places different demands for growth upon the child, which help him learn new adaptive or coping behaviors. These new behaviors may enhance his participation as a family member upon his return home. The child's absence from the home permits the parents to renew their energies and modify their plans for him. Thus Lawrence (see page 64) achieved independent toileting skills while away from home for a short time. His parents modified their plans for him as well as their behavior toward him, for they enrolled him in school and agreed to learn new interventions to use at home.

Periodically, parents and other family members who are with the retarded child regularly should assess and evaluate the patterns of interactions that develop within the household. The social worker should assist the family in identifying any behaviors that have developed that are unhealthy for the family as a unit. Overinvolvement with, or overindulgence of the retarded child by any family member should be identified and redirected, for such behaviors stunt the growth and development of both participants in the interaction. Excessive parenting should be noted and circumvented, for it tends to stifle the retarded child in his effort to take risks—to grow.

As the years go on, emotional and value conflicts that are not related to the presence of a retarded child may develop around any family member. In these instances the family should receive the same social work interventions that would be available if there were no problems with retardation.

In the case of Suzie (see page 55), her mother had become involved with her to the point that Suzie received care from no one else, and the mother had little energy or time to spend with her husband and other children. Suzie had acquired few skills and was becoming increasingly burdensome and physically difficult to manage. Suzie's lack of progress was a concern to her father, but he was even more concerned about his wife's health and well-being and their emotional alienation from each other. As is indicated in the report, the mother's overinvolvement with Suzie may have been prompted by her guilt about her "gut" feelings of resentment toward the child. Some of the mother's feelings about her own sexuality had surfaced, and she was experiencing Suzie's presence as her punishment for enjoying her sexual relationship with her husband.

Suzie's parents were in need of counseling in order to deal with some of the issues that were putting a strain on their marriage. The unhealthy relationship between Suzie and her mother needed to change in order for both of them to grow. Suzie needed opportunities to develop certain self-care skills within her range of achievement potential, and her mother needed to reestablish herself as a wife and as a mother to her other children.

It is recognized that the continuous, unrelenting responsibility for a *very* dependent retarded family member will provoke crises down through the years. The parents and family should be assured of social work service on a regular basis and at times of crises.

Managing the Child's Behavior

Social workers must be prepared to model for, instruct, guide, and support the parents as they develop and sustain the attributes needed to work effectively with a retarded child. The ability to be patient and to permit the child to repeat and practice, repeat and practice must be learned, for it is through this laborious routine that the retarded child will achieve the ability to perform certain life-sustaining behaviors for himself. Parents should be encouraged by the social worker to discuss their child's progress with the various educators and clinicians, and in consultation with these professionals to determine the goals for their child. The social worker should function, if needed, as a liaison between the school or clinic and the parents in order to interpret the professional recommendations; to model for, teach, and monitor the parents as they strive to follow the recommendations; and to provide consultation to the family as they introduce these recommendations into a schedule that takes into consideration the needs of all family members. Frequently the social worker will need to interpret the family situation to the educators and clinicians so that realistic recommendations are made to the family. Little is accomplished if recommendations are so comprehensive that the result is an overburdened parent who is not able to meet other equally important demands.

Six-year-old John needed speech therapy, which could be provided three times a week by a clinic in the northwest part of the city. Physical therapy was available at a hospital in the central city. John's mother was notified by the appraisal clinic of scheduled appointments. A six-week follow-up revealed that John had received no service. During a home call certain conditions became apparent. John's family lived in public housing some distance from the speech clinic and the hospital. John's father worked days and needed the family car to get to work. To get to either treatment site involved two or three buses (and hence transfers and periods of waiting) for John, his mother, and two other children, who were preschoolers. The family could not afford a cab.

In the case cited, John's mother was not uncooperative, but rather a timid woman who did not realize that she could assertively seek the additional consideration she needed in order to implement John's treatment plan.

Sometimes social workers, nutritionists, or public health nurses can be of service to parents by providing tips to improve home management through the introduction of schedules and routines that affect nutrition, health habits, cleanliness, and household organization. The use of prosthetic devices or unusual equipment designed for the mentally retarded child may be introduced and monitored by the social worker.

Social workers share responsibilities with other disciplines to ensure early intervention and stimulation of the mentally retarded infant and preschooler. In later years the worker should encourage recreational experiences for the growing child to enhance his school and home life. Parents may seek the worker's advice in the selection of toys and equipment that are appropriate for solo play.

Parents may wish to discuss procedures to provide maximum stimulation for an inactive, passive child. They may need to be encouraged, prompted, and reinforced in the use of speech, stroking, and touching with the child who appears unresponsive. They may need to learn techniques for spoon-feeding a child who has difficulty swallowing or simple body-movement games to exercise an otherwise inactive child. They may need to be encouraged to move the quiescent, passive child from one location in the house to another—from bed in the bedroom to couch in the living room to a support chair in the kitchen in order to provide the child with a sense of the rhythm of the day in his home.

As the child matures, the parents may seek advice and support as they deal with his or her emerging sexuality. Masturbation and menstruation are typical of the topics parents may need to discuss in order to learn how to guide and train their child toward socially acceptable behaviors.

Parents may need to learn how to manage negative behaviors the child exhibits that are upsetting to them. Behaviors such as thumb sucking, stubbornness, head banging, rocking, extreme perseverance in any other action can become annoying and cause tension in the family. Parents need to be helped to understand that such behaviors are usually the result of the child's feeling insecure about his environment and that they should be ignored even as energy is directed toward making the child's situation more secure. Social workers should teach and support parents as they learn to ignore tantrum behavior and reinforce acceptable bids for attention.

Parents should be encouraged to utilize any programming or training the school will provide them. The child should have an opportunity to interact with a special educator in his own home or, preferably, the local school setting, so that he can experience learning new skills from a person who is trained to teach retarded children. Perhaps of greater importance, the child should have the opportunity to interact with as many different individuals as possible so that he can learn to be separated from his parents and take another step in the process of maturation. Finally, the parents will appreciate the respite they can experience when their child is in the care of other responsible adults.

The school social worker should assist the parents in building a cooperative relationship with the classroom teacher and aides that will prove beneficial for the child. Techniques of training that are introduced in school must be consistently followed at home, and particular skills or behaviors unique to a family situation should be respected and perpetuated in the classroom. If necessary, the social worker may provide the liaison service to enable this mutual support to exist. The school social worker will cooperate with the educators, psychologists, therapists, and support staff as they plan with the parents for the educational experience of the retarded child. Occasionally, the school social worker will attend such meetings as an advocate for the parents and to provide support to them as they present a point of view that may be in opposition to the recommendations prepared by the school staff.

Concerns of the Siblings

Brothers and sisters share with their parents the concerns and conflicts that are a part of the retarded sibling's impact upon the family. They worry about how to tell their friends, and whether the information will make a difference in their interaction with peers. They struggle to accept and wish to discuss the situation with the parents as full family participants, not as protected children who are provided half-truths. Usually they wish to share in the care of the retarded child, but not to the extent that this interferes with their own lives. The siblings seek guidance as to how to set and maintain limits in order to protect themselves from manipulation and exploitation by parents as well as the retarded child. Adolescent and adult siblings frequently will express concerns about having a retarded child themselves and may seek genetic counseling. Older siblings may have concerns regarding parental expectations in terms of future care and financial support of the retarded child.

Emotional concerns may develop for the brothers and sisters as a result of the parents' attitudes and behaviors toward the retarded sibling. They may resent the disproportionate amount of attention the retarded sibling receives. Parents may put pressure on them to achieve to make up for the deficiencies of the retarded child. For example, in the family situation involving Donald and David (see page 39), their brother, Jason, was negatively affected by the twins' excessive demands upon their parents. Initially Jason had attempted to model his parents' behavior of consideration and kindness, but eventually he became resentful because he experienced minimal parenting for himself.

To the extent possible, siblings should be encouraged to join their parents in all sessions—consultative, educational, or therapeutic—that focus upon stabilizing the family milieu for the mentally retarded child.

The foster mother was impressed the day an entire family arrived at her home to check it out for appropriateness for a thirteen-year-old family member. The brother and two sisters were as concerned for their brother as the parents for their son. Down through the years, Andrew's brother and sister have maintained an interest in him comparable to that of his parents.

Another example of sibling concern reflects the complications that are brought into problem solving when the family is scattered over a large part of the country.

A man in his mid-thirties requested a consultation because he was concerned about his twenty-two-year-old sister, a moderately retarded twin, who lived with her elderly parents in an Eastern city. Her twin and three other sibs were high achievers and high earners who lived in other parts of the country. The siblings worried about their sister and were anxious to have her provided for, as none of them wished to invite her to live with them. The man informed the social worker that his sister had been carefully isolated from other retarded people, for his parents had difficulty in acknowledging her disability. Consequently, she was ill-prepared for a future without them. He stated that he had heard of group homes in his Midwestern city and was curious about whether there were similar placements in his parents' locale. He wanted to discuss the best way to convince his parents to help his sister make a life adjustment while they were still able and well.

Frequently the siblings are anxious to ensure the retarded person's future security, for they realize that such a burden could put their personal plans in jeopardy.

Sexuality

Most parents find it difficult to discuss sex or sexuality with any of their children, so it is especially trying to face such a discussion with a retarded son or daughter. In many cases parents prefer to deny the sexual interests or needs of the retarded child until the issue is unavoidable—usually because of some overt behavior or incident that is objectionable to the family. Most parents hope and pray that their children will not be the victims of "sexploitation" but do little to protect them from such experiences other than provide them with a list of don'ts: e.g., "Don't talk to strangers" or "Don't get into anyone's car."

Some parents arrange secretly to have their daughters sterilized or put on birth-control pills.

A physician and his daughter came to the agency to request counseling about the future placement of his daughter. He was approaching retirement and he wanted to know that his mildly retarded thirty-eight-year-old daughter would be comfortable. During the interview, the physician asked to speak to the social worker alone and subsequently revealed that no one had to worry about her getting pregnant because he had persuaded a friend to perform a hysterectomy on his daughter when she was twelve years old. He was glad that he had done this, for there had been occasions when his daughter had been discovered having sexual intercourse in the recreational center. He stated that he had taught her nothing because she could not understand.

The father had succeeded in protecting his daughter from unwanted pregnancy, but unfortunately *not* from exploitation or inappropriate sexual expression. He had denied a mildly retarded woman factual information to replace the street knowledge she had picked up from poorly informed peers and/or experience.

Obviously, a social worker should have no part in such a violation of personal rights. It must be the responsibility of the worker to understand, interpret, and support the laws of the state where the client resides.

Sterilization is becoming the method of choice for many American men and women and should be an option for the mentally retarded as well. However, the mentally retarded person must be protected from involuntary sterilization. Many factors could cause a retarded individual and his or her family to consider sterilization: desire to avoid pregnancy, inability to care for a child, and/or inability to use other forms of birth control.

Whatever the reason for considering sterilization, the persons involved in the decision should carefully consider their assumptions and feelings. Sometimes family members need to be reminded that mentally retarded individuals grow and develop throughout their entire lives and may achieve competencies as adults that will counterindicate the decision of sterilization. Many states have procedures designed to protect individuals from unwanted sterilizations. Frequently court action is required before a person may be sterilized. The court will make a decision in the best interest of the mentally retarded person, using in its deliberations reports prepared by a physician, a psychologist, and a social worker. Regulations and procedures differ from state to state. Thus the practitioner must assume the responsibility for obtaining information as to current statutes in the state where the client resides.

A social worker also has the responsibility to encourage the parents to approach the issue of sexuality as a positive learning experience. Parents must be encouraged to consider sexuality in terms of the rights, privileges, and responsibilities of being a man or a woman, a boy or a girl. They must be helped to recognize the need for their children to learn how to interact with others in a responsible manner. It should be pointed out that every individual has the right to know about himself, his body and its functions. The retarded child or adult has the right to learn about how his body will develop and change and how it is different from, or similar to, that of other individuals. The parents have the responsibility to interpret to their child the social-sexual expectations of their family and community in the most concrete and specific terms. Retarded adults need to learn the "street language," even if it is unacceptable in the home, since knowing the language is necessary for self-protection. A person needs to know how to say "no" to unwanted overtures, and he must learn this in contrast to knowing when to say "yes." Parents need to recognize that withholding such knowledge is no protection for their children, but makes them even more vulnerable.

As the social worker attempts to change parents' attitudes, he should suggest materials and methods to provide this valuable learning experience for their children. Guidelines for sex education programs are available for the use of parents and educators (Gordon, 1976), as well as a pamphlet, *Ten Heavy Facts*, designed to appeal to adolescents (Gordon, 1971). The concerns of sexual relationships and birth control for the mentally retarded have been addressed by prominent sex educators (Kempton, Bass, and Gordon, 1973; Gordon, 1976). Parents should become familiar with the sex education provided in the school or training center. If necessary, parents should urge the staff of such agencies to develop a curriculum, for children and young adults should have the opportunity to learn and discuss sexual issues with their peers as well as in the family setting.

I have been a director of a project called "Training and Technical Assistance in Human Fulfillment for Developmentally Disabled Persons," designed to develop the awareness, knowledge, and skill of parents, care-givers, and professionals so that they can deal more realistically with the issue of sexuality and the retarded individual. Under this project, hundreds of parents have been provided with the opportunity to meet with others to address this issue. Parents are encouraged to consider sexuality and its expression as a sign of normalcy in their children. They are urged to accept the idea that every individual should have the opportunity to develop responsibility for his own behaviors—those he initiates as well as those he permits. Parents are given an opportunity to participate in problem-solving exercises in order to prepare them to deal with behaviors such as masturbation and curiosity about the opposite sex as they occur without shock, fear, or embarrassment. Ten videotapes have been produced by the project to promote acceptance of the sexuality of the mentally retarded by parents and professionals. They are described in the Appendix.

Parents and professionals from every walk of life have concerns, apprehensions, and misinformation about human sexuality—their own and that of others. Frequently they have heard myths about the sexual interest and behavior of the mentally retarded—e.g., the retarded are "oversexed" or "undersexed" or "impotent" or "aggressive." The fact is that the whole range of sexual interest and expression is present in the mentally retarded population just as it is in the general population. Parents need to learn that sexual desires and curiosities are normal for everyone, including the retarded child. The individual with retardation can learn socially acceptable ways to handle his sexual interest. Not teaching him does *not* protect him, but rather sets him up to learn from trial and error or from unsuitable models.

Social workers should encourage parents to consider the need for early education about sexual concerns. The social worker should model for the parents the regular and frequent use of the words for *all* parts of the body. Why do all the body-part identification games that parents play with children omit the genitalia? Children should be permitted the privacy of toileting and bathing as a prelude to the privacy of masturbation.

Most parents and professionals are committed to the idea of providing as "normalized" a life as possible for the retarded. Intrinsic to a "normalized" life-style is the right to be sexually expressive—alone or with a partner of choice who is willingly involved. Yes, there are limitations. Yes, there are rules about privacy and mutual consent between participants. But there can be no denying the right of the mentally retarded to sexual knowledge and expression.

Separation Needs and Placement Options

Sooner or later, parents of a retarded person must permit the individual to move into a life separate from the family. For some children the profound nature of their retardation indicates a placement out of home in order to ensure a twenty-four-hour-a-day monitored, medically supervised regimen. Other children, because of gross behavioral complications, may need to be placed in an institutional setting for treatment and training. Most children, however, should be able to live with their families until they reach adulthood, and at that time should be encouraged to leave home to take up a life of their own with people of their own age and interest as part of the "normal" life experience.

Parents and siblings should be engaged in anticipatory planning with and for the mentally retarded individual. The family situation, the age of the retarded person, and the immediacy of the need for placement will determine at what point a social worker should be involved in this process.

Parents have the responsibility for placing their child into any type of residential setting. Professionals may recommend the child's removal from his home in order to ensure maximum opportunities for him. However, only in instances of neglect or abuse may the professional *insist* upon the child's removal and subsequent placement in another residential setting. In the event of conflict between parents and professionals, the court is called upon to render a decision.

The social worker must be available to the parents as they plan for their child. Parents need to be aware of the choices available. They need to participate with the social worker in an assessment of their child's progress. An objective reevaluation by an interdisciplinary team is needed to determine the current status of the child's mental, physical, and emotional health. Such a process should provide information as to the prognosis for the child: the expected level of maturation, achievement, and/or social accomplishment. The parents need to be provided with a complete schedule of the interventions that will be required in order to assist the child in achieving his potential. The family must participate in a candid assessment of themselves and their capacity to provide the type of interventions required. Support services available from private and public agencies must be evaluated in terms of accessibility to the individual and his family. In every instance parents should be encouraged to maintain the child in their home until he is an adult if they are able to provide the interventions necessary for his growth and development *and* also maintain a stable home environment for each of the other family members. The care of the retarded person should not be at the expense of another family member's mental, physical, or emotional health.

As the social worker assesses the family situation in regard to placing the young child outside the home, there are certain questions he should be prepared to answer for his colleagues who are involved in the placement process:

Are there circumstances present in the home that will impede the provision of good care to the retarded family member?

Are there circumstances such as terminal illness, mental illness, desertion, separation, divorce, or abandonment to be considered?

Is there evidence of hardship present in the family (e.g., underemployment, or a large number of dependent children)?

Is there evidence of improper, inadequate care for the child?

Is there reason to believe that the child is in danger of injury or abuse?

To support a child's placement away from his family is an action that must be approached with deliberation and caution. All factors must be considered and the various alternatives thoroughly explored, so that the individual and his family will act in the best interest of each person concerned. Once the parents' request for placement is received, the admitting agency will determine eligibility. A case conference attended by staff from the admitting agency and the placement agency is conducted. The client's needs and the agency's ability to meet these needs are discussed. An admitting plan is prepared, and all interested parties (including parents) review the document and agree to its content. Once this process is complete the client is considered admitted for placement and may be put on a waiting list for an available space. If the waiting period is lengthy, any participant in the admitting process may request a case review as the placement date approaches.

Perhaps conflict is faced by the parents who *must* institutionalize their child. There is a high expectancy that the profoundly retarded child will live in a setting other than his home as he approaches adolescence and adulthood. However, many families find it impossible to cope with the increasing demands of the twenty-four-hour care demanded by the profoundly retarded infant. Few families are financially able to provide this care within the home setting, and so most must look to the community and/or the state to assist them in the responsibility. A social worker must be prepared to discuss institutional programs with the parents of the mentally retarded.

While it is true that the profoundly retarded individual is more likely to be institutionalized for a long period of time, parents should not assume that the institutional placement is necessarily for the individual's lifetime. Only those individuals who are grossly dependent on professional and semiprofessional care will remain in such a placement. The intent of the institution is to provide an intensive training program designed to help the individual achieve as many self-help skills as possible. No longer are institutions expected to provide perpetual care.

Parents need to become familiar with the residential alternatives available to their retarded child. The institution has long been recognized as a place of last resort for the mentally retarded individual. Historically, institutions have provided custodial care and minimal training in rural settings. This image of the institution is no longer accurate. Under optimal conditions, the modern institution has the staff and the commitment to use the newest and most innovative methodology on behalf of the residents. Everything in the modern institution is designed to promote remediation and management of the complexities of mental retardation. Institutions are utilized as training sites for professionals from diverse disciplines. Mutually beneficial relationships have been established between institutions and universities or learning centers. An institution can be the most adequate setting available to a retarded individual in terms of physical plant, equipment, and professional staff. Such a setting is capable of providing remediation and training to the mentally retarded individual that will prepare him to rejoin his family or live in some other small-group setting. It permits the competencies of several professionals from diverse backgrounds to be focused upon the treatment of an individual with greater intensity and consistency than would be possible if these resources were not concentrated in one physical site.

On the other hand, the size of the institution and the regimen required in such a setting may result in an experience for the individual that appears to lack personal warmth and caring. Institutions are frequently criticized for the impersonal and regimented manner in which staff relate to the residents, who are frequently viewed as patients. Parents are aware that this type of experience can be detrimental to a child who has lived in a less structured home. They may question whether such an environment is a good choice, for they do not perceive it as a nurturing milieu in which the child can grow and develop as a social being with positive attitudes about himself. Frequently parents resent the research and experimental techniques employed in an institution and worry that their retarded child will be treated like a "guinea pig." Yet they believe they must give permission for experimentation to occur in order to obtain the institution's services. Since institutions are dependent upon governmental funding, the parents may worry about the possibility of budget cuts and the resulting curtailment of staff and services. Parents may wish to discuss the possibility of their child being abused by staff members or other residents.

Parents need to weigh the advantage of the intensive training provided by the institution against the disadvantage of an impersonal milieu in which the child must live. An important consideration for most parents will be that as residents and taxpayers in a state, they are entitled to service for their child at minimal expense. Whatever the parents' decision about the institution, the admittance of their child into the program will be subject to his eligibility (on the basis of level of functioning) and the existence of a vacancy.

Some parents may wish to consider placing their child in a private institution as an alternative to a state-supported one. Usually such facilities are smaller and there is more opportunity to provide an individualized experience. Frequently the private institution is partially supported by a religious denomination, and the tuition may be subsidized. Parents may appreciate the atmosphere of a facility maintained by a church-related program. Admittance to such an institution is easier to achieve, and the family in stress may choose the private setting as an immediate solution to a crisis situation. But not all states have such facilities, and frequently the location of the residence serves to limit parental visits to see the child. It is not uncommon for such institutions to operate on a "make them happy" philosophy, so infantilization is apt to occur.

There are additional residential alternatives for the parents to consider within the community itself. Foster-care homes, group homes, and residential treatment centers are placement possibilities that deserve attention.

Such facilities come under the general heading of community placement and have certain characteristics in common. Small residences that are located throughout the community are supervised and monitored by private or social agencies. The number of residents is limited (depending upon the type of facility and level of functioning of residents), and the emphasis is on a family-style atmosphere. Such community facilities are dissimiliar from the institutions in that they are not self-contained, but rely upon community resources for all supplementary services (e.g., clinical, educational, and recreational). The emphasis on small groups in homelike settings using community resources tends to support the implementation of a "normal" life-style for each individual.

Foster-care homes provide the greatest intimacy and exposure to family life. A single parent or a married couple take training and are subsequently licensed to provide a residential placement within their own home. The home is checked to assure its safety and adequacy in terms of structure, room arrangement, and equipment. Usually it is located in a neighborhood where there are no other such homes in close proximity. The number of children placed in such a home depends upon the skill of the foster parent, the size and makeup of the household, and the level of functioning of the foster children. There may be one to three foster children placed in such a home at any time. The advantages to this kind of setting are that in such a situation of intimacy a child can be raised by a parenting person who is able to be objective and realistic about his strengths and weaknesses. The child's progress is monitored more frequently and objectively than if he were living with his biological parents. Biological parents are encouraged to visit their child in his foster home and to take him to the family home for short visits. Some parents, however, have difficulty accepting the idea of a foster home for their child, for they experience it as an indication of their ineffectiveness.

Group homes may be located in any neighborhood in a community. Three to twenty-four individuals may live there, depending upon the level of functioning of the residents. The workers in the home are perceived as staff, even though they may live in the house. As employees, they provide a certain degree of intimacy and warmth but do not assume parental roles. There is a relatively high degree of staff turnover in group homes, which disrupts the continuity and consistency of the programs. Sometimes, in order to control the expression of sexuality in a coed group home, residents are encouraged to consider themselves as brothers and sisters. This is perceived by some parents as an advantage, whereas other parents do not support this idea, for they do not see it as preparation for adult life.

Residential treatment centers are the largest of the community placement facilities—sometimes accommodating as many as one hundred individuals who require a high degree of care. All staff members work scheduled hours, and none of them live in the center. Although community resources are used, clients are frequently taken as a group to use them; for example, a busload of clients may attend the Shriners' circus. Efforts are made to simulate a home by the use of single or double bedrooms and family-style dining and recreational areas. Parents often experience such a residential center as very similar to any one building on the campus of the nearby state institution. Often the individual who meets the criteria for placement in a residential treatment center is so dependent that there is minimal contact for him out in the community, even though the building is community-based. Many parents question the advantages of this kind of placement.

Community placement (i.e., foster homes, group homes, or residential treatment centers) is now considered an alternative to institutional placement. Parents may expect the same kind of guidance and financial support from governmental agencies in the maintenance of their child in such a placement arranged under their authority. There are some opportunities for private placement into community placement settings in which parents assume the entire financial responsibility, but this is not usual.

Social workers should encourage, assist, and support parents in their efforts to accept and implement the placement of their grown child in a "normalized" environment—an environment that provides for privacy and a sense of personal dignity, as well as the opportunity to live with peers. The smaller the setting, the more intimate the atmosphere and the more "normalized" the life experience can be.

The following vignette describes a typical dilemma.

George H. is thirty-two years old and lives with his elderly mother. When George was young, the family decided against a placement outside of the home and moved to a rural section where George could grow up healthy and inconspicuous. The family had few social contacts and George had minimal exposure to any educational or training program. Shortly after his retirement, George's father committed suicide, and George, then age twenty-six, discovered his body. Little is known of George's feelings or behaviors at that time. Partly because of her loneliness and partly out of concern about the future, the mother belatedly permitted her son to participate in an adult activity program, and she began to go out in the community more frequently. She reluctantly let George take job training, but gave him little support as he learned such skills as how to cross the street, use the phone, and recognize coins. She adamantly refused to consider George's move to a group home to live with other retarded people who worked in a sheltered workshop, even though George very much wanted to do this. George was not permitted to use the phone, watch TV, go to the movies, or date because his mother believed such activities would get him into trouble. She refused to discuss future plans for herself or George. She could not recognize that her own advancing years and increasing physical frailty and vulnerability were reasons to permit George more independence and freedom—at least the use of the phone.

George and his mother were locked in an unsolvable situation. He did not feel up to defying his mother, for he was very dependent on her. She was not able to release him to go and live his life, for she was just as dependent on him. Her entire life had been spent trying to protect George and keep him inconspicuous. She would have no reason to live if he began to move into a more normalized life-style.

Other families have reacted in a very different way: they have helped their young adults find their own way and make their own friends. They have worked to maintain casual, comfortable, supportive relationships that permitted the adult with retardation the maximum opportunity to continue to develop, even as they weaned themselves from a mutual dependency that would ultimately need to end because of their death.

Future Planning

Most parents care about their children and want to be actively involved in planning for and ensuring a safe, secure, happy, and fulfilled life for them as they reach their adulthood. Parents worry about the financial arrangements that must be made to guarantee a life of dignity and opportunity for the mentally retarded adult. The social worker must be prepared to counsel, guide, and model for the parents as they are involved in future planning with and for their children.

The parents need to be informed of the benefits available to their young adults from the Social Security Administration in the form of Supplemental Security Income (SSI). SSI is financial assistance in the form of a monthly income that is available to the aged, blind, or handicapped who have little or no resources. All mentally retarded individuals eighteen or older should be assisted in applying for these benefits. Mentally retarded individuals under age eighteen and living with parents who have a low income may also qualify for SSI benefits. Adequate income is provided to cover room, board, and supervision for the mentally retarded living in a licensed foster-care facility or group home. If personal care is required, this is covered as well. Limited funds are also available for personal needs—e.g., clothing, incidental grooming products, recreational costs. Any recipient of SSI is automatically qualified to receive Medicaid, which is a joint federal and state program that provides essential medical services.

Parents need to be informed about the eligibility requirements for SSI. The SSI recipient cannot have financial resources in excess of $1,500. Financial resources include cash in the bank, money held by others for the recipient, stocks, bonds, and real estate. In addition, there are rigid limits upon the earned or unearned income that a recipient may claim. Any substantial monies earned or received from annuities, pensions, insurance, interest, or gifts will result in reduction of the SSI allocation. In the event of the parent's disability, retirement, or death, the mentally retarded person may be eligible for Social Security Benefits (SSB) as well.

It is important for parents to be aware of these guidelines, for they will have a bearing upon their decisions as they consider bequeathing properties or large sums of money to a dependent adult. Any large inheritance could cause the mentally retarded person to lose his SSI benefits.

Parents, regardless of their age or the age of the child, should be encouraged to prepare a will as a way of protecting the retarded individual as well as the other members of the family. Frequently parents have the opinion that their financial assets are so limited that a will is unnecessary. The worker should help them recognize that the ownership of a home is sufficient reason to write a will. Parents need to be told that in the event of a death without a will, properties will be arbitrarily divided among the heirs, according to the regulations of the state, without any consideration that one of the heirs may be a retarded adult who is totally incapable of managing funds. If the mentally retarded individual is in an institution when the parent dies without a will, the state is in a position to assess the estate for his care, thus imposing a possible hardship on other family members. Parents need to be informed that the laws governing intestacy (lack of legal declaration of property disposition at time of death) cannot be modified to consider the mentally retarded heir, and that it is incumbent upon them to make adequate provisions for each of their heirs in advance of their deaths.

Some parents may wish to consider appointing a testamentary guardian for their mentally retarded child. A testamentary guardian is named in the will as a person who is prepared to assume responsibility for a minor upon the death of both parents. Such guardianship is nullified when the minor reaches his or her majority (eighteen in some states, older in others). If the parents have been legally appointed guardians of an adult son or daughter who is mentally retarded, they may name a testamentary guardian for this child. Usually this request will be honored by the court in the absence of a challenge from other interested persons, or until an evaluation of the retarded person may be completed.

As parents consider planning for the future security of the retarded son or daughter, they may wish to petition the court for guardianship of the individual as he or she becomes an adult. The social worker should be prepared to discuss the many aspects of guardianship with the parents.

Guardianship is a legally recognized relationship between a competent adult and a minor child or handicapped adult, referred to as a ward. The guardian is appointed by the probate court in response to a petition from a parent, friend, relative, client advocate, or agency staff member. To support the petition the court requires evaluative material about the ward's mental, physical, social, and educational needs, and his ability to care for himself and to make decisions on his own behalf. The court may decide that guardianship is not necessary, is necessary under certain conditions, or is necessary without any conditions.

The court may decide that the ward needs a guardian for his estate, someone to manage his property. In such a case, the guardian takes possession of all or some of the ward's property and is responsible for its management. Frequently such guardianship is provided by an attorney or a staff member from a banking institution. With such an arrangement, the ward is able to make all decisions except those having to do with large expenditures of money.

The court may decide that the ward needs a guardian for his person. Under these circumstances an individual is appointed to supervise the ward's personal needs by making sure that he has adequate housing, supervision, education, recreation, and other growth opportunities. There is no financial responsibility implied or assumed.

The court may decide that the ward requires a plenary guardian of person and estate, which means that the ward is viewed as totally incompetent to care for himself or his property. Plenary guardianship has serious and far-reaching implications, for it means that the ward can make no decisions on his own behalf and must always have the consent of the guardian. For example, a ward under such a guardianship may not enter into a contractual relationship such as obtaining insurance, a driver's license, or a marriage license. He may not consent to or prevent surgery upon his own person, spend money, change his residence, travel, change his educational, vocational, or recreational plans, or bring court actions. The fact that the ward may never initiate a court action will prevent him from initiating a reversal of the plenary guardianship. Obviously the court is extremely cautious about appointing plenary guardianship and such appointments are made only in cases of extreme incompetence or profound retardation.

The option to appoint a partial guardianship permits the development of a highly individualized plan which is less harsh and restrictive than some of the other possible arrangements we have discussed. The court decides in which areas the individual is incapable of self-care and decision making because of his disability and gives the responsibility for those areas of incompetence to the guardian. Partial guardianship provides for as much freedom of choice and responsibility as possible. This type of guardianship is more apt to focus on the maturational needs of the ward rather than the convenience of other family members.

The social worker must help the parents realize that not all mentally retarded adults need to have guardians. They must be helped to recognize the impact such an infantilizing arrangement may have upon the adult who is struggling to achieve a life-style that is as "normal" as possible. Parents should be helped to recognize that for many adults with retardation the interest, support, and advocacy provided them by friends, relatives, and agency staff will be sufficient to underpin their existence in the community as adults, and the appointment of a guardian may be unnecessary if not counterproductive.

The social worker is in a position to help the mentally retarded adolescent or adult demonstrate to his parents his readiness and willingness to be involved in planning for his own future. The retarded adult is very often able to take responsibility for developing his own security by his active participation in planning for his education, vocation, living arrangements, and social and recreational activities as well as learning to manage his income and attend to his health needs.

Parents need to understand that their legal status as parents of a retarded child is no different from the legal status of parents of the nonretarded child. When a person reaches the legal age of majority, as defined by the state of residence, legal guardianship is terminated regardless of the level of functioning or competency of the individual. In other words, parents are *not* automatically guardians to an adult who has retardation, although many parents believe otherwise.

Yes, there are times when guardianship is indicated, and in those instances legal counsel should be obtained. However, in most instances the move toward guardianship should be considered carefully, for every responsibility or right given to a guardian is a responsibility or right taken away from the retarded individual. Removing rights and responsibilities from an individual is an effective deterrent to his achievement of maximum maturity and independence. It should be noted that guardianship orders may be dismissed or modified by petition to the court.

The laws governing the appointment of a guardian vary from state to state. Thus, it should be the responsibility of the social worker to become familiar with the unique situation in the state where a client resides. It is important for the social worker to be aware of the diverse resources available to the mentally retarded adult to utilize in his efforts to achieve independent functioning under the least restrictive conditions. Many chapters of NARC (the National Association of Retarded Citizens) have developed legal services to assist retarded adults as well as their families. The social worker may need to be prepared to advocate for the retarded adult within the family system as well as in the larger community.

Individualizing the Parents

Usually the parents' first contact with the social worker will follow the traditional pattern of an initial contact with an agency with a service request. The parents initiate contact because they identify an immediate need, problem, or crisis. They may have been referred and thus may have more or less anxiety as they approach the new worker, depending upon earlier experiences. They may be meeting a social worker for the first time in their lives and be unprepared or unfamiliar with what to expect. As in any casework situation, the social worker remembers to "start where the client is" and asks the parents to give their reasons for initiating the service. It becomes the worker's responsibility to gently support the parents as they provide as much information as possible in order to clearly describe their perceptions of the situation or crisis in which they find themselves. The worker must respond by indicating his or her ability, given the restrictions of the agency or clinical setting, to address the parents' concerns and under what conditions.

If the case is inappropriate for service the worker must not drop the parents, as it were, but rather make an effort to direct them to the proper resource and support their efforts to use that resource. A caution is in order though; frequently parents will steer themselves to the proper agency and worker but then state reasons that will force them to be rejected. Many parents find it extremely difficult to acknowledge the "real" reason they are seeking help. A description of an initial contact made by an elderly mother with the social worker in an activities center will serve to clarify this point.

At the time Marie (see page 35) started to use the activity center, her mother asked to see the social worker for urgent reasons. She told the worker that she was very concerned about her husband, who had just retired, for he had nothing to do. He was always around the house and was getting on her nerves. She indicated that her marriage had been shaky for years and that she was unsure about her future, for she was old, ill, and totally dependent on him. She reported that he had always been a good provider and money was no worry, but "now I'm not too sure."

When the worker pressed the mother for details about Marie's place in the family, she blurted out her heartbreak of years of responsibility for Marie with no emotional assistance from the father. She explained that her husband had experienced Marie's existence as an insult and had told her that either Marie or he would leave the home. The mother could not permit him to leave, since she needed his help to provide for the other children. The father agreed to pick up all the expenses of caring for Marie with the understanding that he would never see her. Thus Marie had spent most of her life in private schools, visiting her mother only when the father was absent from the house. The other children had little to do with Marie and were not cooperative with their mother in respect to anything that had to do with their retarded sister. Now that the father was retired and was home all the time, the mother could not have Marie come to the home, and this posed problems. For several weeks she had met Marie's bus and taken her to a neighborhood restaurant to visit. Marie had enjoyed eating out but could not understand why she could not go home. The mother expressed her regrets. "I should have left him years ago. Now I can't. He doesn't love me; Marie does, and we don't have any money without him."

During two sessions the worker was able to help the mother accept the limits of the agency services available, to focus upon Marie and her needs. The mother accepted service under those terms, and the sessions began to focus on considering the different ways the mother-daughter relationship could be maintained without further complicating the mother's situation at home.

The social worker realized that the mother-daughter relationship would be affected by any decisions in the family concerning the marital relationship and retirement plans. The worker assisted the mother in initiating and maintaining a relationship with a denominational family-service agency, where the focus of the casework sessions was the mother's problems as the wife of a retiree.

This vignette provides an example of the evasive manner some individuals must use in order to seek assistance. Initially Marie's mother was not prepared to discuss her feelings of despair about her daughter, but wanted to focus on a topic that she found more acceptable.

Sometimes the social worker's initial contact with the parents takes place when he informs them that their child is retarded. Sometimes a team of clinicians is involved in the informing process. In either event, the social worker must assume responsibility for providing the parents with several sessions over a short period of time in order to give the support needed by most parents at that time. Parents should have ample opportunity to express their anger, despair, and frustration. This is not the time for a structured session full of client-focused facts and interventions, but rather a time to understand what the parents are feeling and permit them to feel it without passing judgment or expressing dismay. It is important to be honest in all statements or answers to questions. It is *not* necessary at this time to call the parents' attention to all the difficulties and challenges that may be ahead. The social worker is not omnipotent or omniscient, and it is well to acknowledge this at the onset. There are some things in life for which we have *no* explanation, and it is human to acknowledge this. The relationship between parents and social worker will only be enhanced by such candor. For many parents the comfort and understanding they need in order to handle their despair will be provided by family and close friends, but they may need support as they reach out to this natural healing source. The social worker must realize that parents need to go through a period of ventilation of feelings in order to gain release from the internal pressures—in order to arrive at the stage of mobilizing their psychic energy to begin to understand, accept, and manage the situation.

Any concrete service the social worker is able to provide the family at this time will accomplish two objectives: first, it will relieve some part of a stressful situation, and second, it will demonstrate the availability and value of social work intervention. As time passes and the parent–social worker relationship becomes established, there will be a need to clarify the problem: the diagnosis of the child's condition and the implications for the child. Discussion of the problem, situation, or diagnosis at this later period will serve to prepare the parents to make discriminating decisions and establish priorities for the actions they must take. As the parents gain control of the decision-making process on behalf of their child, they begin to acquire stability based upon their discovery of their own coping skills. Gradually the parents will ask for more facts about the cause of their child's disability and methods of managing it.

During the process of casework treatment with parents, they gradually raise the following issues: the cause of retardation (or the acceptance of no known cause); implications of the diagnosis—what to expect; confusion as to parenting skills and fear of their inability to meet the unique needs of the retarded child; lack of understanding of the treatment recommended for the child; available resources in the community. Social workers may need to be assertive in introducing the discussion of future pregnancies and the need for genetic counseling if there is any likelihood that the retardation is genetically caused.

For some parents, a therapeutic process may be indicated. Unresolved conflicts may surface for them at the birth of a retarded child and should be treated accordingly. The therapeutic process for these parents should proceed as in any other situation, with the birth of the child viewed as the event that brought to light a conflict that would have needed attention in any case.

Parents should not be treated as patients or "sick" people who need to feel guilty about the birth of their child; rather, they should be approached as adults who face a difficult, stressful challenge. It is true that during the lifetime of a retarded child a situation or crisis might develop that would be appropriately treated by therapy or counseling for the parents, but the contention is that a situation or crisis could arise in the lifetime of any child that would prompt such an intervention.

One could ask the question "How often do professionals expect parents to experience guilt because of their own guilt feelings?" That question could be followed by another: "To what extent have institutions been developed and maintained through the years because of the expression of guilt on the part of the parents and professionals alike?"

It has been my experience that the need for therapeutic interventions for the parents is almost without exception based on unresolved conflicts that *preceded* the birth of the child and surfaced at that time. Most of the parents with whom I have worked are not neurotic individuals, but persons in deep sorrow over an extremely distressing situation. In recent years the literature has supported this point of view (Olshansky, 1966).

There is no particular therapeutic or counseling style that should be used with parents in need of intervention. The therapist should make the decision about appropriate approaches on the basis of his ability and the parents' style of communicating. The therapeutic position or style is of little consequence if the therapist has negative feelings about mental retardation or lacks understanding of the condition and its impact upon the child's future growth and development and ultimate adaptation to society.

If the purpose of the agency is to serve the mentally retarded, that must be the *primary* focus for all interventions of every clinician, including the social worker. If the parents' problems are very deeply rooted and will presumably demand a great deal of time, it is appropriate to refer them to an agency equipped to provide long-term individual or family therapy. A case concerning a middle-aged retarded man and his father will illustrate this point of view. It is included in some detail, for it describes interventions with both members of the family.

Harold, a thirty-five-year-old man with mild retardation, initially came to the attention of the social worker in a vocational training project for mentally retarded adults. Casework services were requested because of the maladaptive behaviors he exhibited in the workshop program. Harold was having difficulties at home, where he was constantly quarreling and physically fighting with his father, age sixty-two. Frequently Harold was in trouble with the police and the neighbors for his inappropriate activities, such as standing in the middle of the freeway attempting to direct traffic, walking around private homes, and disturbing customers in local stores, bars, and restaurants.

Harold had many skills. He could read a newspaper, write, manage money, carry on a conversation, use public transportation, and completely take care of his own needs. He had successfully performed janitorial jobs in numerous settings but had lost them because of his socially unacceptable behaviors. Frequently he made inappropriate sexual overtures to men and women, and he had exposed himself to teenagers on two occasions.

Harold had lived all his life at home and attended special classes in the local school until he was sixteen. He was especially attached to his mother, who had died when he was thirty-three. He had an agreeable relationship with his father and older brother until his mother's death. The older brother did not live in Harold's home but in a nearby community. Harold, even though mildly retarded, had presented no problem to his family until his mother's death, when his behavior began to deteriorate.

It appeared that for more than thirty years Harold had been accepted by his family, the neighborhood, and the community. Harold's father reported that his wife had been the mainstay of the family and had kept the other family members in good shape. When she died the father and his sons were at a loss as to how to manage, and the situation in the home worsened until Harold and his father reached the stage of screaming and fighting with each other. The father was overwhelmed by his grief over his wife and could think of no alternative for Harold other than to have him put away. Harold screamed his resistance to being institutionalized and kept insisting that his father needed help to sort out his thoughts. The social worker initially involved with both Harold and his father succeeded in referring the father to an agency that could provide services to him as a senior citizen.

There were several factors to consider: the need for partial guardianship for Harold in order to help him wisely use the fund his parents had arranged for him subsequent to their deaths; the need to protect Harold from unnecessary medication or institutionalization as his father's answer to the situation; the need to protect the father from Harold's physical abuse and verbal harassment; the need to provide housing for both Harold and his father where each of them could receive help in meal preparation and taking care of their clothes; the need for the father to deal with his feelings of bereavement.

As indicated, two different social agencies collaborated to provide service to the family. This was not an easy task. Harold was able to sustain a relationship with the social worker assigned to him. On the other hand, his father was clever in the way he sabotaged relationships and attempted to forestall any resolution to the situation other than to have his son committed to an institution.

The situation came to a head when Harold accepted an invitation to take a job in a community-based, church-sponsored group home for aging and developmentally disabled church members in another state. Harold assumed some responsibility for janitorial work in exchange for his board and room. These arrangements, in addition to the small income entrusted to him, under the supervision of a partial guardian (whom he selected), served to place Harold in a situation where he was in control of his life. The final contact before the case was closed revealed that Harold had made an excellent adjustment to his new situation. The father continued in counseling in his own community, where he tried to accept his wife's death and his ambivalence about Harold's new situation.

Social work interventions with Harold extended over a period of eighteen months. Frequently there were daily phone contacts. He needed a great deal of support from the social worker in order to learn to make a decision and to act upon it. The worker wisely provided some tangible assistance once decisions had been made, helping Harold shop for new clothes and pack his belongings and providing the transportation to the new home six hundred miles away. For a few weeks following the move, the social worker was available to Harold as he adjusted to his new life-style.

The worker encouraged Harold to take responsibility for his own actions, his own decisions, and his own life planning. He made himself available in an intense, consistent manner while Harold practiced his new behaviors.

Apparently, while Harold's mother was alive he had been treated with benevolent acceptance—hence infantilized and not encouraged to assume responsibility. At her death a crisis came to the family. No family member recognized Harold's strengths and capabilities to function on his own behalf. Fortunately Harold had a skillful advocate at the time he needed him. In a later chapter casework with mentally retarded clients will be discussed in greater detail.

In summary, casework with parents should be time-limited and directly related to the reltionship of the parents to the mentally retarded child. Parents must not be permitted to develop a dependency upon the social worker or the agency. A collaborative relationship must be established between the parents and the social worker or agency that has as its focus the attainment of maximal growth and development by the retarded person. There may be several periods during the life of the retarded individual when the parents will need and request additional series of regularly scheduled contacts with the social worker. Each of these series of contacts should be time-limited.

Parents should not be permitted to develop a lifelong dependency upon a worker, an agency, or a system.

Group Work with Parents

One way to develop a collaborative relationship with parents that is free of dependency upon the social worker is to encourage them to join a group with parents who have similar concerns. Parents may choose a group for many different reasons (e.g., companionship, empathy, social involvement, education, training, or counseling). The social worker should place parents into a group experience after careful consideration of many factors: age, style of communication, sociocultural and economic background, age of the retarded child, level of the child's dysfunction, availability and convenience of the group's location and time of meeting, current attitudinal level of the parents (aggressive, dependent, anxious), and their commitment to participation. The social worker should explain the purposes of the group as an opportunity for parents to gain insights into their own situation, develop an understanding of the child and his needs, make friends with other parents with whom they can mutually share, and learn specific techniques of child management.

Parents should be placed initially in a group (no more than sixteen members) that addresses situational concerns. Some of these concerns are: normal patterns of growth and development; variations of these patterns as manifested in the children; stimulation and early intervention or training; behavior management; family management; impact of a retarded child upon siblings; future needs and plans; legal issues; sexuality; placement alternatives; and evaluation of agency services.

In the process of group meetings many topics will be introduced and discarded. This is viewed as healthy, for even though a group may reject a certain topic at a given time, the fact that it was introduced serves to implant an idea or introduce an attitude. Frequently parents of young children will reject the topic of sexuality as being of no interest to them, but as they become aware that parents of older children are confronting the issue they begin to accept the sexual needs of their children.

In early group sessions the worker should deemphasize the need for parents to address their own needs for personality change and support meetings that not only deal with specific issues but provide ample time for the participants to interact with each other informally. This gives the worker an opportunity to assess the parents' strengths, weaknesses, behavioral styles, and preferred relationships within the group. Over time this becomes valuable information, especially if the decision is later made to provide a more intense group experience. Frequently it will become apparent that there is a need for a fathers' group or a siblings' group. Consideration should be given to scheduling simultaneous group meetings in order to encourage the participation of all family members. Some parents' groups arrange to meet while their retarded children are in a program activity at the same location.

During the early session the social worker should be responsible for introducing and reinforcing norms for group behavior. This is not to be perceived as a formalized statement of "do's and don'ts," but rather as an informal presentation of ways that most people find helpful in making the group experience productive and worthwhile for each participant. Parents need to hear it stated that everyone is entitled to his own attitude or opinion, and that each person will be respected for believing and thinking as he does to the extent that he respects every other person's right to have his own attitude or opinion. It should be stated that everyone is in the group to learn and to contribute to other people's learning as well; therefore, it is expected that everyone will listen carefully as well as share.

The worker needs to be sensitive to the dynamics present in the group. He should avoid becoming the "answer man" or "instant bank of information." Rather he permits the group ample time to share information, experiences, and ideas as long as the discussion remains goal-directed. Sometimes the group will need to be quiet in order to process some particularly difficult information, and the worker should be slow to intrude upon this time. One way to break into such a silence may be to acknowledge the reaction of the group and to ask if there is anything more that needs to be said or done. It is important for the worker to remember that the parents will benefit as they begin to experience the power of the group and their contribution to that power. To be a part of such power is dignifying to the participant and contributes to his self-respect.

It is usual that some members of an educationally oriented group (fourteen to sixteen members) may be better served, or additionally served by having an experience with a smaller group (eight to ten members) in which they can focus upon exploring their feelings, attitudes, and behaviors with and about their retarded children. Once again, the group should be formed with utmost care to ensure a worthwhile experience for each member. If the group leader identifies parents who are willing to explore psychodynamics that are not related to their retarded children, a referral should be made to a more appropriate clinic or agency.

Here is a description of an evolutionary group process:

A random group of parents (mostly mothers) met in a small city once a month with a school social worker to receive information about activities and opportunities available to their children. Initially the meetings were informative, with the social worker making announcements, distributing materials and answering questions about school policy. After several months the parents asked for the opportunity to discuss lifelong planning. The school social worker arranged for another social worker with a broader orientation to serve the group. Three sessions were held to move the parents through a process of recognition of issues related to future planning for *every* family member, the unique complications of planning for/with mentally retarded family members, resources available to them, and areas of lack of service. The process helped the parents recognize the importance of interventions they could initiate immediately in their families in order to start the life-planning process. Three additional sessions were designed to help the parents learn new ways of home/child management that were ego-building for every family member. At this point the parents requested sessions for the families as units to continue to learn how to be positively involved with and on behalf of the child with retardation. Up to this point the parents had relied upon the social worker to be directive in the process. Now the worker invited and encouraged the parents to assume more responsibility for the design of the meetings. They did this and evolved a series of three supper meetings for families, including the mentally retarded child. At this point the social worker called for reinforcements, and three colleagues joined in the implementation. After a family-style potluck supper, one worker provided a recreational experience for the retarded participants, the second worker met with the siblings, the third met with the parents of young children, and the fourth met with the parents of older children.

These experiences were productive; the parents and siblings began to discuss their concerns, anxieties, and frustrations with amazing candor. With one exception, they felt good about the process and what was happening to them in the group. Many individuals reported a change for the better in communication patterns at home. However, one mother was very distraught, and her anguish became more and more openly shared. She was perceived by the worker as vulnerable, and an arrangement was made for her to have an extra-group interview. The worker determined that the woman's concerns were rooted in dynamics unrelated to her son, though the presence of her son complicated the situation. She was referred to a family-service agency for psychotherapeutic counseling.

During these family sessions, one worker observed some behavior on the part of one of the children that made him suspicious of child abuse. This information was relayed, and the school personnel and the family situation were monitored. Fortunately, the worker's suspicions were unfounded.

Ultimately leadership emerged from the parents themselves. They arranged a Saturday "marathon" in order to involve those fathers who had not attended the sessions. Under parent leadership, two individuals were recruited to the group who were not parents but had a great concern for children with disabilities. Family recreational experiences were planned in order to develop relationships over "fun" activities as well as the commonality of retardation. Group members began to talk of becoming their own network of support—their own extended family, as it were.

This is not an exceptional group process. Many parents across the nation have had similar experiences. Sometimes these parents' groups become structured and task-oriented. Many of the NARC chapters started in such a manner. The many ways parents have made an impact upon systems and agencies on behalf of their retarded children is now a matter of history. As a result of "parents' power," the judicial, legislative, educational, and social systems have made great strides toward improving the conditions of the mentally retarded.

Unfortunately, not all group processes are smashing successes.

A denominational school serving mentally retarded boys engaged a social worker to work with the parents of sixteen-year-olds who were about to graduate from the program. The school wished to prepare the parents for some of the issues they would need to face with their sons as they became men in a less protected environment. As a way of preparing for the initial session, the worker spent considerable time talking to the staff of the school and learned of their concern about the boys' sexuality. It was the staff consensus that this was the biggest hazard the young men would face as they returned to their individual communities. On the scheduled Sunday, the naive social worker opened the parents' session with the statement, "Well, it looks like we need to address the issue of your sons' sexuality."

Many practitioners question the validity of having a single session for a group of parents, for they believe it may be a waste of time. In the instance cited, the session was undoubtedly harmful. It was not intended to be a one-session experience, but no parents came back to the second session! It was clear that they had been turned off by the young worker's brash approach and insensitivity to their needs at that particular time. One could question how comfortable the social worker was with the topic of sexuality if he needed to approach it in such a brusque, no-nonsense manner.

The social worker must be sensitive to the community environment from which the parents' group originates. Parents who live in a middle-class suburban area will have different expectations of the group experience than those who come from deprived or poor communities. Generally, middle-class parents will be more used to interacting with professionals and will expect to be involved in a democratic group process. Parents from deprived situations have had little experience in affecting their environment or the systems within it. They may require more direction from the group worker. They may look to the professional to be the authority and may question the professional's competency if he or she refuses to accept this role.

Frequently parents from a deprived community are themselves of borderline intelligence and need to learn the basics of child management. They may need assistance and modeling in order to identify the problems they must resolve. Innovations must be designed and utilized to simplify this process for undereducated parents without jeopardizing their self-respect. The pamphlet *You and Me* (Barnard et al., 1977) was designed to help undereducated parents understand child deveopment in order to be able to recognize problems at an early age and to know when and where to seek help. The manual *Fostering Children with Mental Retardation* (Dickerson, 1977) was written to assist the undereducated, low-income foster mother in her efforts to provide a growth-producing home environment for the mentally re-tarded children placed in her care.

Whatever method is used, social workers must remember the treatment goal: "to enable the parents to maximize the life experiences of their mental-ly retarded child." Social workers must accept the responsibility to help the parents learn to do for themselves without developing a chronic depen-dency. The parents will gain respect for themselves to the extent that they gain control over their own lives. Using that self-respect and self-control, they will seek the guidance and support of social workers as they need it during the many years of parenting a handicapped child. Social workers should avoid falling into the trap of becoming so necessary that they create a dependency that further hobbles the parents of a child with special needs, who already have enough to manage.

CHAPTER 6

The Mentally Retarded Individual as the Primary Client

As STATED IN CHAPTER 1, until recent years social work practice focused on healing the family of its despair and disappointment over the presence of a mentally retarded child. This healing process was supported by the provision of custodial care for the retarded family member. Today most practitioners accept the concept of normalization as it applies to the mentally retarded. Thus, the individual who is mentally retarded is perceived as the *primary* client. As a result of this refocusing, the priorities for social work intervention need to be realigned. Therefore, it seems relevant to reexamine the goals of social work.

The primary goal of social work with the mentally retarded individual, as with any client population, is to enable and assist the client to achieve his maximum potential. Most people have a sense of their capabilities that has been partly shaped by their interactions with others in the enviroment. The mentally retarded client is at a disadvantage as he attempts to consider his potential. The condition of retardation tends to blur his perceptions and confound his understanding. Because of his depressed cognitive skills, he is frequently in situations where he is not accepted and thus receives distorted feedback. Interaction that is tainted with avoidance or patronization behaviors on the part of others intensifies the confusion he may experience. Thus, the first challenge to the social worker is to affirm for the client his capability to grow, change, and progress toward expanded accomplishments. The social worker must give the client a strong message of expectation of growth and change. He must support any indication of the client's desire to be in control of himself and his environment. Through this process, the worker can help the mentally retarded client develop recognition of his potential.

The social worker must accept the reality of the client's retardation without condemnation, patronization, infantilization, undue sympathy, or guilt. He must be able to perceive, acknowledge, assess, reinforce, and maximize the client's positive qualities and behaviors, and he must also be able to identify socially dysfunctional behaviors—such as screaming, lying, stealing, and inappropriate touching—that the client, through training, may be able to extinguish or modify. The social worker must be committed to the concept that the individual with retardation is first of all a person who has a right to a fulfilled life in the community, and that the condition of mental retardation is not an adequate reason to obstruct the person's right to such a life. A life of fulfillment in the community implies that the client must have access to funds to provide adequately for health care and a suitable home. Transportation, education, a vocation, recreation, and social opportunities must be included as basic to a fulfilled life.

In order to accomplish such a goal, the social worker may need to support a client in his efforts to stay in the community, out of an isolated, institutional setting; or the worker may need to assist the client in his efforts to become deinstitutionalized and return to the broad community of his family and relatives.

The Client's Right to Services

A client who is mentally retarded has certain rights that are common to all people regardless of the conditions that shape their lives temporarily or permanently. Recognition of the right of a person to command or demand respect because of his humanness is basic to the practice of social work and need not be justified here. It is sufficient to assert that the acknowledgment of and response to all other primary human rights results from the acceptance of an individual as an individual. Like other community members, the person with mental retardation has the right to treatment, training, and support services.

The retarded client's right to treatment includes the breadth of medical, dental, and psychiatric services. He should have access to health screening, routine physical examinations, immunizations, medical care when ill, medications, drug counseling, a tonsillectomy, dental care, reparative or plastic surgery, cataract treatment, glasses, a hearing aid, braces and other special equipment, physical therapy, occupational therapy, psychological testing, speech and hearing therapy, psychiatric therapy, nutritional counseling, genetic counseling, and family planning.

The mentally retarded client has a right and a need to be trained or educated throughout his life experience. This means that the client must have access to evaluation, appraisal, and assessment services at every stage of his life when his level of accomplishment indicates a need for redirection or a greater challenge. During his lifetime a client with mental retardation could experience any or all of the training opportunities now available: infant stimulation, early intervention, homebound program, special classes, special programs in a general education setting, behavior modification; pre-vocational, vocational, and skill development; job counseling, job placement, work evaluation, sheltered employment, and retirement counseling.

Frequently a mentally retarded client has acquired certain dysfunctional or antisocial behaviors (not unlike his nonretarded siblings). He is entitled to discipline, limit setting, and training in order to modify such troublesome patterns as physical or sexual abuse of self or others, destruction of property, rebelliousness, tantrums, and violence.

Treatment, training, and discipline are basic to the individual's exercise of his right to develop as a unique human being who has awareness and knowledge of self. This in turn contributes to the individual's ability to acquire responsibility for and control of his own behavior, including making decisions and solving problems related to his own life experiences.

The mentally retarded individual must have easy access to a safe, comfortable, attractive living situation where supervision is provided depending upon his needs. He should have transportation, when necessary, so that he can keep appointments and fully participate in the various activities of the community—religious, recreational, educational, vocational, and social. He should be supported in his efforts to establish, maintain, and develop social-sexual relationships. He should be supported in his participation in programs or services uniquely developed to meet the needs of the multi-handicapped.

The social worker must help the retarded client have the opportunities to take risks, to make mistakes, to succeed or fail so that he may achieve his maximum potential (Perske, 1972). Too frequently the child, adolescent, or adult with retardation is further handicapped by parents, relatives, and professionals who persist in lovingly protecting him from possible injury or harm. Such overprotection stifles the trial-and-error process that is a critical part of the development of self and competence. Rather, the approach should be to guide, encourage, and teach the retarded individual to strive for improvement of self through the acquisition of skills.

During the individual's early life, the school may be his primary resource. In later years the work-activity center may become the primary resource. Throughout his entire life span, social agencies must be an available resource, to coordinate or complement other resources used.

Self-Perception and Self-Respect

Self-respect is based upon self-perception, or knowledge of self. "What am I? Am I crazy?" were questions posed to me by Zelda, a twenty-two-year-old woman recently returned to the city after years of institutional life. Zelda knew she was different from the other people who lived on her block, but she did not know how or why. At first I was reluctant to address this topic with her, perhaps because I believed she would never understand. Zelda persisted in her questioning and I tried to answer. The results of the process have had such a powerful impact upon the ensuing years of my practice that I present the highlights of the experience below.

Zelda persisted in her questions: "What am I? Am I crazy?" My canned response—"What do you think?"—moved us nowhere. One day she showed me a picture of her brother, and I, wishing only to make social conversation, asked her to tell me about him. I experienced her description as accurate and perceptive. An idea came to me. Using a primitive lighting arrangement, I was able to get a rough profile of Zelda reflected on the wall. I traced it onto a large piece of paper. Zelda and I discussed the profile. She described her ponytail and why she preferred the hair style. She commented that the drawing "makes out like I'm white, and I'm a black girl." Over a period of time, using several different photographs, Zelda described herself to me, her interests, her concerns, her highs, her lows. I responded to her statements as honestly and precisely as I could, giving her feedback as to my perceptions of her, and my assumptions as to how others perceived her. Gradually Zelda pieced together a picture of herself.

Zelda and I started on a new line of discovery. She identified a well-known black performer, and I was able to get a photograph of this woman. We spent many sessions talking about the woman and how she appeared. Finally I asked Zelda to tell me some of the differences between her and the actress. We discussed obvious and assumed differences, including making a list of the actress's accomplishments. "She can drive a car . . . make clothes . . . read music . . . tell time."

Our discussions took a new direction and we began to talk about retardation, which I explained as a "condition in your brain that makes it hard for you to learn." First, I made sure she knew the location and function of the brain. I tried to use words that were familiar to her as I said, "Your brain is like the boss of your body. It tells it what to do." I explained that sometimes the brain was damaged or hurt because of illness or accident and could not be repaired or made well. Finally Zelda understood that she was mentally retarded because of something that had happened a long time ago, perhaps before she was born. She began to accept that some things she could not do, such as read and write, were because of this retardation.

It was much more difficult to help Zelda understand mental illness and comprehend why other people would call her "crazy." I tried to help her accept the fact that ignorant people often confused mental illness and mental retardation, and that she must overlook their remarks. It helped her self-esteem to learn that some people didn't even try to learn all the ways people can be different from one another. She took this to mean that she was accomplishimg something by learning the differences when ignorant people did not. "But what *is* crazy?" she persisted. In desperation I said, "Crazy is a way of saying a person is sick in his head or brain, and is not capable of being in control of himself, or bossing himself, any more. If a person is sick he can be treated and perhaps get well. A retarded person is not sick and cannot be treated to get well. I cannot make you get over retardation, Zelda. I can't take it away from you. I can only help you to do as much as you can for yourself."

As I have reflected upon our many sessions together, I have come to realize that our relationship became stronger and more productive after the day I tried to interpret the concept "crazy." Zelda realized that I was having as much difficulty communicating with her as she was with me. The distance between us diminished as we recognized each other's frustration in trying to share ideas about important topics and feelings. We became more respectful of each other's efforts. Zelda was a member of a group of five men and women who met at the activity center. I asked her if she would be willing to share some of the materials we had used to help her learn about herself. She agreed and volunteered assistance as I introduced the use of profiles, photographs, and pictures to the other group members. The innovation proved even more effective in a group process, for the members could provide feedback to each other in addition to the insights I could provide.

I have used variations of this process many times since then. It has proved helpful to young adults as they have tried to negate the unfair distortions they have of themselves as a result of dehumanizing treatment by others.

My work with Zelda and many others has brought me to realize how important it is for the mentally retarded person to achieve some level of understanding about his handicap. Many parents and professionals find it difficult to address this concern, perhaps because of their ambivalence about the condition of retardation. I believe it is important for an individual to understand his retardation as a condition of his personhood and as a factor in understanding his sexuality. Sexuality is a universal phenomenon that is basic to the physical and psychological development of all people. Any handicapping condition that impairs the physical and psychological development of an individual impacts upon that person's sexual development. Unfortunately, disability and its relation to sexuality is frequently regarded as a taboo topic and hence is avoided by professionals and parents alike. To avoid discussion of these critical concerns for the client is to contribute to his confusion about his personhood. The result is that the client is beset with anxieties, fears, anger, frustration, and depressed feelings that further distort his inaccurate image of himself.

Even as Zelda needed to understand her handicap in order to develop an awareness of herself, Phillip needed to learn about his oneness, or separateness from other individuals. Phillip came to live with my family when he was sixteen. He called himself and everyone else by his last name. It took many months for him to learn to use correctly the names of the other six family members. As he used the names, he also learned the concepts of "foster father," "foster mother," "friend," "teacher," and "mother." As Phillip's circle of contacts grew larger, he learned the names of several other individuals. He began to understand how each individual was connected to him and what that person did for him that was unique. Now Phillip understands that Jim is a neighbor, a friend, and a teacher who lives next door. He knows that Jim as a teacher is different from Mr. Chen, his teacher at the training center. At age twenty, Phillip understands a great deal about himself because he has learned about important other people in his experience.

Sometimes mentally retarded individuals need assistance in their efforts to persuade parents and siblings to treat them as adults. Following is a description of such a situation and the social worker's resolution.

Annie, a pleasant, timid thirty-six-year-old, attended a pre-vocational program. She was capable of many independent behaviors in the community. She demonstrated competency in the use of buses, elevators, escalators, and revolving doors. She attended to traffic signs and recognized landmarks. However, she was fearful of attempting any of these behaviors unless an authority figure was with or near her. Annie understood that many vocational and recreational opportunities were available to her once she could go to and from home and work by herself. The vocational trainers asked the agency social worker to work with Annie to overcome her fear, which was hindering her efforts to achieve independence.

The social worker met with Annie for several sessions in order to develop a relationship of trust between them. Some of these sessions were conducted informally in a variety of settings so that the worker could assess Annie's competencies with someone other than the pre-vocational trainers. The social worker began to realize that Annie's fear of trying certain things by herself was being sustained by certain remarks she heard from her mother. The worker decided that in order to help Annie acquire the confidence she needed to move around the community independently, she would need to help the mother change her attitude about Annie's right to such achievement. Thus the worker set two objectives for her involvement with Annie: first, to provide support and encouragement to Annie as she learned to use the bus alone, and second, to assist the mother in accepting Annie's right to do so.

The social worker talked with Annie about the need to meet with her mother so that together they could help Annie acquire more skills. She treated Annie as an adult when she asked her permission to have such a meeting. Annie's mother was ambivalent about the social worker's goal of helping her use the bus alone. She shared her daughter's fear that some harm would come to her if she did so. On the other hand, she was sincerely pleased to learn of the vocational opportunities that were available for her daughter.

Finally, with reluctance, Annie's mother agreed to cooperate with the social worker in a plan to help Annie learn to ride on the bus alone. A series of experiences were designed to permit Annie increasing independence over a period of several weeks. For the first experience, Annie's mother accompanied her to the bus stop, several blocks from home, and the social worker met the bus at Annie's destination and accompanied her to the agency. Over a series of several trips, Annie learned to leave her home, get to the bus stop, get on the correct bus, arrive at a busy intersection, and proceed to the agency all by herself.

At first the social worker would call Annie's mother to report on her arrival at the agency or confirm her safe return home. This provided the opportunity for the worker to discuss many issues with the mother. In this manner, she learned of the mother's failing health. She was able to help the mother recognize that Annie's increased independence could relieve her of some concerns in that she would not need to be out in all kinds of weather to accompany her daughter.

It was not easy for Annie to take a risk, overcome her fear, and ride the bus. However, the gradual steps toward independence designed by the social worker permitted her nervousness to give way to confidence. The fact that the worker promised Annie a reward when she accomplished her first trip alone from home to agency was a practical inducement.

It was learned that Annie coveted a pair of red tights which were much more fashionable than the white anklets her mother provided for her. The red tights proved to be the strong reinforcement necessary to support Annie as she dared herself to do things by herself.

Subsequently, Annie achieved considerable independence in the community and earned a rainbow assortment of tights. Annie asked the staff to treat her as an adult and call her Ann. She succeeded in convincing her mother that she could go by herself on the city bus to and from home, work, and the recreational center. She has since refused to wear white anklets and insists that her family call her Ann.

Annie/Ann is typical of many individuals who need help to establish themselves as family members and community citizens deserving of respect. Parents and professionals may provide protection and security to the point of convincing the retarded individual that he is less competent than he really is.

Frequently mentally retarded individuals appear self-centered and behaviorally focused in the present. It seems difficult for some of them to deal with issues of time, cause and effect, and delayed gratification. The inability to make conceptual discriminations complicates the retarded person's ability to cope with the demands of the community and may result in dysfunctional behaviors that are misunderstood by the community. The retarded individual, in turn, is at a loss to understand the community's misunderstanding or lack of perception. The result of this breakdown in community understanding is that the retarded citizen may suffer intensified alienation and dependency.

Because of retardation, the adolescent will be unsure of himself and his place in the family and community. He may have an image of himself as a much younger person than his body size and maturation indicate. Usually he will have had fewer opportunities to take the typical risks of childhood, perhaps because of parental overprotection or motoric or sensory impairments. Whatever his history of risk taking, the adolescent with retardation must cope with the complexities and behavioral expectations of puberty. He must face these changes and accept these demands with an unsophisticated, underdeveloped perception of himself. Adolescence is difficult at best; it must be a nightmare for the mentally retarded teenager who lives in a world of mixed messages and half-truths that he is ill-prepared to manage. The involuntary acts of menstruation, erections, and nocturnal emission must provoke anxieties for teenagers who have only recently achieved independence in toileting.

Fortunate is the child who lives with a family that views his retardation as but one aspect of his personhood. Mental retardation must be acknowledged, discussed, and confirmed. It must not become the primary characteristic of a child that serves to shape all parental behaviors toward the child. The mentally retarded individual needs affirmation of his personhood from his parents and others in the community so that he may develop an awareness of self, a respect for self, and a purpose for self. To learn about one's self is basic to the acquisition of knowledge about, and respect for, other individuals. The humanizing process depends upon this learning about self, others, and relationships.

Too often children are observed in clinics who have little sense of self. They respond minimally to the outside world, and as a result many parents have given up responding to them. Parents and professionals must continue in their efforts to individualize this type of child by calling him by name and talking to him about his person, his body, his toys, his clothes, and his space. Every attempt must be made to help him establish a connection to others. To help an individual discover, develop and maintain an awareness of self is a behavioral goal based upon the philosophical conviction of every person's right to respect.

The Right to Treatment

During infancy, early childhood, and adolescence parents monitor the medical, dental, and psychotherapeutic needs of each of their children. To monitor the treatment needs of the mentally retarded child may be especially demanding because the multiple problems that may accompany retardation require a comprehensive approach. As with other children, every effort must be made to help the retarded child understand the reason for a particular medical regimen and the expected outcome if it is followed. Like any normal child or adolescent, the retarded individual should see the doctor or dentist alone so that he can begin to acquire the responsibility for maintaining his bodily functions. The retarded individual should not be subjected to discussions *about* him in his presence, but rather should be a part of deliberations that concern him, so that he may be prepared to cooperate on his own behalf. Sometimes the social worker must advocate for these rights to be extended to the retarded client. Professionals and parents become accustomed to acting in behalf of the client without recognizing his need to learn to assume responsibility for his behavior in treatment-oriented interactions.

As maturity approaches, the parents should support their retarded child's efforts to assume responsibility for following through on any treatment demands. When possible, the individual should keep appointments without parents. He should be helped to learn how to report his concerns to the professionals. Siblings, friends, and the social worker may be useful supports to the retarded individual during such experiences as he moves away from relying upon parents. Professionals who are accustomed to practice with mentally retarded citizens are skillful in providing reinforcements to the patient as he struggles to learn about his condition, his treatment, and his medication. Infantile, resistant behavior must not be tolerated in the doctor's office or the dentist's chair, for such indulgence serves to perpetuate the infantilization of the retarded individual.

The following excerpts from case logs demonstrate the support social workers provide to a client in need of medical or dental treatment.

During the home visit I learned that Mrs. Thomas did not know where to take Mark for immunizations, as there is no clinic in her village. I referred her to the _____ clinic in the next community. She said that she would be able to arrange her own transportation.

The social worker drew upon her knowledge of community, county, and state resources to identify a clinic convenient for Mrs. Thomas. She provided her with the information and made sure she was able to use it. She treated Mrs. Thomas as a responsible person and began to establish her own credibility.

Tom's parents need a dentist for him. The family dentist prefers not to treat Tom again because he acted so badly last time. I urged Tom's mother to contact the NARC chapter for a list of recommended dentists in the county. I also suggested that when she selected the dentist, she accept his recommendations as to the best way to prepare Tom for the experience. Based on past history, I suspect that Tom's mother may contribute to his negative experience at the dentist by her insistence upon standing beside him.

Although Tom's mother was provided with the information she needed to locate a dentist, the social worker did not address the important issue of Tom's behavior in the dentist's office. The worker seemed to have recognized Tom's behavior as the important factor to consider if Tom was to receive dental attention, but all she did was to ask the mother to accept the dentist's recommendation of the best way to prepare Tom for the experi-

ence. This was a feeble attempt to confront the issue of the Mother's infantilization of Tom, and it only served to obscure the issue. The interaction
between the mother and the social worker would have been more honest
and productive if the worker had asked the mother to consider how she, as
well as Tom, could improve behavior at the dentist's.

The foster mother reported her irritation because the dentist had given Robert (age sixteen) a toy watch for "being a good boy in the chair." I agreed with her that the dentist
had some attitudes that were outdated. We discussed her responsibility to share her
concerns with the dentist.

The social worker supported the foster mother in her wish to have Robert
treated in a manner appropriate to his age. It was appropriate for the foster
mother to discuss the incident with the dentist. It is hoped that the social
worker recognized the responsibility to educate the dentist also.

[July 1975] Helen had three seizures at the work activity center today. I called the group
home to discuss the situation, only to learn that Helen had refused to take her medicine for several days. No one had reported it to the case manager assigned to Helen.
When I reached the case manager, we agreed that Helen should be taken to the emergency room at the hospital. I explained to Helen what had been decided and proceeded to drive her there in my car. On the way to the hospital I asked her why she had
refused to take the medicine. She told me that she wanted to get pregnant and that she
believed the pills were preventing this from happening!

[August 1975] Helen is back on her seizure-control medicine. I'm not sure that she be-
lieves me when I tell her that she is not on birth-control pills. She has the idea that any
kind of pills will keep her from becoming pregnant. There is no indication that Helen is
or has been sexually active. I have decided to concentrate on helping her learn some
facts about her own body, pregnancy, etc. I shall investigate the resources at Planned
Parenthood to see if there is an educational group she may join as well.

In the absence of a nurse in a school or adult activity center the social
worker may be asked to handle medical emergencies. Helen's case is typical
in that many individuals were involved in the decision to hospitalize her.
The group-home manager, not necessarily a trained person, has the responsibility of dispensing and monitoring the use of medicines. The case manager, a social worker from a state or county mental health agency, is responsible for coordinating all services provided the retarded person who
has formerly lived in a state institution. Thus, the social worker in the activity center acted in a cooperative and knowledgeable manner when she contacted the group-home manager and the case manager. She acted in a supportive way toward Helen in that she accompanied her to the hospital and
discussed the situation with her. Although the log does not indicate it, we

can assume that the worker shared Helen's confusion about the purpose of the medications with the group-home manager and case manager so that each of them could help Helen get a clear understanding about seizures and about seizure control as being different from birth control.

The activity center's social worker followed through on her concerns for Helen by determining that she had resumed the medical regimen although she still was confused about birth control. The worker used their existing relationship as a starting place to open frank discussions about basic sexual facts. The plan to refer Helen to a group to reinforce her learning experience is appropriate. It is hoped that such a group included women who were not retarded, so that Helen could learn from women who shared her need for knowledge but were able to model a broader range of behaviors and interest than those to which she was exposed at the activity center.

The group-home manager requested some service for Jess. It seems that Jess has been bragging about his encounters with the streetwalkers in the neighborhood. The manager is concerned that Jess may have picked up a venereal disease. Contact with Jess resulted in him repeating the story. Since Jess is streetwise and can find his way around the community, a referral was made to a nearby clinic. Jess was able to follow through on this and is receiving treatment for VD. Jess was invited to join a men's rap group to learn some facts about sexuality.

The worker treated Jess in a way that encouraged independence. His non-judgmental manner enabled Jess to acknowledge his sexual encounters, and the worker was able to explain the risk of contracting venereal disease. He gave Jess the information he needed to act on his own behalf to obtain medical treatment. The worker maintained his interest in Jess's welfare and made sure that Jess did follow through in the medical regimen. Of greater importance, the worker gave Jess the opportunity to join a group of his peers so that he could continue to learn other things that would enhance his independence.

This and the preceding examples demonstrate some of the many ways in which a social worker can support the mentally retarded individual in obtaining the treatment services he may require at a given time. In almost every instance, the worker supported the clients in their efforts to assume responsibility for their own behavior, and enlisted the cooperation of the parents in these efforts. The following example describes the support I was able to give a mentally retarded woman in need of psychotherapeutic services. Selected excerpts from the log notes are presented.

[Session 1] Gertie, twenty, has been attending the activity center for many weeks. She is a petite, attractive woman who wears very large, very long clothes. She has the habit of using several large safety pins to reinforce all the zippers and buttons on her clothing. None of the zippers are broken and the buttons are intact, so it appears that the huge pins are used as a precautionary measure. Her unusual garb makes Gertie appear odd. This, in addition to her screaming out at people who get too close to her, is causing a problem for her in the center. She is not apt to be considered for pre-vocational training at this time. Individual counseling was recommended, and twice-weekly sessions commence as of today.

[Session 40] Today Gertie really astonished me. "How many holes are there in me where a man can put his thing?" I was at a loss to handle her question but must have mumbled something because with even greater urgency she repeated the question as she pointed toward her pubic area. I told her there were two holes where it was possible for a man to place his "thing." I explained that usually a man put his penis, or "thing," into a woman's vagina, or "pussy." However, sometimes a man could put his penis into a woman's anus, or "asshole." Gertie was bewildered by my answers, so I tried other street-words with which she might be familiar. Finally I took a pencil and drew a simple picture of a woman's genitals, and pointed to the location of the vagina and anus.

[Session 41] Gertie wanted to talk again about "where a man can put his thing." Again I drew a picture and used the factual statements I had made last week. I suggested that when she went home she could take a hand mirror into the bathroom, close the door, and all by herself look at her body and locate her vagina and her anus. Today she wanted to talk about "which hole I use when I go to the toilet."

[Session 42] Today Gertie again wanted me to draw a picture of "my holes." As I did so, she blurted out "That's the one where the old man put his thing" and pointed to the anus. "What do you mean, Gertie?" "That's where the old man put his thing in the hospital." She proceeded to tell me of something that had happened to her a long time ago. While in the hospital for some reason, Gertie had been the victim of an anal rape. Gertie recalled that no one had discussed it with her. She went on to say emphatically, "That's what made me a retard, and that's why I had to live at_____(institution)" I told Gertie that she had shared some very disturbing information about herself and I knew it was painful to discuss it; we did not need to talk about it any more today, but we could talk about it again at the next session and as often as she needed to.

[Final session] During the past eighteen months there have been over one hundred sessions with Gertie. Session 40, when she began to ask questions about sexual intercourse, was the breakthrough. I was able to verify from old records that Gertie had been a victim of anal rape as a pre-teenager. The old records revealed that Gertie had been referred to a hospital for some minor treatment just prior to her admittance to the state institution. Her admittance to the institution had been planned for some time and the incident in the hospital was coincidental. However, there was no indication that any attempt had been made to discuss the experience with Gertie. Gertie's recall and perception of the experience was that no one had discussed the rape with her other than to say it was awful, and that as a result of this "awful" incident she had been placed in the institution.

During the ensuing sessions, therapy has focused on relieving Gertie of guilt for an incident over which she had no control. In addition, Gertie has been helped to see that her institutional experience was because of her slowness to learn, not the rape incident. Many of the sessions have focused upon Gertie learning about her body parts, male body parts, intercourse, and pregnancy. Gertie has been supported in her efforts to come out of her shell and she has dispensed with her cumbersome, bulky clothes and unnecessary pins. Gertie is still loud and apprehensive if some people get too close to her. However, increasingly she permits others to sit near her or touch her.

Gertie is scheduled to start pre-vocational training and will see another social worker on a less frequent basis. She has accepted my leaving and realizes that I will not be at the agency any longer.

To work with Gertie was as much of a growth experience for me as it was for her. I had not anticipated her question about sexual intercourse and my initial response was awkward. Fortunately, Gertie did not perceive my awkwardness as shock or rejection and we were able to sustain our discussion. Gradually I learned the street language with which she was familiar and I was able to teach her some of the preferred terms for body parts. Soon we were able to communicate about sexual concerns without embarrassment. I remember feeling very intrusive when I suggested that she use a mirror to learn about her own body. However, it proved to be a risk well taken. It was helpful to review the old records and learn that Gertie's report of anal rape was factual, since this provided me with specific information I could use in the ensuing sessions. During the sessions we talked about the mistakes that other people had made by not discussing Gertie's feelings with her. Gradually she accepted the idea that her family and the hospital personnel had intended to be kind but had misunderstood her retardation. They had ignored her feelings because they did not realize that as a retarded person she had feelings.

It must be recognized that the treatment process for people like Gertie may be unusually repetitive and may require innovative methods of covering the same ground over and over. However, the unusual demands are not sufficient to support denial of treatment to the mentally retarded individual. Some retarded individuals are eager to develop insights into their behavior. With patience and perseverance, the therapist may enable this to happen.

The Right to Training

A mentally retarded person may spend much of his youth in a public school setting. Parents rely on the schools for much of the education and training their retarded child will receive. The social worker must be knowledgeable about the school and its programs in order to provide adequate service to the mentally retarded individual and his family. To provide that background, the services of the school will be described in some detail.

Like other children, the mentally retarded child must have the opportunity to attend school with his age peers in order to develop the necessary skills to benefit from human relationships. Through the development of such relationships, a child has a better understanding of himself as a family member and as a community participant. Within the school setting the child may develop safe, healthful habits. He will have the opportunity to develop academic and social skills that will help him to earn a living and enjoy leisure time.

Educators recognize the need for special programs for children who have physical, mental, or social problems so severe that they cannot be educated in the regular classroom. These special programs have the identical goal as the regular classroom programs—to help the child develop his capabilities to the maximum degree. To achieve this goal for and with the mentally retarded student demands an individualized process. As with all other students, the educators must provide an experience for the retarded student that permits the integration of life experiences with academic demands and social opportunities.

As of September 1975 the Education for All Handicapped Children Act (P.L. 94–142) ensured the education of all retarded individuals through age eighteen (in some states this has been extended through age twenty-five). This law requires that an agreement be reached among parents, teachers, and school administrators on behalf of every retarded student. The agreement, which is intended to individualize the program for each child who has special needs as a result of physical, mental, or social problems, identifies annual goals for learning in the areas of language development, social skills, motor skills, and self-help skills. Provision is made for regular evaluation, and consideration is given to the child's maximum use of the regular classroom activities, with special programs designed to meet those needs that cannot be met in the regular classroom. The agreement defines the duration of services and identifies the person responsible for coordinating them. Often the school social worker is expected to be a part of the process of designing and implementing the Individual Educational Plan (IEP) for the retarded child.

Educators may become involved with the retarded individual at an early age (in some states this may be within weeks of the child's birth). This involvement may take the form of providing home training experiences to the parent and child two or three times weekly. These experiences may be continued for several months or years until it is feasible to transport the child to the school facility for a program that may vary in length from half a day or three days a week to an all-day, daily schedule. Transportation is a problem for many families, for the school facilities may be located many miles from the family home, so bus service may be provided on a limited basis.

For the severely and profoundly retarded preschooler, the educational plan will focus on helping the child to achieve the various levels of performance that usually occur for the normal child by age five. The teaching will start at the simplest step and progress sequentially. For example, in the area of sensory-motor development, the child will be encouraged to acquire a range of behaviors from the primary behavior of holding his head erect to the complex behavior of throwing a ball. In the area of self-care, the child will be toilet-trained as well as taught acceptable feeding habits or table manners. Educators have designed many strategies to encourage severely retarded children to develop communication skills, beginning with encouraging a response to sounds up to the complex behavior of saying words. These are but a sample of the range of activities that are introduced and encouraged in the early-stimulation, early-intervention programs, intended to deter further retardation by focusing upon the development of basic strengths.

The moderately retarded "trainable" child usually attends a special kindergarten, where he may continue to stabilize certain behaviors such as independent toileting and following directions. Usually a child is considered ready for such a class when he is reasonably continent, walks without undue risk to others, responds to simple language, and makes his wants known. It is expected that a child in a trainable class is emotionally stable to the extent that he will cause no major problems for others and that his own problems will not be intensified or worsened by the experience.

During the years a child attends a trainable classroom he will have frequent opportunities to learn in a one-to-one situation. He will be taught to recognize his own name and to correctly identify objects, shapes, and colors. He will be encouraged to paint, draw, color, sew, and work with wood and clay. He will develop some understanding of the concepts of time, distance, and money. As the child or adolescent develops competence in these tasks, he develops self-confidence. He learns to pay attention, cooperate, share, and make choices. He begins to take responsibility for himself in groups and learns to be dependable. As these behaviors and attributes are learned and refined, the mentally retarded individual begins to develop pride in himself, and his manners and grooming are positively affected. The young man or woman who has spent many years in a trainable-classroom experience will probably be a good candidate for a work-training program. The moderately retarded individual is usually capable of performing a concrete, repetitive task with great efficiency and endurance.

The mildly retarded child may receive no special attention from the school until kindergarten, for retardation may go unnoticed until then. Such a child (referred to as "educable") will probably attend a regular classroom until he is eight or nine years of age. By that time the retardation will be evident in his inability to keep up with the academic demands of the classroom. From that time on the individualized educational plan should ensure a maximum learning experience for him which will include as much time as possible in the regular classroom, even as his special needs are met by special programs. The mildly retarded adult may develop amazing social behaviors that permit him to move with ease throughout the community.

Since the individual will have had extensive exposure to the nonretarded population, his conversational skills will usually be well developed and he may have a range of interests comparable to those of his nonretarded siblings and age peers. When he completes school he will be a good candidate for job training. At best the mildly retarded person will be able to read simple directions, comic books, and books designed for the fifth or sixth grade level. He may be able to recognize money and manage numbers well enough to make purchases.

As young adults proceed through special educational programs they may be referred to pre-vocational-training experiences. More and more schools and training centers are deemphasizing academic achievement for retarded teenagers and young adults and instead placing instructional emphasis upon helping them develop the personal and social skills necessary to maintain employment. Men and women must be taught to follow directions, attend to tasks, remember instructions over a period of time, evaluate their own work performance as to quantity and quality, and ask for help when required. The schools can help students learn to be dependable, punctual, and congenial in a work situation, and thus become better candidates for vocational training and subsequent employment.

Every individual must have an educational experience appropriate for his unique needs. Most educators believe this goal is philosophically acceptable, but many educators find it impractical if not impossible to achieve. Financial support has not moved into the educational system to the extent necessary to implement the intent of P.L. 94–142. Many professionals and support staff are ill-prepared to provide the highly specialized training experiences required by developmentally disabled students. There are many teachers who are resistant to the mainstreaming of developmentally disabled children in the regular classroom for any part of a school day. Parents are frequently ambivalent about their preferences for their children. Sometimes they want them to have exposure to the normalcy of a regular classroom and sometimes they want the protection and security of special education. Sometimes students are graduated prematurely from schools that can't cope thus losing maximum educational benefits. This is a dilemma for the schools, for the parents, and most of all for the mentally retarded student.

The school social worker must assume responsibility for addressing this dilemma as an advocate for the student and as a liaison between the school and the family. In the absence of a school social worker an agency social worker may serve as advocate for the family. Parents have a right to expect and demand a good education for their child. The school must respond fairly to such demands within the limits placed upon it. The social worker is in the position of interpreting the concerns and priorities of the family to the school, and of the school to the parents. In practice this means that the social worker must have a thorough understanding of the educational system as an entity—its strengths and limitations. He must be aware of the needs of each individual student. In addition, he must assess how these needs may be similar to or different from parental preferences for the student. It becomes the responsibility of the social worker to ensure open communication between school personnel and parents in order to meet the needs of the student while acknowledging, clarifying, or otherwise handling the differing preferences of the family. In each instance the needs of the retarded student must be the primary consideration.

Frequently social workers provide the necessary bridge between the parents and school staff by conducting forums, affinity groups, or workshops. Such group activities permit the participants to learn to communicate, advocate, and cooperate in order to achieve improved school experiences for children. "Special People—The Home-School Team" was the title given to a series of workshops conducted for parents and professionals of the Wayne County Intermediate School District, which serves much of metropolitan Detroit. As the social worker who conceptualized and coordinated the workshop I recruited the cooperation of an audiologist, a regular classroom teacher, and a special educator. The four-member team presented a twelve-hour workshop in several school settings. The interdisciplinary team as well as the design of the workshop proved to be successful in opening up communication between parents and school staff.

Not all efforts to establish and model communication need to be this ambitious. In some instances it may be more effective for the social worker to arrange for one or more informal meetings between parents and staff to discuss the concerns of one child.

Within the school setting, the social worker must help the student have the best school experience possible. This is accomplished by helping the student to: (1) accept the behavioral norms or expectations of the school setting; (2) practice behaviors in the school that will be transferable to, and acceptable in, the family, neighborhood, or community; (3) develop ego strengths based upon self-awareness, self-respect, and responsibility for personal behaviors; (4) discuss issues pertaining to self with someone other than family members; and (5) manage crises.

In order to meet the needs of the mentally retarded student, the social worker must develop and maintain a relationship based upon trust and acceptance. There must be sufficient contact between the student and worker to provide for constant, consistent reassurance and modeling. Such relationships may be nurtured by developing one-to-one contacts, through the formation of groups, or by a combination of both processes. Following are three examples of social work interventions with students in the school setting.

Terrence, an eleven-year-old boy with severe mental retardation and hearing impairments, communicated in signs and gestures. The social worker was called into the classroom because Terrence's overt masturbation was a concern for the staff. The worker determined that the interventions up to that time had been limited to the adult placing Terrence's hands upon the table and making the sign "No." The social worker arranged to spend several hours in the classroom observing Terrence, his peers, and his teachers. She learned from the teachers the signs and gestures Terrence could use. She became accustomed to his way of communicating his needs and wants. She recognized his independence in the areas of toileting, dressing and eating.

The social worker learned that Terrence had no commonly understood gestures or signs in his vocabulary for many parts of his body including his genitalia. He used original gestures to indicate his toileting concerns. The worker encouraged the teachers to teach signs for the following words: "penis," "rubbing," "alone," "bathroom," and "feels good."

Over a period of weeks the teaching staff consistently responded to Terrence's behavior by using the specific signs to communicate "It feels good to rub your penis. Go to the toilet and do it alone." The worker accompanied the gestures or signs by leading Terrence into the toilet.

In this situation the social worker introduced objectivity into the classroom. She assessed the situation, the classroom dynamics, and Terrence's level of performance. She initiated an intervention that acknowledged Terrence's awareness of his body, gave permission for self-pleasuring without inducing guilt, and directed the behavior to a place where it ceased to be socially offensive. In the process, the worker learned that the teaching staff did not have the complete lists of gestures and signs developed for the use of the hearing-impaired. She took the initiative to obtain these materials for them and through informal discussions persuaded the staff to use the recommended gestures for body parts and body functions.

It should be noted that in the instance described the classroom toilet did provide privacy. Many school toilets do not. Therefore, there is a danger in teaching a boy that masturbation is permissible in a school situation that is in fact public, for such behavior may increase his vulnerability to unwanted sexual attention. It would have been a better intervention for Terrence's future social-sexual adjustment if he had been encouraged to masturbate at home.

The second example of intervention in a school setting concerns a group of boys in a religious school.

The six members [boys fourteen to sixteen] asked me if I would ask Father _____ [the school principal] if they could have a dance and invite girls. I asked them why they didn't approach Father _____ and ask for themselves. They had several reasons why that was not possible; "He won't listen," "He doesn't like us," "The other social worker would ask him for us," and "He'll listen to you." I told them that I thought they were old enough to have a dance and ask girls, but I couldn't be sure if they couldn't even discuss it with Father _____. I encouraged them to approach the principal by themselves, and added, "If he gives you permission, I will help you plan the dance.."

After a couple of weeks of agonizing, the boys got it together to ask Father's permission. He gave it to them today. They are back on me now to make good on helping them have a dance. (I'm ashamed to tell them that I had prepared Father _____ for their request. I suddenly realize I did not have to do that, and by doing it I was infantilizing them. Damn, damn, when will I learn.)

The worker's candor is refreshing. How easy it is to infantilize men and women who are retarded. She acted wisely when she insisted that the boys be assertive on their own behalf. Fortunately, the boys never learned how she had sabotaged their efforts, and she would never forget the lesson *she* had learned. There are some practitioners who will argue that it didn't hurt to guarantee a successful experience by "greasing the skids," "making it easier." I would challenge that such guarantees are not honest preparations for the harsh realities of life.

Following are selected excerpts from a group log.

[Session 4] The group of teenagers (three boys and one girl) met again today. Harvey and Rich were supportive to Betty as she again discussed her hatred for her stepmother and fear that her father would send her away. Mac sat off to the side and listened to his radio. When I asked him to join the group he told me "I don't want to listen to her."

[Session 5] Betty got into the whole thing again about her stepmother and father. Harvey and Rich are beginning to lose interest and Mac stayed only to enjoy his radio, which he cannot do in class.

[Session 6] . . . brought in a film today from the "Inside-Outside" series. I told the group I thought that the film would give us all something to talk about. The film has to do with separation, and the group members quickly identified with the characters and began to discuss how each one must have felt. We took turns pretending we were a particular character in the film and that seemed to make discussion easier. Even Mac joined in, and only at the end did Betty want to talk about her family situation again. The members asked if I would bring the film to the next meeting. "This one, or another one?" I asked, but they were adamant about wanting to see the same film again, so I agreed.

[Session 9] tried another film today—having to do with divorce—it certainly opened up a whole discussion. I didn't know that Mac's parents were divorced years ago, and Mrs. J. is his stepmother! Maybe it wasn't boredom that made him remove himself from Betty's discussion.

[Session 12] The group is really growing together. They look forward to meetings. I have told them I will be leaving at the end of the school year and they are beginning to realize that this is another opportunity to consider the sadness and promise of yet another separation. They really made me feel good today when they told me that they hoped there would be another social worker, because "we don't talk like this—about friends and staff—anywhere else."

The social worker acted upon her knowledge of her clients and their interests when she used films to initiate a discussion about feelings. It was a concrete nonthreatening, impersonal intervention. She created an environment of trust, candor, and acceptance. Too late (session 9), she began to consider Mac's boredom as a possible defense mechanism. Mac, like other people, may have appeared bored because he was fearful of greater involvement, which could expose him to hurt, ridicule, or rejection. She learned an important lesson: mentally retarded clients should have the right to have their behavior considered from as many angles as other clients.

The entries in the group log shed light upon the need for the mentally retarded adolescent or young adult to have safe, consistent experience in discussing with his peers concerns and issues related to the development of meaningful relationships. Since the retarded adolescent usually lives in a family where he is the only one with the condition, he may have little opportunity for slow, deliberate, repetitive discussion about his concerns. This can be provided for him by affording him a group experience with peers. It should be recognized that most nonretarded adolescents benefit from peer-group experiences as well.

These are but a few examples of how the social worker may function within the school setting. The demands are numerous and the potential for innovative practice unlimited. However the social worker may function within the school, the practice focus must always be upon supporting the retarded student in exercising his right to an education.

The Right to Self-Discipline

In this book, discipline is defined as training that leads to self-control and management of one's own behavior. It is perceived as a positive concept and does not imply punishment. Self-control (discipline) and self-knowledge develop concurrently and must be established in order to achieve an adult life of responsible self-expression and fulfillment. Too many clients have been denied positive training in self-control and self-knowledge because they are retarded. What foolishness! To help a person develop self-discipline is the ultimate of loving and caring.

With the exception of profoundly retarded individuals, every mentally retarded client with whom my students and I have had contact has been capable of developing a degree of self-control and self-knowledge. Retardation may limit the extent to which control and knowledge may develop, but it does not preclude the developmental process. For parents, care-givers, or professionals to functionally obstruct the development of self-control and self-knowledge is to add the handicap of improper, inadequate socialization to the disability of mental retardation. Every time an interaction with or on behalf of an individual is negatively influenced by the term "mentally retarded," the interaction risks contamination by infantilization and patronization. Self-control can be taught to severely retarded individuals. Discipline can be developed in an experience that provides acceptance, structure, and supervision.

Acceptance is behaviorally expressed by parents and professionals as they provide consistent, patient guidance. Acceptance implies fair treatment, tolerance, and loyalty. Acceptance is enhanced by humor and forgiveness. Acceptance is glorified when love is also there. When an individual knows he is accepted, he trusts the acceptance and the opportunity to experience, achieve, and grow.

Structure can be provided by the establishment and by maintenance of routines and limits within the environment that ensure privacy, safety, and learning opportunities. Routines provide the mentally retarded individual an opportunity to achieve maximum control of his own behavior because of the stable, regular demands that exist in a routine. Repetition of a behavior increases competency. Basic limits must be maintained in any environment, and the condition of mental retardation must not be perceived as a reason to exclude any person from adhering to basic limits. Limits have to do with everyone's safety and survival, and may be simply stated: (1) no one may hurt anyone, including one's self; (2) no one may destroy or damage property; and (3) no one may threaten or intimidate another. *Limits cannot be negotiable.* They represent the firm extremes beyond which behavior will not be tolerated in any environment. There can be no deviation from the expectancy that limits will be maintained. All children must learn to adhere to these limits in order to live their lives in a free society rather than in a confined setting, such as a prison or an institution for the mentally retarded.

Limits must not be confused with rules. There are few limits, but many rules. Rules are situational, developmental, negotiable, and reversible. Rules are statements or expectations that are agreed upon by certain individuals in particular situations. For example, a house rule for teenagers could be "Bedtime is 10:30 P.M. on school nights." As the teenagers complete school, the bedtime rule would become obsolete.

In 1693, John Locke wrote *Some Thoughts Concerning Education.* His ideas are as relevant today as they were then.

> Let therefore your rules to your son be as few as possible, and rather fewer than more than seem absolutely necessary. For if you burden him with many rules, one of these two things must necessarily follow: that either he must be very often punished, which will be of ill consequence, by making punishment too frequent and familiar; or you must let the transgressions of some of your rules go unpunished, whereby they will of course grow contemptible, and your authority cheap to him.

The mentally retarded child or adolescent will spend most of his time within two environments, home and school. It is critical that each of the environments provide an opportunity for him to develop personal discipline.

The social worker is able to function as a liaison between the two environments as they coordinate their efforts to provide consistency and constancy to support his efforts.

Each environment must be familiar with the behavioral expectations of the other. In school the expectation may be that the children will remove their own coats. Tommy's mother needs to be aware of this in the home and have the same expectation. If Tommy's mother helps him when his teacher does not, confusion will be added to Tommy's other difficulties. A simple example, but typical of the kind of information that may be unrecognized as important to share. The social worker must be responsible for identifying these areas of potential misunderstanding and must intervene to modify the situation. The following excerpt from a case log provides another example:

I asked Mrs. Stone to describe a typical day. I told her I would complete a simple outline as she described it, so that I could share the information back at school. She told me about the previous school day. I guided the discussion to correspond with my prepared outline so she gave information about the home routine in the following time units: 6:00–8:30 A.M.; 8:30–11:30 A.M.; 11:30 A.M.–1:00 P.M.; 1:00–4:00 P.M.; 4:00–6:30 P.M.; 6:30–10:00 P.M. This helped us get an understanding of how she experienced the demands placed upon her by Jeff and the other children. Mrs. Stone recognized the fact that the period between 4:00 and 6:30 P.M. was the most difficult time for her. "Everyone wants something, and that is also the time that Jeff always soils himself!" Mrs. Stone shared her frustration about Jeff doing well in school about toileting—no accidents. "Why must he do it at home?" We talked about some of the things she could do to relieve the pressure she felt during that part of her day. I suggested such things as preparing as much of the supper as possible *before* the kids came home, teaching them how to prepare their own snacks, giving herself some time in the early afternoon. I assured her that I would find out how the school was managing Jeff's toileting, and would talk to her in a week.

In this case the social worker used a technique that helped the mother consider her family situation in an objective manner. She helped Mrs. Stone pinpoint her problems and consider them in terms of some of the things she did that caused results she did not like. Thus, she was helped to acknowledge her own role. The worker helped the mother become a better planner in the management of her home, thus achieving more control of the situation. This design would result in Mrs. Stone becoming less of a reactor in the late afternoon. The worker provided immediate suggestions to support the mother in changing *her* role performance and thus making an immediate impact upon the home. Thus, the stage was prepared to allow an objective approach to handling Jeff and his toileting accidents.

To achieve independence in toileting is a major step in the development of self-control. Other examples of such behaviors are feeding, bathing, dressing, ambulating, and exercising. Behavior modification has proved a successful approach to use in teaching those behaviors that lead to self-control (Azrin and Foxx, 1974). Materials have been developed to teach parents how to apply the principles of behavior modification (Benassi and Benassi, 1973). The social worker should be familiar with specific resources as well as the general principles underlying this treatment approach (Bandura, 1969; Hardy and Cull, 1974).

When determining behavioral goals for a client, it is useful to consider the following questions:

1. What is the desired final outcome?
2. Is the outcome possible?
3. Can the desired behavior be described in specific terms?
4. Can the particular learnings be specified that need to be achieved in order to reach the final outcome?
5. How will goal attainment be recognized?
6. What behaviors or strengths does the individual demonstrate that will support this endeavor?
7. What behaviors does the individual demonstrate that may be impediments to goal achievement?

Consideration of these questions should serve to focus training toward the achievement of behaviors useful in adult life. The ultimate aim of all behavioral training for the development of self-control is to help the individual achieve a fulfilled life as an adult member of society. All new behaviors introduced must build upon those *appropriate* behaviors that are already part of the individual's repertoire. Frequently parents and professionals need to be reminded that they are training children to be adults, not perennial youth.

Since the social worker may enter a retarded individual's life at any stage of his development, he must be prepared to assess the individual's behavioral performance in the situation quickly and "start where the client is" to enable him to gain control of himself in his environment. A social worker assigned to a group home for deinstitutionalized men had an interesting experience:

During my regular visit to the home, the house manager [female] asked for help with Sam. He had moved into the home eight days earlier. For three days Sam had such an offensive body odor that other residents were complaining. The house manager could not understand what was happening because Sam bathed every night and had put the correct number of soiled clothes in the laundry. She asked if I could do something. I asked Sam if he would mind if I watched him the next time he took a bath. I told him I wanted to figure out why he smelled so bad.

Sam agreed. I sat on the stool and watched Sam carefully remove his clothes, climb into the bathtub and turn the water on. He never sat down, but using his hands he splashed water on his body, rubbed soap upon himself and splashed more water upon himself to rinse. He never did get totally wet, lathered, or rinsed. Evidently this procedure had been going on for four baths. No wonder he smelled! I told him to put in the plug, sit down, and fill the tub with water. I then taught him to take a bath in a tub. He shyly told me that he'd never seen a tub before.

This excerpt from a student's record prompted several smiles when the case was discussed at a staffing. "First you put in the plug!" became the catch-phrase in that agency when the workers wanted to remind each other to start at the beginning. The student earned the respect of everyone concerned because of his wisdom in permitting Sam to be responsible for himself, and teaching him the next thing he needed to learn.

Not all situations are so easily resolved. Retarded individuals are unusually vulnerable to accusations regarding behavior. Sometimes they are held accountable for behaviors that are viewed as normal mischief when other children and adolescents indulge in them. Normal children growing up in a family are permitted a certain amount of self-protection or retaliation. Often this is denied the retarded child for a variety of reasons, most of them invalid. Thus, the retarded child who may have had no opportunity to learn the acceptable ways of asserting himself, retaliating, or clearing the air must contain his irritation and annoyance and become more frustrated. This constant frustration may lead to emotional problems that further complicate a difficult situation.

Parents and others often express concern over the following behaviors: unevenness of skill development, short attention span, lethargy, hyperactivity, overreaction, lack of social skills, and clowning. None of these behaviors is unique to individuals who have retardation, and all are subject to modification. Frequently the retarded individual or others in his environment will have concerns related to such behaviors as unexplained aggressive acts, rebellion, lying, stealing, wandering, obstinancy, overt sexual curiosity, offensive sexual behavior, or sexploitation. Reports about, or apparent manifestations of, such behaviors must be checked for accuracy, for it is not uncommon for behaviors of the developmentally disabled to be misinterpreted simply because the individual has been labeled retarded. However, assuming that negative bias is absent, parents and clinicians must learn to respond to these concerns. Two examples are presented to demonstrate the need for caution.

A frantic call yesterday from _____ [residence for twelve boys and girls, ages eight to twelve]. The housemother is extremely agitated because Doug is masturbating. She is afraid that he will molest the girls. "What will I do if he comes into my room?" was the final statement in her outburst. I agreed to stop by on my way home.

Upon my arrival, the house seemed calm, supper was almost ready and the children were putting their toys away. Mrs. S. explained that "he always does it just before supper." I stayed through the supper hour and observed no unusual behavior on anyone's part. I agreed with Mrs. S. that perhaps my presence had made a difference. Mrs. S. calmed down and when the relief worker arrived we sat over coffee and talked. She described Doug's pattern of behavior. He usually disappeared just before supper. She would call him for supper and get no response. Always she would find him in the linen closet, where he would be hiding and masturbating. She would yell at him "Don't be dirty" and insist he come to supper. I asked her if she knocked on the linen closet door, and she answered "Of course not." She was very upset with me when I remarked that it appeared that Doug had been considerate in that he had gone to a private place. I suggested that in the future she should knock on the linen closet door, remind him that supper was ready, and tell him to come immediately or he would miss it. I told her I would come back in a few days to discuss with the entire staff some of the issues related to sexuality that would need to be addressed, but that I did not support any punitive action against Doug for this behavior.

There was nothing in Doug's behavior that was abnormal, and he seemed to be behaving with discretion. The housemother's perception of his behavior was distorted, perhaps because of her lack of knowledge about normal sexual development or her misconceptions about the sexuality of mentally retarded individuals.

A different type of dilemma was presented to a case manager who provided social work services to several adult male residents living in a board-and-room facility.

Mrs. Thomas called today to tell me that Andrew and Wally would need to move out of her house because they had sexually used Paul, another client. I went to the house immediately. She reported she had caught the three men acting "funny," and when she confronted them Paul had blurted out, "They made me do it." I asked to talk to each of the men. Andrew and Wally acknowledged that they had had sex with Paul and had done so frequently. They stated he had been a willing partner. Paul told me, "They made me do it—lots of times." He was afraid to see Andrew and Wally and stayed in the kitchen. Since Mrs. Thomas was about to throw Andrew and Wally out on the street, I was forced to move them, although they contended it was unfair. Mrs. Thomas permitted Paul to stay because she sees him as the victim. I really question this. . . .

The worker had no choice but to move the men to another facility. Perhaps the men were fortunate that the home operator did not call the police. However, it was unfortunate that Andrew and Wally were spared the initial confrontation with their parents. The social worker responded to their pleas and saw their parents on their behalf. In retrospect, it was clear that Andrew and Wally should have had the encounter themselves so that they could begin to experience the responsibilities of adulthood as well as the privileges. The social worker initiated counseling with each man in order to help him learn to deal with his sexuality without the exploitation of others. It was impossible to initiate training for the home operator so that she could become more comfortable with issues concerning her residents. In subsequent months Paul asked to be moved to where Andrew and Wally lived because he missed them. He admitted that saying he had been forced was a lie he told because he was afraid of Mrs. Thomas. Immediately the social worker initiated counseling with Paul to help him deal with his sexuality.

There is no *one* way to solve a problem, handle a conflict, or relieve stress. The more experience an individual has in dealing with such pressures, the better prepared he is to do so. The process of growing up includes learning to decide, choose, and cope. The mentally retarded individual must not be denied the opportunity to experience this critical part of achieving self-control. The extent to which the retarded individual may achieve responsible adulthood is directly related to the extent he has been permitted to take a risk, to fail, to try again, and to learn.

A retarded individual does experience more frustration than a normal individual. It is regrettable, but nothing is gained by attempting to protect the individual from his frustration. He must be taught to handle it in a socially acceptable manner. The retarded individual is no different from any other person in that he must accept the reality of frustration, handle it, and move toward problem resolution or stress relief.

Some retarded individuals develop the ability to persevere with patience and tolerance and do achieve a level of happiness and contentment. They learn to accept themselves with respect and are able to push themselves to the utmost of their potential. Others become resentful and bitter, perhaps because of lack of support in their struggle to understand and control themselves in relation to their environment.

It has been stated elsewhere in this book that professionals and parents err in having low performance expectations of the mentally retarded. It is reemphasized here. Professionals and parents tend to have diminished expectations of the mentally retarded person's potential for personal discipline and self-control.

Social workers must learn to model a different way of working with the retarded citizen. They must prove that overprotection is infantilization. Overprotection stifles the desire to grow and learn and weakens self-confidence and self-respect. Social workers must demonstrate that every individual, including the person with retardation, learns from failure as well as from success. Everyone should have the opportunity to take risks, make mistakes, challenge the limits, and accept the consequences. To stand responsible for one's mistakes is not punishment but the mature way of making restitution, or earning the right to try again. We must stop doing *for* the mentally retarded and demand that they do for themselves to the utmost of their ability.

The Right to Human Fulfillment

Fulfillment is the common goal for all people, since it is the realization of the potential of the individual to express those characteristics common to all people. Humanity is characterized by social-sexual interactions that must be learned by each individual in order to have individual fulfillment occur. The rights, privileges, and responsibilities inherent in an individual's role in relation to another person's role must be learned. In acquiring behaviors that lead to acceptable social-sexual interaction, it is essential for an individual to learn the specifics of sexuality. Every individual has sexual needs and urges. The mentally retarded person is no exception. Everyone must learn about himself in order to be in control of himself. Self-control allows for expression in socially acceptable ways.

To be sexual is a lifetime process. At the time of birth, the infant is identified as male or female and from that moment is treated differentially. The child's name, clothing, and toys are obvious examples of the differential treatment. For an entire lifetime, all interactions are influenced by the sexuality of the people involved. In the earliest stages of infancy the baby experiences the differences between the soft curves of Mother's breast and the firm flatness of Father's body. Through the entire life experience every interaction will be influenced by the gender of each participant. Certain privileges and responsibilities are intrinsic to certain relationships. The fulfilled human being must learn how to manage these diverse relationships with respect for himself and others.

From the day of birth, parents have the privilege of directly teaching and training their child about his sexuality and indirectly influencing him by their own behavior. They may choose to do this openly, joyously, and in a manner that permits the child–youth–adult to experience himself as having pride in his sexuality. Some parents are afraid, timid, or embarrassed and choose to withhold factual information from the child. However, when the parents are hesitant to share, the child acquires many ideas about sexuality *because* of this denial. Some adults have the opinion that to withhold knowledge about sexuality will prohibit sexual expression or protect the innocent from exploitation. All evidence proves the fallacy of such an opinion. To be knowledgeable about sexuality is the best protection against casual expression or sexploitation.

In those instances where parents refuse, negate, or balk at the responsibility to meet their child's need for education and training in sexuality, the social worker must advocate for the client's right to know and learn. This advocacy may take the form of providing education and training for the parents, so they may address the concerns of their child, or working directly with the client to provide important support to his growth and development.

As an individual's life progresses, he or she has many facts to learn about his or her own body: its parts and functions; variations in male and female bodies, and shapes and sizes; maturation, conception, pregnancy, and birth. Under optimal conditions the parenting person provides information, answers questions, and encourages curiosity in the normal course of daily events. For example, body parts and bodily functions can be introduced and discussed during bath time.

More important than facts, attitudes about relationships and behaviors are modeled, reinforced, and discouraged every single day in every environment. At an early age children learn about touching—they differentiate between the touching one may receive and give within the family and the distance that must be maintained outside of one's intimate circle. They also learn from statements or innuendos the parents' attitudes about how and where they may explore their own bodies. Attitudes about touching are the first of many with which the young child will be imprinted by his family, peers, teachers, and strangers. Attitudes will be developed about hugging, kissing, dating, going steady, marriage, sex in and out of marriage, fantasy, and homosexuality. All these attitudes and many more will develop within each individual with or without parental permission or guidance.

Parents must be helped to recognize that to avoid their responsibility in this regard places an unnecessary handicap on even a normal child. For young people who have retardation, the absence of such guidance and training makes their vulnerability even *more* serious. Social workers must accept the responsibility to influence parents to guide their retarded child as he puts together his knowledge about himself and learns to relate to people. There are many interventions that an innovative worker may introduce, such as encouraging privacy for each family member.

Every person should have a space and time where he is undisturbed. If possible, a child should have his own bed and a place to store precious belongings. Every child should have some things he does not have to share—a toy, a shirt, *something!* A child must learn about privacy in contrast to "in public." In order to learn *my* ownership of *me*, I must learn it in contrast to *your* ownership of *you*. I have a toy—you have a toy. I have my bed—you have your bed. I can be in my bed alone—you can be in your bed alone. I have privacy away from you—you have privacy away from me. Even without understanding the concept, the most severely retarded individual can learn to experience and control the *contract* of privacy. When a child has learned to sleep alone and toilet independently he has learned to demand privacy. He is capable also of respecting the privacy of others. And he has learned self-control, or discipline.

By providing privacy for a child, parents guarantee privacy for themselves. Parents who provide privacy for a child give a strong message to him: "I respect you and your need to be by yourself, and you respect me and my need to be by myself." Unfortunately there are still school programs that are not respectful of a child's right to privacy. Too many children are receiving toilet training in the classroom in a public fashion. It is common to see a classroom with several children in various stages of undress "going potty" simultaneously, and with teachers and aides walking around checking on each individual's success. Such training is poor preparation for the expectations for toileting in our society. Adults do not "go potty" publicly under constant monitoring. It is time to advocate for the children in such classrooms.

Children must learn to recognize the need to toilet and how to toilet alone. They need to learn the correct words for their anatomy and its functions. Not to provide this basic information and training merely sets the stage for behaviors to develop that will be considered offensive when the toddler is an older child. Overt masturbation, partial undress, and baby talk are not desired public expression. Retarded children do need a longer period of time to learn fewer lessons, but it doesn't make sense to permit behaviors to develop that will take costly training time to extinguish.

The social worker must be aware of the subtle invasions of privacy that are likely to be perpetrated against a retarded individual because he is less able to object. For example, in a residence for sixteen men and women, staff walk into the various bedrooms unannounced, without knocking. When confronted, the response is "They don't mind." It may be necessary to monitor a woman's menstrual cycle. However, it is an invasion of her privacy to ask questions about it in front of other residents. The social worker must recognize, confront, and redirect such interaction.

In order to help a retarded person learn to control and express his sexuality in a socially acceptable manner the worker must be prepared to respond to situations as they happen, in addition to scheduling interviews and meetings that provide more formalized guidance.

The following excerpts describe some informal situations that have occurred.

Sandy had $2.00 to spend today. I accompanied her to the drugstore where she bought a large box of sanitary napkins. She said that at the house everyone had to share from a big box, and the housekeeper doled them out. When we returned to the center, she borrowed a pen and wrote SANDY in big block letters on the tab of every *single* napkin.

Later I spoke to the housekeeper and suggested that the women be permitted access to supplies without having to find her. I was told that the women would be wasteful and careless about disposal if permitted to own or store their own sanitary napkins. A clear example of infantilization!

I did not accept the housekeeper's position and explained that the residents had a right to have personal grooming aids. The housekeeper was adamant and stated that she was following the home operator's instructions. After confirming this statement with the home operator, I initiated advocacy proceedings on behalf of the women residents. Once the home operator realized that the female residents were prepared to move if not given certain privileges, she relented and permitted each resident to own her own sanitary supplies.

The social worker was not in a position to provide counseling or a training program to the staff of the group home. She did begin to document other cases in which clients' rights had been ignored and staff had maintained unwarranted control of situations and people. In due time she presented this to the licensing agency as evidence that operators and staff in general needed to be trained.

Following are selected entries from a case log:

Opal is so offensive at the training center that the other people make fun of her. If she is not busy every moment, she has her hands up her skirt. When staff remind her to stop, she soon forgets.

We've noticed that Opal likes to stand by a certain bulletin board and play with herself. I asked her what she liked about the photographs displayed there. She pointed to a snapshot of a former staff member. She told me how much she missed him since he had moved. I asked what she would do if she had the photograph. She said she'd sleep with it under her pillow. I tried to be supportive as she acknowledged she would rub herself.

I discussed an idea with my colleagues, and we decided to give Opal the picture of Mr. _____. I asked her into the office and explained that rubbing herself was called masturbation, and it was OK. I told her that she got into trouble and people didn't like her because she masturbated where they could see her. I told her she could have the photo if she would try to stop masturbating at the center. I warned her to keep the picture to herself so the housemother would not find it and the other women would not tease her. We talked about the fact that masturbation was OK, to have the picture was OK, and to keep a secret was OK.

In this instance the worker provided information to Opal and supported her right to enjoy her own body in privacy. She introduced her to fantasy and gave her permission to have a secret. The worker was wise to obtain support for herself and her actions by discussing the plan with her colleagues. An entry two years later from Opal's case log may be of interest.

Opal has developed fine work habits. She attends to the task at hand, sorts accurately and quickly. She is responsible for the telephone in that she answers it and pages the person being called. Although she is unable to write, she has demonstrated her ability to remember short messages. She has learned two different bus routes and travels independently.

The entry continues for some length and concludes with the statement that Opal will be considered for job-training. No mention is made of sexual acting-out. One can assume that Opal has become discreet, for she certainly appears to be socially acceptable.

Gloria came into the office today to say that she was pregnant. That was a surprise: I was sure her records said that there had been a tubal ligation years earlier when she had aborted. I asked her why she thought she was pregnant. She said she hadn't been "screwing . . . but last weekend, when I went to that family party in _____, my cousin, Rob, kissed me and put his tongue in my mouth, and Susan [another group-home resident] says I'm pregnant."

Gloria, like many other retarded women, is sexually active yet has little knowledge of her own body. The people she lives with have many misconceptions about sex, and the women tend to perpetuate each other's ignorance. Gloria responded positively to the worker's invitation to join a group to learn more about sex, how to make contact with other young people, and how to date.

Twenty-four young adults were deinstitutionalized and placed into group homes several blocks apart. The men and women were eager to spend time with each other in addition to meeting at the adult activities center. The following plan was implemented. Two male workers trained the male clients to use the phone to call the women and to use the bus to visit the women's home. At the same time, two female workers trained the female clients to receive calls, prepare the house for guests, and make refreshments. Every Monday for twelve weeks the men accompanied by two staff members, rode the bus to visit the women. The experience was fun and the young people learned certain social graces in a safe situation. The women encouraged the men to entertain them, and the plan was reversed. Soon the young adults were beginning to couple and were asking permission to date independently. Since the weather was pleasant, the group as a whole had several outings to various settings easily accessible to them. A park, zoo, museum, theater, and bar were explored. In each instance the young people learned how to get there, how to pay admission, and how to behave in the situation. By the time the group had disbanded, after twenty-four sessions, most of the young people had learned how to date and enjoy some of the recreational opportunities in the city without any staff support. A few of the men were still unsure of themselves and incapable of initiating a relationship, but all showed marked improvement in personal grooming and use of simple courtesies.

The staff treated the entire experience as a group opportunity. No individual relationship was singled out for special support, fostering, or "matchmaking." No pressure was placed upon those individuals who wanted to be present but did not want to dance or play games. Some of the group members were frustrated by the lack of privacy and the absence of a place to go and "make out." Others were grateful that this opportunity was not available. Although the group members did evaluate their experience, the focus was on discussing the things they had learned and the places they had been. There was no opportunity for them to deal with the larger issues that they were confronting in their lives. They did not have an opportunity to discuss their feelings about the dilemma in which they found themselves. Each of them was in a life situation that permitted few social opportunities and no opportunity to be alone with another person, for whatever reason.

The staff viewed the sessions as successful in that each group member had acquired social skills, but they were frustrated by the recognition that they had helped the young people learn behaviors that they were incapable of developing further. They were "dressed up with no place to go." There was *no* private place for couples. There was *no* support from the agency, community, group homes, or parents to develop such a private place for couples. In spite of the negative aspects of the experience, there had been marked improvement in the group members' adjustment to community placement as a result of the training and guidance they had received.

For many clients sexuality becomes an issue only at times of crisis. Social workers must be prepared to respond at these times. Sometimes parents and professionals will consider certain behaviors as deviant because the participants are mentally retarded. Two clients who live in a coeducational setting for adults are hardly deviant because they are discovered in the laundry room, half naked, exploring each other's bodies! That kind of behavior happens in college dormitories and is not considered deviant. In instances where a mentally retarded individual is engaging in behavior that is within the range of behaviors permitted a nonretarded person, this fact must be pointed out to the concerned parents. Parents are fearful that their children will be exploited. Sometimes they worry that they may be oversexed. These attitudes tend to distort their perceptions of behavior. Of course the young people found in the laundry room need help. They need to learn about mutual consent, places of privacy, and how to protect themselves from intrusion. They certainly do not need therapy for sexual deviancy!

There *are* instances of bizarre sexual behaviors, and each of them must be evaluated and treated in a highly individualized manner. Any individual, regardless of his IQ, must be treated or punished if he engages in sexual behavior that is harmful to others. Rape and child molestation are sexual crimes that must be treated as such regardless of the individual's retardation. Frequently noncriminal but bizarre behaviors may be redirected so that the individual is no longer vulnerable to criticism or ostracism. Following is an example from log entries written by a social work supervisor.

[July] A young man asked to see me. He would not give his name. He lives across the street from _____ house [residence for men]. He and his housemates have witnessed

Billy G. exposing himself on several occasions. The informant told me that he had stopped Billy on the street, learned his name, and where he went for training. He had come to see me so that we would do something to protect Bill G. from arrest or worse.

[October] I thought that Billy G. was no longer exposing himself. He has been attending a man-talk group and there have been no unusual incidents until tonight. When Mike walked across the park on his way to work, he looked up to see Billy exposing himself at one of the windows in the activity center. Mike immediately confronted Billy. He refused to talk with us.

[October, a week later] Mike insisted that Billy talk to the two of us as a condition of continuing to use the center. The session started by Mike making a firm statement that exposing oneself would not be tolerated in the center. "It's against the law, and if the cops catch you it may mean jail." Billy was surly during this part of the session. Mike softened his style somewhat and went on. "Everyone gets turned on, but they don't let the whole *damn* world know about it." He went on to ask Billy G. what were the things or situations that aroused him. During the discussion Billy kept looking at me, and both of us were uncomfortable. I volunteered to leave, thinking he might do better without a woman present. Mike insisted I stay, because as a fulltime staff worker I would always be here. After some skillful interviewing Mike learned that Billy was afraid to approach another person for sex—in fact he was afraid to touch anyone. He stated, "They told me at _____ [state institution] that if I messed around I'd go to Hell and I'd always be retarded." Mike comforted him as much as he could and suggested that the two men meet again in a few days.

[later] During supervision we discussed Billy G. and his problem. We conjectured about the impact a porno movie might have upon him. Mike believed that Billy could attend a movie, select a remote seat, and conceal any arousal he experienced. He thought Billy could learn to go home, recall the movie in the privacy of his bed, and successfully masturbate. Mike agreed to design a plan to help Billy learn this process.

[January] Mike says the plan worked. Certainly there has been no other incident.

The male worker in this case demonstrated sensitivity and street wisdom as he worked with his client. It is assumed that by redirecting the client's behavior the client has a better chance of surviving in the community without arrest or alienation. There is much more that could be done to help Billy rid himself of incorrect and crippling ideas. However, he has been sustained in the community. His interest in porno movies is one he shares with countless other community residents who are not retarded.

Most mentally retarded women are biologically capable of pregnancy, but that does not mean they are attitudinally or behaviorally ready for parenting. Parents of retarded women typically worry that their daughters will have unwanted children. They often see only two solutions to the dilemma

for their daughter—abstinence or sterilization. Either solution is impractical. It is difficult to force abstinence upon another person, and sterilization
of another person is difficult to achieve in a way that is medically safe, legally endorsed, and psychologically acceptable to all concerned. With training and counseling, most retarded women are able to be responsible for
their own bodies and can decide whether or not they want to become pregnant. Retarded women appear to make decisions from the same range of
choices as other women: birth control; abortion; whether to place a baby
for adoption or keep it; and sterilization. A few examples of work with retarded women about the issues of birth control and pregnancy:

Several of the women in the home have been talking about birth control. Ever since Linda got pregnant it has been a topic of great interest. Planned Parenthood has agreed to
provide some group sessions so the women can become familiar with the choices.

Thelma is not only pregnant, it looks as though she has a venereal disease as well. I
talked with her about being a high-risk mother and she said, "It's hard enough for me
without a kid—especially if it isn't OK." I described several options to her and she was
adamant about wanting to get "rid of it." I accompanied her to make the arrangements
and will go with her for the abortion. She was referred for treatment for the VD.

I've decided to help Sally arrange to be sterilized. She has been discussing it for weeks.
She is aware of her habit of "sleeping around," and doesn't want to get pregnant again.
The abortion last year was uncomfortable. I am convinced that this is the thing to do
because Sally made an appointment with the M.D. and kept it to herself. The doctor
told her to come back and bring me, to discuss the idea. I guess if she can take all those
steps she is ready to make the big decision. At least I will go with her.

Carrie delivered a normal son last week. Bobby looks like his father, which will complicate life for Carrie. It will be hard enough for a single parent who is retarded—but a
white woman with a black child in that neighborhood! She wants so much to raise Bobby. The visiting nurse will see them Monday, Wednesday, and Friday, and I've agreed to
drop in on the other days. I guess between us we can teach her to be a mother. I gave
Carrie my home phone number, as well as the telephone numbers of two other staff
women. Just in case. . . .

The social worker gave Carrie considerably more than a phone number.
For a period of two years she became a surrogate parent to Carrie and was
in daily contact with her. During the first few months after Bobby was
born, the worker arranged to drop in at Carrie's apartment every evening
on the way home from work. As the months went on, the visits became less
frequent and Carrie relied upon the phone for support. During the two-year
period Carrie learned to shop, cook, clean her apartment, and do the laun-

dry, as well as take care of Bobby. Carrie learned to introduce games and toys to make sure that her son had the stimulation he needed to grow and develop.

There were a few minor emergencies, like the day Bobby swallowed the wheel from his toy car, or the time the toilet overflowed and the janitor could not be found. Of greater importance, Carrie needed to have some time away from Bobby. Finally Carrie approached an elderly neighbor in the apartment building and arranged an exchange of help. Carrie did simple household chores for the elderly neighbor in exchange for some baby-sitting.

The visiting nurse and the social worker cooperated to teach Carrie the many skills she learned. The worker provided the hours of discussion that were required to help Carrie learn to make decisions and act upon them. Early in the relationship, the worker told Carrie that she would never do anything *for* her, but would help her learn to figure things out for herself.

When Bobby was about twenty months old the social worker told Carrie that she needed to cut down on the frequency and length of their conversations because she was planning to.marry in a few months and would be moving out of the city. Carrie and the worker spent the next several months handling their feelings about termination and planning for Carrie's increased independence. The worker supported Carrie's growing reliance on her elderly neighbor and helped her begin to use the services of another social worker. When the social worker was turning over the case file to the supervisor, she commented on Carrie's profound love for her son and her desire to continue to be a good mother. She shared her concern that Carrie would need guidance for the next several years so that she could continue the adequate parenting that would be needed. The worker expressed her confidence that Carrie could manage with less and less professional contact.

Carrie did not have a permanent relationship with her son's father, but some retarded individuals do move into permanent relationships, if not marriage. Barbara, a moderately retarded woman who had a seizure disorder as well, met a man at a neighborhood bar. They became friends and began to date. Soon they decided to live together. Barbara suggested that he come to meet her social worker.

Barbara's lover came with her today. He appears genuinely interested in her. He told me about his work in a factory and said that he had named Barbara as the beneficiary of his insurance policies. He asked for information about how to treat Barbara when she had a seizure. He is talking about marriage and wanted to know if I would help him get her rights restored. I asked him why he would want to marry a retarded woman and he answered "Why not?" He went on to say that she treated him well, was a good cook, and kept the apartment clean. He wasn't interested in having children, and they could look after each other.

Retarded individuals are apt to establish the same kinds of relationships as other individuals. Many of them are successful, some are not. Some retarded people are sexually curious but inactive; some of them enjoy their own bodies and the use of sexual toys. Some enjoy homosexual relationships and others are heterosexual. Some retarded individuals are openly involved, and proud of their competency in managing social-sexual bondings. Most retarded individuals are forced by society to be ashamed of, and clandestine about their sexual preferences and behaviors.

The important fact to recognize is that most mentally retarded people are as concerned about, and interested in, expressing their sexuality as any other segment of the society. However, no other segment of society is so systematically denied the right to human fulfillment. It is hypocritical for parents and professionals to expect children to learn the responsibiltiy appropriate to their personhood as adults and then turn around and deny them the privileges of their personhood. It is as though the society has a special message for the mentally retarded citizen:"Do your best. Learn to conform. Be like the rest of us, but remember that you are not to enjoy life. You are asexual." To deny a person the expression of sexuality is "neuterization," the final terrible stage of infantilization.

Social workers are no exception to the rest of society. Many of us are fearful of honestly confronting the issues of sexuality with our clients and their families. This probably is due to insecurity about our own sexuality. Whatever the reasons, they are irrelevant. Social workers must face up to the challenge and work to ensure every client's right to human fulfillment.

In September 1979, funding for a three-year project of national significance, "Service to Aging and Aged Developmentally Disabled Persons as a Basis for Training and Technical Assistance," was awarded to the Institute for the Study of Mental Retardation and Related Disabilities at Ann Arbor, Michigan. Although the project is in its infancy, the practice experiences indicate that older clients wish to discuss such issues as separation from family and friends; the death of family members and friends, and their feelings about their own deaths. It appears, from this small sample, that these issues are at least as interesting to the older retarded clients as their concerns about independent living and use of community resources.

In the past, many mentally retarded individuals have been shielded from the deaths of family members. Too frequently they have been protected from a reality of life—to grieve and accept the death of a loved one. This is yet another example of the infantilization that is perpetrated upon the mentally retarded.

CHAPTER 7

Helping the Retarded Adult Achieve Maturity

THE YEARS OF MATURITY SHOULD PROVIDE AN ADULT with the opportunity to increase and expand his self-knowledge and his range of behaviors and to achieve a life pattern that permits various degrees of independence within the community. Very few individuals, retarded or otherwise, achieve total independence. Rather, most individuals appear to establish interdependent relationships with selected other people. These relationships permit an individual to be independent or dependent in some instances and interdependent in still others. As with the so-called normal population, mentally retarded adults must be permitted to experience interdependence, independence, or dependence in an individualized way.

As indicated in Chapter 3, there are four categories of mental retardation, based upon intelligence and adaptive behavior. Eighty-nine percent of the mentally retarded population are classified as mildly retarded and usually can achieve an independent life-style. Moderately retarded individuals who make up 6 percent of the client population, can usually achieve semi-independence. Severe mental retardation is the diagnosis given to 3.5 percent of the client population. Individuals who experience this level of impairment can acquire many independent behaviors but require a supervised, protected environment. Profoundly retarded individuals (1.5 percent of the population) who live to adult years are so extremely handicapped that skilled nursing care is required to sustain life. Generic social workers provide case-management services to ensure maximum human fulfillment to these totally dependent clients as well as support services to their families.

134

The social worker must advocate for the profoundly retarded client so that he may live in the least restrictive environment possible. Within this environment, the client must be encouraged in every conceivable way to participate in the usual activities of the broader community. As we have repeatedly stressed, it is no longer acceptable for professional social workers to condone minimal custodial care for profoundly retarded individuals. Rather, they must accept the challenge to model for, teach, train, and support paraprofessionals, volunteers, and other care-givers in the use of improved techniques that enhance the client's human experience.

This chapter places its emphasis upon the 98.5 percent of the client population who are capable of achievements leading to ever-increasing self-care and independence.

The Right to Maturity

In spite of a condition that limits the development of skills and adaptive behaviors, the mentally retarded individual eventually comes of age and faces the challenge of adulthood. He must meet the years of maturity uninhibited by infantilization but with the assurance of supports necessary to maintain the conventional standards of a secure, happy life. He must be guaranteed psychological, social, and economic services to foster his developing adequacy and independence.

The severely retarded individual remains visible throughout his life and services are available to him, but mature retarded individuals are not recognizable as a homogeneous group, for they differ greatly in chronological age, mental age, legal status, and social adaptability. Mild or moderate retardation is not so easily identified in the adult, and many individuals with the condition are absorbed into the community. Unfortunately for the retarded adult in a city, he may get lost among the street people. He may be erroneously perceived as just another alcoholic, hoodlum, or vagrant. The fact may be overlooked—as has been said repeatedly—that the retarded man or woman, like any adult, has certain basic needs related to income, health, residence, vocational opportunities, recreation, relationships, and crisis management. Each of these needs will be discussed in terms of unique demands related to retardation.

INCOME

As indicated on page 84, any adult with mental retardation is eligible for financial assistance in the form of Supplemental Security Income (SSI). The monthly income, while not generous, does provide monies to cover room, board, and supervision for adults who live in a licensed facility such as a group home. Limited funds are available to cover incidental grooming, clothing, and recreational costs. There are rigid limits on the earned or unearned income a recipient may claim without placing his SSI income in jeopardy. At present, these outside financial reserves are limited to $1,500. This limitation can discourage the mentally retarded adult from seeking employment. Frequently parents and professionals, as well as the retarded adult, believe he can never earn enough money to risk losing his guaranteed monthly income.

HEALTH

Any recipient of SSI automatically receives Medicaid, which covers essential medical expenses. For the chronically ill the Medicaid program is generally adequate. Individuals who have complications such as epilepsy need careful monitoring for their entire life. Medicaid coverage for dental maintenance and repair is very limited.

RESIDENCE

Residential choices are limited for the mentally retarded person. If he receives SSI, he must live in a licensed facility. The options available in the community under such a stipulation have been described in detail in an earlier section (see page 78). Such facilities may be adequate, but they do not permit the individual to choose the kind of setting that best suits him. Too frequently his own space consists of a bedroom shared with one or more persons in a house or home where several other retarded individuals live. There is security in such an arrangement but little opportunity to exercise any options.

VOCATIONAL OPPORTUNITIES

The retarded adult has a difficult time entering the mainstream of the American world of work. There are many barriers that confront him when he attempts to make his way into competitive employment. Architectural limitations are a reality, but negative attitudes on the part of employers and fellow employees are an even greater obstacle. Many employers are reluctant to hire mentally retarded individuals because they believe job training will be lengthy and costly. Sometimes employers express concern for the retarded individual's safety and the effect this may have upon company insurance. Usually the job for which the retarded person is qualified will attract other applicants who are not retarded. The mentally retarded person is often the last to be hired and the first fired.

As a whole the community finds it difficult to permit the mentally retarded to gain access to a range of jobs. Nevertheless, there are notable exceptions, and some mentally retarded men and women are satisfactorily performing a variety of jobs ranging from machine operators to gardeners, welders, or messengers. Mentally retarded individuals have proved competent on the assembly line as well as in the more traditional role of janitor or domestic.

Like the rest of us, those retarded individuals who establish themselves as members of the work force earn the tolerance of their fellow employees, and sometimes their respect. There are some individuals who are able to earn an adequate income and do not need financial aid from the government. These individuals become mainstreamed into the American way of life and cease to be singled out because of retardation. Generally they would have been considered educable or trainable during their school years, but as adults they have become absorbed into the larger community.

Unfortunately, there are some adults classified as educable or trainable who are not encouraged by their parents to acquire this kind of independence. In families with a history of high achievement and substantial financial success it is frequently an embarrassment to have a member who is in a low-paying, low-status job. For example, a professor and his wife who lived in the cultural milieu of an Eastern university campus found it unacceptable for their daughter to be employed as a domestic in a nursing home. They preferred to have her live at home, without a job, where she could be with "her own kind" of people.

On the other hand, some families discourage the retarded adult from seeking gainful employment because they are fearful that the SSI monthly income may be placed in jeopardy. They do not believe that the retarded person could possibly earn more than what the government provides. Some parents are apprehensive about their adult children taking work because of the risk of injury or worse.

In addition to unwillingness on the part of the employer and reluctance on the part of the parent, the mentally retarded adult may have concerns of his own. Frequently he will be anxious about a new situation. He may lack confidence and feel inadequate or ill-prepared to try a job.

The social worker can be extremely supportive to the adult retarded client who wants to acquire a level of maturity by moving toward the independence that comes from work. Sometimes the social worker must advocate for the adult and initiate a referral to a service setting where he can receive vocational training. The social worker may cooperate with a rehabilitation educator or counselor to move the retarded individual through a series of experiences that will lead toward the goal of employment. Sheltered workshops, rehabilitation centers, and job training centers are steps along the road to the greater independence of competitive employment.

The vocational educator or counselor will focus primarily on helping the future employee develop appropriate attitudes about work as well as marketable skills. He will turn to the social worker to help the client with other aspects of his life that must be stabilized in order to guarantee the development of a good candidate for employment.

Specifically, the social worker can provide the vocational educator with important information about the client. He can evaluate the client's readiness for training, learning style, maturation, patterns of behavior under stress, and management of interpersonal relationships. The social worker is able to describe the client's use of leisure time, which may provide important clues for future vocational interests. The worker is able to assess the family situation or other living arrangements. Thus, the vocational educator will have a sense of the support or lack of support he may expect from the client's home environment.

Once the client is prepared to enroll in a work-readiness program or accepted in such a program, the social worker will use any or all of the following interventions: introduce the client to the setting; teach him how to get from his home to the training site; meet with the vocational staff; arrange an initial meeting between the student and the staff; plan the student's first experience; follow his progress; interpret to his family; and counsel the client in such areas as crisis management, frustration control, and facing new situations. The social worker may need to help the adult client learn how to improve his appearance, hygiene, manners, and other social skills so that he will be more acceptable in a job situation.

The social worker should be familiar with the usual training methodology of the vocational educator. He should recognize that the educator will use concrete examples and demonstrate many tasks to the client in a one-to-one learning situation. The vocational educator will appreciate the reinforcement the social worker can provide the client as a result of this familiarity with his way of work.

Often a retarded adult develops adequate work skills but has no idea how to use the money he has earned. The social worker can help the client learn to manage his money so that he begins to enjoy the pleasures and rewards that result from his work. The social worker may be called upon to help the client learn to accommodate his life-style to meet the scheduled demands of employment. For example, Richard lived in a group home where meals were served at regular hours that did not coincide with his work schedule. The social worker helped Richard learn how to prepare his breakfast and pack his lunch. She introduced him to a new routine of bathing when he returned home in midafternoon, so that he would be refreshed and clean for dinner.

Frequently the social worker may need to help the client modify some troublesome behavior so that he can maintain his job.

Prince, a charming, well-mannered, quiet man, was often tardy and sometimes filthy when he arrived to run the elevator in an office building. He was in danger of losing his job, and the supervisor contacted the social worker for help. After some questioning it was learned that Prince was helping neighbors with yard work before he came to his salaried job. The worker helped him to use an electric timer. He would set it to ring to remind him to stop the yard work, take a shower, and go downtown—a simple enough solution, once the problem was identified.

One day, the social worker was called to a small plant where George was employed. George was a highly productive worker, and regularly during the work day would be ahead of the nonretarded people beside him on the line. He would be asked to rest for a few moments in order to let the other workers catch up. Frequently he spent this time masturbating at the work station. The supervisor did not know what to do, because George was retarded. The social worker asked him what he would do if George were not retarded. "I'd send him home for a day or two, until he learned better." The social worker convinced the supervisor that that was exactly the message George should receive as well.

In recent years there have been dramatic strides in the development of vocational programs for the mentally retarded. The successful programs have demonstrated the need for close cooperation between the vocational instructor and the social worker, not unlike the cooperation that exists between the educator and social worker during the school-age years.

The social worker should support the client as he tries to convince his family that he must be permitted to join the work force and experience all the responsibilities, privileges, and rewards that are part of the experience. In a larger arena, the social worker should be part of the effort to educate the community to the meaning of mainstreaming mentally retarded adults into the vocational scene. Social workers who are involved with school-age clients and their parents should make every effort to help everyone concerned plan ahead, just as planning takes place for the nonretarded school-age child.

RECREATION

Adult activity centers continue to be the most available resource for out-of-residence programs. Voluntary agencies, service groups, and churches have designed new services and opportunities to meet the religious, recreational, and leisure-time needs of the retarded. In my suburban community there are many choices available. A group of churches cooperate to provide an ecumenical religious experience for retarded individuals. The adults have one session a week as a group, and it is hoped that each person will attend the denomination of preference for the regularly scheduled service. The

YWCA sponsors a social club for dancing twice a month. Three different service groups sponsor canteen programs on three different weeknights. A bowling alley provides league bowling at reduced rates. A parents' group sponsors a weekly schedule of events emphasizing enjoyment of the arts. At first glance this may appear to be a generous list of choices. Compared to what was available in the 1960s, the activity list *is* impressive, yet all of the opportunities listed are designed for the mentally retarded citizen's exclusive use and thus perpetuate his alienation from the community at large.

RELATIONSHIPS

The mentally retarded person often finds himself limited to choices of personal relationships because of his living conditions. It is a usual procedure for staff to make room assignments on the basis of available space rather than individual personality needs. Thus residents are expected to live with one or more roommates in same-sex situations that may not suit them. Sometimes men and women develop homosexual relationships because of preference, and sometimes because of availability. In some facilities, that are promoted as coeducational men and women do live under the same roof sharing common rooms but *not* bedrooms. The usual expectation in such a facility is that men and women will live as brothers and sisters! Of course incidents happen, and they are handled with discretion as one or both participants move away.

There are notable exceptions. Some courageous professionals have advocated for the adults and have developed residences where each person has his own room and is permitted to use it with impunity. The League for Goodwill Industries in Detroit sponsors two residences in two former convents, one for male residents and the other for women. Each resident may use his or her room as freely as one would use a hotel room. He or she may have guests at any time for as long as desired, as long as the rights of others are respected. There are similar accommodations elsewhere in the nation. Many of them do not advertise their liberal policy for fear of community retaliation. Many are located in communities where the local college or university permits coed dorms.

CRISIS MANAGEMENT

Lack of friends and lack of living options function to limit the choices men and women have to establish relationships of permanence—relationships with sexual commitment. The result is that we have forced thousands of men and women into clandestine, sordid experiences that only serve to further alienate them from the mainstream and cause them to lose respect for themselves.

Like other people, the mentally retarded individual may experience a crisis when he feels unable to manage his life and its demands given the resources he has available. The crises in a retarded person's life are not different because of his retardation, they are merely more complex. Like other people, the mentally retarded individual must learn to cope with success and failure.

In spite of the dearth of support services, many retarded adults do live contented, semi-independent lives. Each of the individuals described in the following examples spent his or her youth in a state institution.

Tom, thirty-nine, has worked for years as a janitor in a hardware store. He met Mary, forty-five, who did similar work in an adjacent office building. As children they had lived in different institutions. As young adults they had returned to their parents' homes, where they lived until marrying two years ago. Now they share a three-room apartment. Between them they are able to do all the household chores, although meal preparation is limited. They are able to manage their money by using a system of envelopes that Tom's father monitors. They ride the bus to work, movies, church, and the park. They worry about who will answer their questions when Tom's father dies. Generally they lead a quiet life and are happy together.

Charlotte, forty, and Jason, thirty-five, have been together for five years. Neither of them knows the whereabouts of any family members. They met in a bar some years ago and have become a team. Charlotte, a streetwise woman, has held a chambermaid job for seven years. Three years ago she got Jason a job as a dishwasher at the same place. For the last several years they have shared a two-room apartment. They pool their funds and manage to make ends meet, even though Charlotte occasionally blows a paycheck on clothes and they both spend a lot of money at the neighborhood bar. Charlotte is the decision maker, and Jason is content with that most of the time. It has been years since they have ventured out of the neighborhood. Their lives are limited to the ten-block area where they are recognized as having a place.

Paul, twenty-nine, is a personable man who can talk himself into jobs. Unfortunately, his stubborn streak has *cost* him several jobs. Nevertheless, he is able to live on what he earns with an occasional "loan" from his father. Paul receives no SSI and wants it that way. He lives in a board-and-room facility where most of the other men are retirees. He enjoys "the old boys" but likes to go where the action is. He spends time at an inner-city bowling alley–bar and occasionally spends the night with a prostitute. Paul moves around the city with ease, stays out of trouble, and has telephone contact only with his father. Once a month he sees the social worker at the adult activities center.

In each of these situations, the individual has control over his own life in that he lives in a place he has selected with a person or persons he chose. He does work that suits him and enjoys the results of his work. The success of the community placement of retarded adults depends largely upon the conditions present in the community: availability of jobs for unskilled or semiskilled workers, housing alternatives, and attitudes of the neighborhood people toward the mentally retarded. Unfortunately, society, if it has any expectations at all, expects that when the retarded person makes a successful community adjustment he will "live happily ever after." If he experiences the same problems and ups-and-downs as the so-called normal population, it is believed that this is because he is retarded.

Some adults have not acquired the necessary skills to cope in the community. They may prove to be undesirable residents in a group home because of personal untidiness, offensive eating and toileting habits, or refusal to adhere to a medical regimen. They may have difficulty with interpersonal relationships and act inappropriately because of this. Unruly, destructive, moody, insolent, quarrelsome people cannot be tolerated in a group-living situation. Some men and women find it difficult to accept the normal rhythm of a community. They may rebel against the expectations placed upon them by job, adult activities center, and residence managers. They may be lazy, unreliable, inefficient, and uncooperative. Sometimes the retarded adult is ambivalent about the conflicting messages he receives from the professionals who urge independence and the relatives who foster dependence.

There are some individuals who have health problems that make life in the community too great a challenge. Physical disabilities, seizures, and nonambulation may serve to provide the retarded individual with a personally acceptable reason for not exerting himself to adapt in the community setting. A few individuals behave in antisocial ways that put a strain upon the nonretarded segment of the community, which has developed a tentative tolerance at best. Sex offenses, theft, and assault should demand retribution from every citizen, the retarded not excepted. However, certain other antisocial behaviors which are tolerated in the general society loom very large for the retarded person. There is less tolerance extended toward the retarded person for promiscuity, unmarried pregnancy, and illegitimate children.

Some deinstitutionalized adults have been so threatened by the reality of community life that they have run away from the group home and tried to return to the institution, which was familiar and safe.

Martin wants to be permitted to return to _____ [state institution]. He hates the city, Mrs. W. [home operator], and the other men. He never gets to see his girl, which he resents because at _____ they were always together and were lovers. "I'm going to break up that damn house," he proclaims. He has made a good start. Mrs. W. called today to report that he broke a window and smashed a toilet over the weekend. This in addition to two fights.

The community social worker collaborated with the institutional social worker to determine a plan for Martin. They agreed that he was experiencing the community as more restrictive than the institution because he did not know how to move around with freedom, and he was with unfamiliar people. It was decided that any intervention should result in Martin's acquiring a preference for community living so that he would put energy into becoming a community person.

Martin was returned to the institution, which pleased him initially, and admitted to a building that housed thirty profoundly retarded adolescent boys. He was restricted to the building with *no* campus privileges except to go to the pre-vocational workshop. He was told he could request a placement review after two months.

Two months passed and Martin requested community placement. The two social workers discussed with him some of his discomfort with his former placement and some of the things *he* had done to make the restrictive experience even worse.

Subsequently, Martin was placed in a setting that encouraged and taught men to live in an atmosphere similar to a college dormitory. He was permitted guests and was helped to learn to use public transportation within the city. It came as a shock to Martin to learn that his former girlfriend was involved with someone else. However, he quickly recovered and made other contacts. He is now employed in a sheltered workshop and attends recreational activities sponsored by a local church. He has friends. Martin no longer wants to go back to the institution. It would appear that he was not prepared for his *first* placement and had received minimal help in learning to accommodate to that setting. When supportive services were available to him, he was able to make an adequate adjustment.

It is true that social workers manipulated the environment on Martin's behalf. They decided he should have an aversive experience at the state institution in order to make the community more attractive by contrast. There was some involvement of Martin in the decision-making process in that his opinions and feelings were elicited and considered; however, he did not experience the right of self-determination to the extent that may be desired in practice. If the end does justify the means, it can be concluded that Martin's life improved as a result of the manipulation. However, caution must be practiced to prevent the vulnerable client from indiscriminate manipulation.

Impediments to Service

A man and woman developed a friendship while living in a coed group home. They asked permission of the house staff to date. The request was denied because of the house rule that residents could not date each other but were permitted to date only outsiders. The man arranged to move, and after the move returned to see his friend and take her out. At this point the couple was told that the woman did not have dating privileges! He would be able to visit her only in the public parlor. The young woman was dismayed and told the center social worker, "Now I see even less of him." When the social worker confronted the house staff with their manipulative practice, she was informed, "We can't have that sort of thing going on here. He was becoming too interested in her, and that would make trouble. Besides, the parents won't like it." It became clear that the young woman was a victim of staff manipulation to meet the expectations of her parents, with no recognition of her needs.

The young woman was receiving many different messages: the center social worker was encouraging independence and decision making, the house staff was talking independence but manipulating her social life, and the parents were infantilizing her.

Parents and staff do manipulate the clients—often overemphasizing needs because these are the needs they are prepared to address. For example, adult residents in one group home asked to have regular sessions with the social worker to learn about sexuality. Sessions were scheduled for Monday evenings. The sessions were discontinued after the third one because Monday was the only evening volunteers were available to take the group swimming. Everyone was expected to go so that the house staff could have two hours of relief time. An exaggerated example? Not at all—a very typical example of how parents and professionals sabotage programs that may be threatening because the retarded individuals receive encouragement to assume responsibility for their behaviors in an age-appropriate manner.

The conscientious social worker may find himself in a situation that seems unsolvable. He may be convinced of his client's right to have dating privileges and wish to help the client exercise that right. Usually the client is too fragile to assert himself, too dependent to risk defying the system that has victimized him for so long. The social worker may decide to confront the staff with the unfairness of their restrictive position. They, in turn, may take the position that they are providing good care and protection for retarded adults through the use of supervision and stringent rules. They may believe that they are relieving the community and the parents of a heavy burden. Finally, the social worker may wish to persuade the parents to support their grown children in their pursuit of independence. Generally his efforts are met with resistance, for the parents are apprehensive about the future for themselves and the son or daughter. They are fearful of losing a good, safe home for their child, which is the last thing they can arrange before their own deaths. No matter where the social worker turns, he will not find support—not from the timid client, the overprotective staff, or the apprehensive parents.

The social worker may wish to urge his client to act in an assertive, if not a defiant, manner. However, it is a lengthy route to reach the solution of this dilemma. The worker must join others of like commitment to educate the community, the parents, and thus the staff so that attitudes will be positively affected. With the change of attitudes, humanistic treatment of others will follow.

Survival in the community is a challenge not only to the retarded adult but to those who are responsible for his welfare. For those retarded adults who continue to live at home, there is the concern about the future, when family stability may be disturbed by illness or death. How adequately will the retarded adult function without parental influence? Should he separate from his family and learn a new life-style while they are alive to support him? For those who live in supervised settings there is concern about overprotection, oversupervision: could it be infantilization? The adult retarded who return to the community after years of institutional living have unique problems to face. Reentry into a complex, open community must be frightening after years of a routinized, monitored, and controlled life. Many of the behaviors that were functional within the institution are extremely inappropriate in the community.

The sociocultural factors existent in the community influence the success or failure of the adult retarded who live there. Also critical are the individuals' ability to adapt and cope, as well as the influence of parents plus caregivers and other staff. Perhaps the greatest impediment to success for the retarded in the community is the failure of professionals to individualize the them and recognize the diversity of their needs.

Most of the aging or aged mentally retarded have as little in common with the young retarded adult as they do with a twenty-year-old in the nonretarded population. The different needs of the aging and aged mentally retarded received scant attention until 1975, when a national consultation-conference was convened in Ann Arbor, Michigan, to address their unique needs. The proceedings of this consultation-conference revealed the lack of demographic information about this segment of the population (Hamilton and Segal, 1975). Subsequently, several university-affiliated programs have been focusing attention upon the aging or aged retarded, and the results of their efforts are beginning to be reflected in the literature (Sweeney and Wilson, 1979).

Casework with the Mentally Retarded

The role and responsibilities of a caseworker with a mentally retarded client are unique only because of the retardation. The social worker must perceive his role in relation to such a client just as he would in any other client relationship: he has the responsibility to understand retardation, even as a worker in another setting would need to understand gerontology or alcoholism.

During the initial stages of the client-worker relationship, it is imperative to establish trust and acceptance. The worker must give this message by establishing eye contact, touching the client, and carefully listening to any statements he may make. The worker may need to teach the client how to engage in a dialogue. The following technique has worked for me. I sit facing the client with our knees touching and take both of his hands and gently hold them. This serves to focus his attention and physically conveys the message of acceptance. I urge the client to look at me when we talk together. When necessary, I will turn his face toward mine. As the relationship becomes established, I am able to provide more physical distance between us.

The relationship must focus upon the reality of the present situation. The client may be unable to make complex decisions for himself, but he may be capable of simple choices when the opportunity for choice is presented to him. The client's inability to make decisions for himself may create a philosophical dilemma for the social worker, who has been trained to ensure the client's right to self-determination. The worker must consciously provide the client with the opportunity to experience self-determination to the extent possible, encouraging him to take risks and make choices. The worker is there to protect him from destructive tendencies and must take this responsibility.

Because of his retardation the client may have difficulty understanding the subtle causes of his feelings and behavior; however, he must be taught to recognize his feelings and the consequences of his behavior. Since the client is likely to act his feelings out, the relationship with the social worker should be strong enough to permit this to happen. The retarded client may view the social worker as an authority, parent figure, or older sibling. He may need guidance and patience from the social worker as he learns to perceive that the worker is different from other adults in his experience.

In each worker-client interaction, the worker must use language that the client understands. He must innovatively and creatively communicate in verbal and nonverbal ways. Every idea, thought, and suggestion must be stated and restated over successive contacts so that the client will retain the concepts introduced. The worker must check his own behavior to avoid patronizing or infantilizing the client. It is difficult to be patient when a simple issue is discussed for the "umpteenth" time. It may be difficult for the worker to permit the client to *be* retarded without experiencing feelings of frustration, guilt, revulsion and despair. The worker should recognize his own negative feelings in order to keep them from obstructing the relationship. It may be helpful to honestly state, "I am unfamiliar with a disability such as you have. It makes me uncomfortable, but I shall learn from you how to overcome my discomfort."

The task of the relationship is to develop a bond of concern about the client's problem. The worker will obtain information from the client and appropriate other sources. The client will experience the worker as clarifier, model, support, enabler, and advocate. The nature of the problem, the data available, and the client's level of retardation will influence the treatment goal and design. In some situations the worker may effect a change in the client's milieu in order to relieve stress. In other situations the worker may support the client as he learns to tolerate stress. In still other situations the client may be helped to change his behavior.

Mentally retarded clients present a range of concerns comparable to any other clientele: health, general welfare, relationships, sexuality, and future plans. But the retarded client may face these universal concerns with a self-perception that is inaccurate, distorted, and deprecating. Thus it is of primary importance for the social worker to focus on helping the client develop a perception of self, retardation, and disability that is similar to others perception of him (see the description of Zelda, page 101). One worker's log reports:

I decided to use a drawing to help Joan talk about herself and her family. I drew a large square and suggested we pretend it was her house. I asked who lived in the house. She listed Father, Mother, Brother, Sister, and Baby. "Where is your sister's husband?" "She doesn't have one." "What is her name?" "Faye." "Brother?" "Jeff." "Baby?" "Just Baby." I had written the names on the paper at random, which did not suit Joan. So I cut up small pieces of paper and wrote the names on them. Thus we were able to move them around. "Mama watches TV, Dad's gone a lot. He runs the bar."

The log continues to describe the gentle, nonthreatening way this social worker helped Joan tell the story of her family and home. There were inaccuracies that she attempted to correct during several sessions: Faye was Joan's sister-in-law, not her sister; Joan adamantly called Charles "Baby" even though he was a sturdy, mischievous six-year-old. Many sessions later a record contained this information:

Joan was very agitated. Nothing I said could soothe her. As a way of diverting her I suggested we talk about the family and use the cutouts. She threw them on the floor and shrieked, "How can Baby do all those things I can't?" I asked Joan if she had ever heard about mental retardation. She became even more agitated, screamed, and ran out into the main room of the center, knocking over some chairs on the way. When I caught her, I took her by the hand and said, "I know you are very angry and you hurt real bad. I am sorry. Please come back to the table and we will talk about it. "Joan permitted herself to be led back to the table, where she sat down and began to cry. She sobbed for a long time and I just stroked her hair. When the sobbing subsided, I said, "I know it hurts and I want to help you understand."

The worker permitted Joan to ventilate her feelings and quietly sat with her, maintaining a physical contact with her, thus silently giving a message of caring. Joan was learning about the handicap that retardation placed upon her, and she was angry about the new awareness. She spent several sessions comparing her skills and achievements with "Baby's."

As the relationship with the worker becomes reliable and trusted, the client may want to become increasingly dependent upon the worker. This must be confronted. The client must come to accept the goal of gaining more control of self.

Nita, a Mexican-American woman, returned to her family after years of institutional life. Although she could not read, write or manage money, she learned to move around the city and found herself a job as a dishwasher in a neighborhood restaurant. Her mother and sisters spoke Spanish, but Nita had used English exclusively in the institution. Perhaps because of the language difficulties at home, Nita asked to see the social worker more frequently than was necessary. The worker helped Nita build relationships within her family and neighborhood and accept responsibility for decision making.

Within the institution, the social worker must be ready to help the client cope with interpersonal relationships—with staff, other residents, and family members. Emotional difficulties may need attention. The client will need help to understand why he is in the institution rather than in the community with his family. It is usual for the client to experience feelings of loss, anger, frustration, abandonment, and bewilderment about his separation from his family. Sometimes his feelings will erupt in rebellion and uncontrolled aggression. Sometimes he will be withdrawn, anxious, or apathetic. Whatever the behavior, the social worker must help the client adjust to the institution and its routines. He must help the client make use of the institution as a place to accomplish certain tasks of growth and development in order to return to the open community. The social worker supports the institutionalized client as he attempts to maintain his relationship to his family while also learning to use the services of the institution. The worker must be available to support the client as he enters into treatment or training programs, makes shifts within the institution, from ward to ward or program to program, and eventually returns to the community.

Vince, twenty-two, was a mildly retarded paraplegic who had been institutionalized for sixteen years. Within the institution, Vince was well liked by staff and other residents.

No visitors came to see Vince and he experienced the institution as home. He had certain privileges including a room of his own. He talked about living in the city someday and enjoyed visiting possible residences there.

When a barrier-free hotel for men was located Vince became apprehensive about leaving the only home he remembered. His apprehension mounted so much that he threatened to refuse the community placement. The social worker spent hours with him and eventually learned that Vince was unhappy about leaving his girl friend. The worker arranged for Vince to learn to use the telephone so that he could call his girl at regular times. Under these conditions Vince agreed to move. The social worker was able to arrange for Vince to return for visits, and the girl friend was helped to visit Vince in his new location.

As Vince became comfortable in the community he began to make new friends and his ties to the institution became less important. Vince went on to make great strides in the community. He attended a vocational rehabilitation program where he received job training and learned to drive a car. Eventually he found a job and moved into his own apartment. He was provided a car with special controls by the Department of Vocational Rehabilitation. Vince's life had changed dramatically. Although Vince broke off his relationship with his girl friend, she was highly motivated by his success and worked hard to acquire behavioral controls so that she, too, could be released from the institution and returned to the community.

Vince's success was due primarily to his desire to get his life together. This desire for self-fulfillment was fostered by a succession of professionals: the institutional social worker, placement worker, residential manager, agency social worker, education counselor, and vocational specialist. Throughout the entire experience the community agency director functioned as an advocate for Vince and a coordinator of the services he received. The advocate/coordinator shared techniques with each of the counselors. Vince responded openly and trustingly to the workers, who were specific and precise in discussions with him. He learned best when behaviors were demonstrated to him; explanations without demonstrations were apt to bewilder him. Perhaps the greatest achievement for Vince was to have a car of his own. Certainly the ultimate tribute was paid to him when a staff person said, "Vince, I have never learned to drive because I've been afraid. I'm going to get over my fear and drive, because you did." An exceptional case? Not at all. Vince is typical of 89 percent of the individuals labeled retarded.

Workers must not hesitate to be directive in their relationships with their clients. True, directive guidance may lead to overdependency. On the other hand, a nondirective process accomplishes little if the client is incapable of using logic and reason. Sometimes the client needs to have access to the concrete wisdom of the worker. For the worker to provide direction judiciously is a practical intervention based upon the acceptance of the client. As long as the worker maintains the goal to enable the client to achieve maximum independence, it is appropriate for him to accept the responsibility to assertively model, guide, and train. A caution, though: the social worker must not permit himself to become the omnipotent authority, for this can only lead to patronization and infantilization of the client.

Some adults with retardation never have had an opportunity to develop any sense of independence and are perceived as chronically dependent. Such clients should not be refused the opportunity to learn as much as possible about choices.

A student worked with several aged, developmentally disabled men and women who lived in a nursing home. The youngest client was fifty-five. Each client had lived in an institutional setting for forty-eight or more years. The clients were considered to be chronically dependent for all of their needs, with the possible exception of independent feeding.

The nursing-home administrator was indulgent toward the young social worker and her elderly clients and permitted her to "do what she could to ease their days." The student arranged to televise her practice, and this documentation showed amazing results. More than half the clients were capable of responding to her attempts to make friends. Given the opportunity, it became apparent that many of them were capable of developing a bond with the worker. To the chagrin of the nursing-home staff, the videotape provided irrefutable evidence that some of the clients could *talk intelligibly* and were capable of relating reactions to information heard on the television and their feelings about some of the staff!

This example is given to emphasize that relationships can be established with most mentally retarded individuals. The more responsive and highly functioning the individual, the more productive such a relationship can be. Peter and Lucy provide us with a rich example of what can happen with excellent interventions.

Peter had lived most of his life in a state institution. At eighteen he was placed in a group home for men in a poor section of a large city. Peter learned street life quickly and began to move around with freedom. He used his allowance for liquor and on two occasions was picked up by the police for drunk and disorderly conduct. In both instances the social worker at the group home was notified. Each time the worker refused to ask for exceptional treatment and instead urged the police to detain Peter overnight. After two experiences Peter decided he didn't like the consequences and accepted the social worker's invitation to see if he could "make a man of himself." Over the next several years, with regular and frequent counseling, Peter did go through training to become a janitor, and subsequently he found a job. By age twenty-five he was self-supporting and had saved $1,000. However, he was unable to manage money, and therefore the social worker was appointed as a partial guardian. Peter had a tendency to be stubborn and occasionally got drunk or was in a fight.

Eventually Peter met Lucy, who lived in a residence for retarded women. They began to date and eventually became lovers. Peter shared the progress of his relationship with his social worker. During the next two years the worker counseled Peter as he made major decisions about birth control, unplanned pregnancy, placement of Lucy in a home for unmarried mothers, declaration of paternity, marriage, selection of an apartment, establishment of a family, and maintenance of a job. The social worker collaborated with the worker from Lucy's group home, the counselor at the maternity home, the visiting nurse, and the job counselor. As each crisis developed, Peter was provided with information about consequences so he could make a careful decision. He thoroughly trusted the relationship with his worker.

Marriage did not prove to be an easy adjustment for Peter because he was possessive and jealous. He abused Lucy and on one occasion hurt his daughter. His social worker informed the protective service in order to serve the best interests of the baby, Lucy, and Peter. It was hard for Peter to accept the fact that his friend had turned him in. However, the worker-client relationship proved to be strong enough to pass this test. Subsequently the court decided that Peter and Lucy could continue to raise their daughter with supervision from a public health nurse, who would teach them appropriate ways of handling the child.

During the seven-year relationship, the social worker had been available for both scheduled and informal contacts with Peter. Telephone calls had been accepted at times of crisis. When the worker left the agency, Peter was functioning as adequately as many of the other fathers in his inner-city apartment complex. It was expected that he and Lucy would become increasingly competent as parents. The worker had taught Peter a simple method of budgeting, and steps were taken to remove the limited guardianship so that he could manage his own affairs.

Group Work with the Mentally Retarded

It is a natural, humanizing experience to interact with people in all kinds of situations for brief or extended periods of time. Most people enjoy this spontaneous process in the activities of their daily lives. Joy, sorrow, excitement, and frustration are a few of the feelings that may affect social interactions. Most people learn to handle a range of feelings as they casually or selectively interact with other individuals. Through trial and error they achieve social acceptance and acquire a repertoire of acceptable behaviors.

This unstructured, casual process of finding "one's place in the sun" is both frightening and an unproductive experience for the mentally retarded individual. Most such individuals receive little support for their efforts to "join the human race." At best, they are rewarded with tolerance, patronization, and infantilization. At worst, they are ignored or isolated. Most retarded individuals accurately assess themselves as misfits in a society they neither understand nor influence. Frequently an individual will reinforce the perception of himself as a misfit by developing antisocial behaviors in reaction to the treatment he experiences. These behaviors serve to increase the distance already existing between the retarded individual and the society as a whole. The irony of the situation is that the mentally retarded individual must take major responsibility for closing the gap between himself and the rest of society. He must refute the label of "misfit" even as he accepts the condition of retardation. By so doing, the individual will develop an accurate perception of himself that legitimates his demand to be part of the total human experience. He must modify any distortions of self-perception in order to develop the social skills necessary for developing relationships.

Group work is an effective way of helping the retarded individual establish himself as a human being with social rights and responsibilities. Within a group the individual can develop a perception of himself that is realistic and dignifying. He can learn new behaviors that will enhance his ability to initiate, develop, and maintain relationships. He can modify those behaviors that intensify his social alienation.

Following is a description of a treatment design used by a team of group workers in service to thirty-six adults with retardation.

BACKGROUND

Many men and women had been deinstitutionalized and scattered all over the city into board-and-room homes. Most of the adults had lived in rural institutions for much of their lives and were ill-prepared for community living. The board-and-room homes offered no program. Frequently supervision was provided by the cook. The adults were unhappy, the neighbors upset by strange behaviors they observed, and the home operators dismayed by the lack of community support. A community agency was assigned a group worker to design a service to address these concerns.

GOAL OF SERVICE

The intent of the program was *to enable these mentally retarded individuals to achieve their maximum potential as citizens in the community.* In order to achieve this goal the following objectives were identified:

1. To provide training and practice in the activities of daily living.
2. To provide social experiences so that interpersonal relationships could be fostered.
3. To introduce community resources and provide support to use them.
4. To provide recreation.

5. To support development of attitudes and behaviors appropriate to the community.
6. To provide a field placement for six graduate students of social work.

PROGRAM DESIGN

The program was designed to serve a total of thirty-six men: six from each of six different board-and-room homes. A student worker was assigned to serve each group of six. Each student had the responsibility of preparing his clients for participation in a weekly six-hour session at a central facility which was generously equipped for diverse activities. Pragmatically, each client needed to learn to prepare to go out in the community by accomplishing such tasks as clothes selection, grooming, and riding the bus to the appropriate stop. The student was expected to provide modeling, support, and guidance until the client could come to the weekly session without assistance.

Once the clients had assembled for the six-hour session, the social workers assumed additional responsibilities in order to facilitate the functioning of the "club," as it was called. More on this later.

When the residents had achieved the entry skills necessary to use the club, each worker initiated a weekly in-house session for the clients in order to maximize the continued use of the club experience. Thus the worker developed his role as the person responsible for guiding six individuals through a process of integration into a larger experience.

The field instructor functioned as coordinator of the entire design. She chaired weekly staff meetings to monitor each client's progress and to modify the program plans as required.

The club's schedule allowed for large- and small-group activities, tasks, and privileges; choices and decisions, discussions and counseling sessions. A typical club schedule follows:

10:00 A.M. Arrival: coffee hour and other social/recreational activities.
11:00 A.M. Group activity: crafts, meal preparation, decoration, shopping, table games and conversation
Noon. Buffet lunch: parties as appropriate
1:00 P.M. Club meeting: business affairs or behaviors discussed
2:00 P.M. Two mens' groups and two womens' groups
3:00 P.M. Social/recreational activities

10:00. The first hour allowed for staggered arrivals and informal conversation. Coffee, pool, dancing, television, records, a piano, and table games were available. Staff circulated and encouraged interaction.

11:00. The second hour included six activities: crafts, meal preparation, decoration, shopping, table games, and conversation. A worker was assigned to each activity for a six-month period. Six participants were assigned to each activity for one month, at which time they were reassigned to another activity. This provided an opportunity for the clients to get to know each of the workers. *Crafts* provided each client with the opportunity to make an article that was age-appropriate and necessitated four stages of completion. The intent was to teach the client patience with the task and develop his ability to wait for the reward, or "delayed gratification." *Meal preparation* gave the clients an opportunity to plan, prepare, and serve lunches for their friends. Efforts were made to encourage meals that were simple, nutritious, and easily prepared. *Decoration* provided an ongoing experience in changing the meeting rooms to reflect the interests of the group members. Various group projects resulted in personalizing the environment and providing the clients with a sense of belonging. Pieces of furniture were painted, posters framed, and pictures hung. Snapshots were taken of each client and incorporated into an attendance chart. Calendars were made to teach seasons, holidays, and birthdays. *Shopping* was an opportunity for clients to learn to use a variety of stores in the community, and to practice using money. This group shopped for special items needed by the club as well as for individual purchases. *Table games* introduced clients to simple games that could be played alone or with one or two others. This enabled the worker to teach the clients to accept simple rules and take turns. *Conversation* was designed to teach social behaviors such as initiating a conversation, accepting a compliment, giving a compliment, and accepting or refusing a date.

Noon. Buffet lunch was served. All special occasions were celebrated with food, including individual birthdays. Individuals were encouraged to sit anywhere for lunch as long as they sat with someone. They learned to make choices at mealtime; for example, an individual would choose the topping for his ice cream from among several kinds. This was an attempt to prepare the clients for the endless choices available in a noninstitutionalized setting.

1:00. The club meeting was for the entire group. Although this meeting was chaired by the program coordinator, steps were introduced to encourage client decision making and problem solving. The members learned to identify some rules for behavior such as "If you can't do it in a public place, you can't do it here." They also were helped to identify acceptable rewards such as "Five minutes, all alone, to use the phone."

2:00. Four groups met simultaneously. Members were assigned to the groups for a minimum of twelve sessions. The groups were formed on the basis of each client's ability to communicate and maintain interaction with others. The intent of this selection was to provide one hour during the day when the more highly functioning clients could address issues that interested them without being limited by the behavior of those with fewer skills. During the course of the program these groups changed membership several times as needs emerged and changed. Ultimately the groups became coeducational and focused on the concerns of human fulfillment.

3:00. The social/recreational hour allowed time for each individual to wind down from the intensity of small-group discussion and to finish the day with a person or activity of choice. It provided the staff with time to meet special concerns which had surfaced.

The schedule of activities described above was carefully maintained for four months so that club members could become familiar with the environment's demands, limits, and opportunities. The four-month period gave the staff time to assess the social skills of each individual.

The team assessed each person's social performance through observation and team discussion. A simple outline was used to focus attention upon behaviors that would support the client's entry into social situations with nonretarded individuals. The outline served to guide the staff to consider the following aspects of behavior: personal grooming, ambulation, communication and mobility (use of bus, elevator, revolving door, escalator, and street signs). It encouraged evaluation of the individual in terms of his relationships by concentrating on his use of the club, the staff, and community resources. Finally, the individual's ability to make choices and decisions was discussed. As a result of this process, a profile which listed social strengths and weaknesses was prepared for each client. It identified negative behaviors considered to be amenable to rapid modification as well as those behaviors that were most aversive to the general public. Two behavioral goals were determined for each person. One was selected from the list of behaviors amenable to change in order to provide the individual with an early success with relative ease. The second goal was selected from the list of aversive behaviors in order to decrease the alienation of the individual from the society as a whole. For example, one client needed to learn to bathe and use deodorant—a behavioral change that is relatively easy to accomplish. She also had a habit of talking very loudly, which called attention to herself and embarrassed her listeners. This behavior needed to change in order to diminish her social distance from others.

Once individual goals had been determined, they were discussed at the in-house small-group meetings. Interventions designed to bring about change were introduced there and at the club meeting as well. Thus the client could work on behavioral changes in a small, intimate setting and in an environment that more closely approximated an open community.

As the interventions were introduced, group norms developed. Progress was publicly recognized and rewarded. Charts were maintained as a visible reminder of achievements earned. Additional charts were developed to determine the quantity and quality of participation of each member in a group. This provided a baseline from which to work to encourage increased involvement.

Gradually small groups moved into the community. Trips were arranged to educational and recreational sites (a zoo, a museum, and an amusement park). As weather permitted, the clients enjoyed picnics, ballgames and swimming. In each instance, the same steps were taken to prepare the clients for the outing so that they could experience social acceptance. *At no time was the community facility prepared for the clients' attendance or participation.* The norm of the club was that "each person is responsible for himself and his behavior." The preparation steps included: discussion of the experience (what to expect, unusual demands, and acceptable reactions); role-playing the situation; and preparation of self in terms of appropriate clothes and equipment.

A club member left the group when either of two conditions had been met: he was gainfully employed or had enrolled in an adult-activity program that provided daily program choices. For those members who terminated because of employment, evening "rap" sessions were provided to reinforce the transition from dependence toward independence.

The model of practice described permitted each client to freely interact with others who shared his goal and concern. The lengthy sessions permitted a relaxed atmosphere where individual growth was encouraged, nurtured, and rewarded. Crises were handled when and where they happened, so that all parties could learn from the experience. Each client had the opportunity to receive feedback about his behavior from other clients, as well as the staff. Stimulation was provided by the creative use of the facility, time, and particular activities. Support was sustained by the structure of a schedule, simple rules, and staff involvement.

The clients demonstrated measurable improvement in social behaviors over a twelve-month period. They made progress toward understanding their disabilities and acquiring compensatory behaviors. The social workers had served the clients in many ways—as enablers, confidants, leaders, teachers, parent surrogates, resources, agency representatives, and community representatives.

The process described was ambitious in terms of staff hours. Six students devoted fourteen hours each week to the implementation of the design, eight of those hours in direct contact. In other words, six students provided forty-eight hours of contact to thirty-six clients. These students put in an additional thirty-six hours in staff meetings, maintenance of records, and extragroup contacts. The one salaried staff person spent twenty-four hours a week to coordinate the design, participate in the club, and supervise the staff. Thirty-six clients received an individualized goal-oriented program, and six graduate students shared in an excellent learning experience for the investment of three-fifths of a supervisor's time.

Small groups that are time-limited also provide growth experiences. Retarded individuals present a variety of behavioral peculiarities that can be addressed in a time-limited group experience. It is usual for retarded individuals to be demanding of attention, especially if they believe they are accepted. Sometimes it is difficult for them to share and to wait their turn to receive the attention of a respected worker.

Everybody wants to talk at the same time, and they all want to touch me, or sit beside me. I can't manage this, and the group will never move anywhere.

I played the piano for them. They all know "Jesus Loves Me" and enjoy singing it. I told the group I would play and sing a favorite song with each person alone. After each solo everyone could sing "Jesus Loves Me." Fortunately, I knew each of the songs selected. Everyone was quiet while Michael and I sang "Michael, Row the Boat Shore." Then we sang "Jesus Loves Me," and on to the next choice. It worked. We had a pleasant twenty minutes. They enjoyed singing and listening. They sat in their chairs and I think I may have found a way for them to share.

The group has come a long way in eight sessions. They have learned each others' songs and enjoy the togetherness of the experience. I introduced an action song in which each person could be a particular instrument. They enjoy this and it forces them to pay attention.

Sometimes the clients have immature or inappropriate expectations of authority figures. They appear to need and make a parent out of every adult. A series of log entries will serve as illustration:

The first discussion was laborious. The young people insist upon calling us "Mama" and "Daddy." Somehow we need to help them learn how we are different.

Since we were having supper together, the members all but fought to sit on either side of "Mama" and "Daddy." Fortunately, between us we have four sides, but that left the other four members out in the cold.

This week we played a game to determine seating and it worked. Also, we told the group members that we would no longer respond to "Mama" and "Daddy," but only to our given names. We explained that *friends* did this.

Tonight we had an informal supper. No table was set, people fixed their own food and sat where they wished in the meeting room. No one wanted to sit near us. So we sat and ate together. Perhaps they are getting the message.

Now the group members think we are husband and wife! At least they know we are not their parents.

Sometimes retarded individuals dress in ways that make them appear odd and the social distance to the nonretarded is increased. Women clients frequently benefit from a "glamour group."

The women went through all the hair-styling books and selected their favorite styles. I explained to them that my friend would be willing to come to the center and style their hair after they had learned to wash their own hair. We planned our next session. Each woman was to bring a towel. I agreed to bring shampoo and rinse.

My friend Sylvia came today and styled hair. Each woman's appearance is vastly improved with the shaping and trimming. They were very excited and wanted to leave early to show off their hairdos at home. They thought I was mean because I insisted that they clean up. Sylvia said she would not come again if they did not do their part. That did it, everyone pitched in.

It is great to see the women respond to the personal attention. Sometimes I think they hunger for touch. Cynthia has developed quite a knack for putting up rollers and she is gracious as she helps other women. Sylvia has a notion that Cynthia could be trained to be an assistant in a beauty salon, doing things such as shampooing, laundry, washing brushes, etc. We shall see how she continues. In any event I will inquire around.

It is true that clients frequently give many signs of having been deprived or denied many experiences they could have had if the community were more accepting. A group can provide retarded individuals with the opportunity to ventilate their feelings of frustration, despair, bewilderment, and impotence.

In group today Olive talked about being Jewish. I asked what that meant to her. She explained that "you don't believe in Santa Claus but instead you play with a dreydl." No one else knew what that was, but she insisted "No Santa Claus—just the dreydl." I asked her if she had played with a dreydl in the institution. "No, but when I go home I do." I asked her how she felt about all the things the other kids were doing about Christmas—decorating the tree, making cookies and gifts. She told me that was OK "but I wish I could play with a dreydl."

No one at the group home knew what a dreydl was, so I called Olive's mother. She explained that in their home they did keep the Jewish holidays and that the dreydl was a very special kind of top that the children were permitted to play with at that time only. We talked about the confusion Olive must have experienced at Christmas time in the institution. I told Olive's mother that I would arrange for Oive to have a dreydl at the holiday party, and that I would do what I could to help her understand the meaning of being Jewish.

Most retarded clients have normal curiosity about sex that may be intensified by the lack of opportunity to satisfy this curiosity. Retarded children
and adults do not have the same access to books, pictures, movies, and peer
discussions that the nonretarded have. Vignettes from the logs of two group
workers will serve to illustrate.

The women in the group were upset by an item that has been on the TV for several
days. A young mother who was mentally ill had poisoned her baby. They asked if they
could have a session without the men in order to talk about the news item and having
babies. This surprised me and I responded by saying the men could be in on this discussion as well. They were emphatic and said they wanted to talk to me alone and the men
could join us later. In retrospect I know they were right in their decision. They wanted
me to talk about women and mental illness.

"The housemother says she is crazy. We're not crazy, are we?" We talked about the
differences between mental illness and mental retardation. Eventually the women
seemed convinced that they were not crazy. I talked to them about retardation making
it difficult to learn a lot of things. I took a pile of blocks and said, "If each one of these
blocks was one thing to learn about being a mother, your mother and sisters could
learn about each one of them. Because you are retarded you may only learn two or
three things about being a mother." They seem to understand the comparison. I asked
them to tell me all the things a mother needed to know about taking care of a baby. I
listed them on the board and then each girl identified the things she could do. Betty
Jane may have summed it up for the rest of the members when she said, "I couldn't
make formula because I can't read. Perhaps I need to learn some more things before I
have a baby." There were many nods of agreement. Laura closed the topic by pro-
nouncing, "Well, maybe I can't be a mama because I can't do things but at least I
wouldn't kill my baby because I'm *sick*! When I asked the women if they were ready to
join the men, they agreed and, "let them look at our list, too."

Many weeks later, the men from the group described above asked for a
special session with the male worker. Perhaps they felt they had missed
something. In any event, the worker agreed to have a session with them
without women, and they identified sexual concerns they wished to discuss.
They told him they wanted a session with the *woman* worker to learn about
women. Her notes follow:

Mike had prepared me for my session with the men. I was prepared to discuss birth,
conception, and menstruation. I was surprised by the first question directed to me:
"Does it hurt?" "Does *what* hurt?" "You know, does it hurt when you're 'on the rag'?" I
took a deep breath and jumped in. . . .

The session ran overtime, but it seemed important to stick with the discussion. Each
member was genuinely interested and respectful. They were shy and uncomfortable,
but they did nothing to embarrass me. They asked if I would talk with them again. I cer-

tainly will, and next time I'm going to tell them about some of the games some women try to run on men. They appear too preoccupied with the fragile-woman image.

Not everyone should work with mentally retarded clients. The demands upon the worker's patience, tolerance, enthusiasm, and understanding never cease. The worker must be prepared to challenge the individual to strive to meet his maximum potential, even as he accepts the reality of mental retardation. Some workers are able to reach past the retardation and establish a relationship with the client that truly validates the humanness in both of them. Such a person was Ron, who provided an exquisite group experience for a group of men and women, all under the age of twenty-five.

Ron and a co-worker provided several hours of group experience each week to six men and six women. The goals of the group were to enhance social skills and develop pre-vocational attitudes and behaviors. Many different interventions were used to stimulate the young people and support them in taking the risks of personal growth. Every relevant topic was initiated and discussed in formal and informal situations. Some of the best exchanges occurred over lunch. Eventually the group members' interests turned to sexuality and human fulfillment. Specifically, they wanted to discuss pregnancy and the birth of a baby. It would have been acceptable for Ron to turn this experience over to his co-worker, but instead he proceeded to discuss the topic.

He shared with the group the information that his wife was expecting their first child and told them the birth of a baby was especially important to him as well. Pregnancy, birth, and conception became comfortable topics for everyone to discuss. The group members constantly asked Ron about his wife's condition, and he dutifully shared its progress. Gradually the focus of the discussions shifted; the young people wanted to discuss parenting—how to be a father, how to be a mother. They talked a lot about the responsibilities of parents and the great need children had for parents. They developed amazing insights and began to recognize some of their limitations in terms of parenting. The young people *really* learned about family from Ron—about the roles, rights, and responsibilities of the different family members. Quite an accomplishment when you consider that all but two of them had lived in institutions away from their families for most of their lives. Ten of the young people could not remember their fathers, and four of them had no contact with their mothers.

Ron's baby was expected at the same time he planned to terminate his connection with the agency. The group members decided to have a baby shower for him instead of a farewell party. They persuaded the woman worker to help them as they prepared a shower, complete with decorations, food, and gifts. Unable to find a card that expressed their thoughts, they decided to create their own. Following is the message they prepared:

Dear Ron—

Your friends think there are three things they wish you would do with your baby
1. love the baby a whole lot
2. keep your baby safe and warm
3. teach your baby to be kind like you.

Good directions for any parent and a powerful affirmation to a man who had done his work well. He had reached beyond retardation and found people.

CHAPTER 8

The Social Worker as Part of an Interdisciplinary Team

Eleanor Whiteside Lynch

"INTERDISCIPLINARY" HAS BECOME a byword of our times. Its definition has been set forth in volume after volume and in article after article. However, in daily practice its meaning has remained elusive. Darnell (1972) defines interdisciplinary functioning as "the internalization of a commitment by each member of the staff of a given institution to moderate the principles and practices of one's professional discipline in order to enhance the ability of members of associated disciplines to contribute to productive joint effort and to take actions consistent with that commitment." He goes on to point out that the interdisciplinary concept is founded on "the fertile soil of interpersonal relationships." Balthazar and Stevens (1971) suggest that "interdisciplinary" carries the meaning of "transaction between or among disciplines." Falck (1977), in discussing "interdisciplinary" as it applies to social work education and practice, states: "Interdisciplinary practice means professional activity by two or more practitioners in an interdependent work relationship, within a common work system and spanning two or more fields of learning and professional activity."

Common to all of these definitions are the concepts of mutuality and sharing. There is a recognition that each discipline's knowledge and skills

162

will be enhanced by those of other disciplines, with the end result being improved service delivery. It is the purpose of this chapter to describe ways in which social workers and special educators can work together with handicapped persons and their families to give meaning to the word "interdisciplinary," ways in which they can share their knowledge and skills to provide a more coordinated and effective approach to students and clients.

Historical Perspective

Special educators and social workers have both worked with handicapped persons and their families since early in this century, but all too often neither discipline has understood the other's role or function. Instead of moving toward one another to explore commonalities, differences, and ways to collaborate so as to improve services to children and families, each discipline has retreated and hidden behind a wall of jargon, misunderstanding, and mistrust. Until recently, social workers in many settings were usually regarded by teachers as "on the family's side" with no understanding of or appreciation for the day-to-day demands of the classroom. After all, since most social workers had never taught, how could they understand what it was really like? But those who had taught were treated with little more respect. Like former teachers who become school psychologists, the school social workers were regarded as defectors from the pressures of the front line. In many other systems, school social workers were given monitoring positions which virtually involved policing—e.g., attendance officer, truant officer, detention officer. In these roles their skills and training were wholly misused. Their tasks were reduced to record-keeping, detective work, and enforcing. In many instances, they knew of interventions which might help the child or family but were pushed by the system to respond punitively rather than therapeutically. Still other school systems had no social workers at all. They were either never hired or among the first to be fired in the years of austerity.

The negativism just described ran in both directions. Social workers were often in a position to see the personality, cultural, and family prejudices that teachers brought to their classrooms and acted out, often unwittingly, on their students. Workers saw the youngsters' homes and families up close and recognized that it wasn't disinterest or lack of caring when somebody's mother missed conferences and PTA meetings. Rather, it was because she had three children under four, no money for a baby-sitter, no transportation, and a husband walking the picket line in the twelfth week of a strike. Social workers were also in a position to see the frequent conflict in home-school priorities and the arrogance of school systems in insisting that their demands must always come first. Ten minutes of quiet teaching time in the home can be hard to find when each parent works a different shift and the oldest sibling takes major responsibility for the daily care of the handicapped child. Workers who visited classrooms also saw that many teachers lacked skill in group dynamics and group process. Under these circumstances it is easy to understand why many social workers chose to identify themselves as child advocates and to take stands that the school considered adversarial.

Although the above description is grim, it remained the rule rather than the exception for many years. Only in the quite recent past have major changes taken place. Some of the changes have come about through legislation, some through modifications in preservice training programs, and some through the efforts of individuals seeking ways to improve services to persons with disabilities.

Group Process and P.L. 94–142

Probably the single most important piece of legislation which has contributed to the teaming of social work and special education is Public Law 94–142, the Education for All Handicapped Children Act of 1975. This law guarantees each handicapped person's right to a free and appropriate education in the least restrictive environment possible. Implementation procedures require that a yearly meeting be convened to develop an Individual Educational Plan (IEP) for each handicapped student receiving special education services. This meeting involves the parents, teacher, administrator, and often ancillary personnel including the school social worker. The IEP and the planning and placement meetings mandated by various states have become important vehicles for social work–special education cooperation. The social worker's training can be used to develop an effective process for conducting these meetings, and his group skills can be used to guide participants through the process. Besides his frequent role as coordinator, the social worker is often relied upon to supplement family information and to help devise educational plans and strategies in the affective domain. In this give-and-take among parents and school personnel, school social workers and special educators have an opportunity to observe each other's skills and to utilize the strengths represented by each in the development of the most appropriate educational plan.

This kind of cooperation was apparent in a recent case:

Wendy was a ten-year-old girl receiving special education services in a program for the trainable mentally retarded (TMR) through a large, metropolitan, intermediate school district. During the past several months her behavior had deteriorated considerably at home and at school. The majority of her classroom time was spent screaming, tossing materials, and assaulting her classmates. At home she sulked and refused to follow family routines.

For the first few weeks of the behavior change, the parents and teacher worked together to try to pinpoint the problem and to develop effective means of dealing with it. When no solution seemed apparent, the teacher asked for a complete evaluation. With the parents' permission, Wendy was evaluated by a team of specialists representing medicine, psychology, education, social work, and speech.

The results of the evaluation ruled out any physical or medical problems which could account for her behavior, and no specific environmental factors that might be contributing to the problem in the home or classroom were identified. Cognitively, her functioning was on the border between moderate and severe mental retardation.

At the end of three months and many failures, the parents and the teacher had reached an impasse. Their early joint concern and cooperation had been forgotten in the frustration caused by Wendy's daily outbursts. Finally, in desperation, the teacher requested an Educational Planning and Placement Committee Meeting (EPPC) to propose that Wendy be removed from her class and placed in a program for the severely mentally retarded where the staff-to-student ratios were higher and where disruptive behavior is seen more frequently. The building principal supported the teacher's position. Wendy's parents were totally opposed to this proposed change of placement, wanting her to stay in the TMR classroom, where, they felt, she at least had the benefit of more highly functioning classmates serving as models. On the day of the EPPC meeting the tension and frustration around the conference table were apparent.

Mr. J., the school social worker, had been asked to chair the meeting and to record the decisions. He had prepared himself by observing Wendy at home and at school, and by talking to her parents, teacher, and other school staff and eliciting their support to try something different at the EPPC. He had carefully reviewed her file and the most recent evaluation material, and had checked the available school resources. When he opened the meeting, he briefly summarized the situation and proposed a problem-solving format which forced all participants to focus on Wendy's strengths and weaknesses, the objectives to be accomplished, and the resources available to assist the school and the family. Through his carefully designed plan and excellent facilitating, the frustration dissipated and both sides were enabled to see that they could accomplish more for Wendy by working together. The meeting ended with an agreement that Wendy would be placed in a special behavioral-treatment room and that her current teacher would be given time to observe the methods practiced there, to advise, and to receive consultation. Wendy's parents agreed to go to a community agency whose staff consulted to the behavioral-treatment room for counseling and training in management techniques. The plan was implemented and reviewed again in six weeks, at which time Wendy was able to be reintegrated in to the TMR classroom, with the full support and cooperation of the parents and school staff.

This is only a single example of how the school social worker can work with parents and special education personnel to develop the best services for handicapped students. Parents and teachers work with their children and students for hours at a time on an almost-daily basis. This close contact, the frustration it engenders when things are not going well, and the tremendous investment that both parents and teachers have in providing the best possible experiences for handicapped youngsters can cause communication to break down. The school social worker by training and by role is in an excellent position to help home and school resume communication By bringing both sides together, developing an effective process, and facilitating the interaction, the school social worker can help both parents and teachers work more effectively on the child's behalf. Although P.L. 94–142 is applied in the school setting, state institutions, rehabilitation facilities, and community mental health settings, all have comparable vehicles for individualizing the resident's or client's treatment program. The social work–education team is equally important in these settings.

Interdisciplinary Assessment

The assessment of handicapped children, adolescents, and adults is a complex task which requires the knowledge, clinical expertise, and experience of many disciplines and the input of the client and the parents or care-givers. Each of us presents far too complex a physical, medical, psychological, and social picture to permit the assumption that any single professional could accurately represent our strengths and weaknesses. To believe that any professional could accurately represent us without asking us our perceptions or talking with our parents or care-givers (if we still have our primary relationship with either the former or the latter) is equally foolish. The same is true for persons with developmental disabilities. Getting an accurate picture of the client's or student's strengths and weaknesses requires an interdisciplinary evaluation which includes that person's input as well as the input of the parents, care-givers, and teacher. This kind of comprehensive team evaluation also requires advance planning and should include ecological assessment (i.e., observations in the home, school, workshop, etc.) as well as assessment in the clinic setting.

In an interdisciplinary team evaluation, disciplinary roles blur, and each team member strives to gather information which will contribute to an understanding of the client/student's perspective as well as the larger picture. In this kind of model social workers and special educators have an opportunity to work closely with each other as well as professionals from other disciplines. The following example serves to illustrate this kind of assessment model.

David was referred to the clinic by his placement social worker for a comprehensive, interdisciplinary assessment to determine his level of functioning and to review his current school placement and program. At the time David was four years old, deaf, legally blind, and living in his fourth foster home. He attended a full-day program for handicapped preschoolers that emphasized self-feeding, tactile exploration, and communication. David's foster parents and the school staff had had problems communicating, and each was angry with the other. All of David's developmental milestones had been delayed, and he had been both abused and neglected in his previous home environments. It was only in this most recent home that he had formed a primary attachment and had begun to make noticeable gains. His social worker from the placement agency was quite involved, and eager to be a part of the team and its evaluation process.

A planning meeting of all evaluators was called two weeks before David and his foster parents came to the clinic. At that meeting the major evaluation questions were listed and plans for gathering the needed information made. For example, instead of doing a formal social work interview, the social worker agreed to serve as liaison to the community social worker during the evaluation process and to support the strong positive relationship that the community social worker had already developed with the foster parents. Since David had only a few sounds and no words, the speech and language therapist decided to gather his information by observing the special education evaluation and by giving the psychologist some specific questions to ask the foster parents in his interview with them. The occupational therapist, the physical therapist, and the pediatrician collaborated so that the pediatrician could do the motor and physical exam herself using the OT and PT as consultants. This kind of "planned teaming" reduces the number of evaluators who must have "hands on," broadens each discipline's expertise, and assists in viewing the client or student as a complex whole rather than a set of unrelated parts.

During the evaluations many team members viewed other evaluator's assessments, asked questions, and provided their observations. After the evaluations, informal interchange continued and formal reports reflecting the conclusions of the mini-teams were presented.

Because of the home-school conflict which had been reported in the referral, information was found to be a serious problem for David's foster parents; it was decided at the staffing to concentrate on helping resolve this difference. The community social worker and the clinic special educator were seen as the most appropriate people to help the school and family work through their differences. Both served as facilitators in a meeting of parents and school staff, with the social worker providing process skills and the special educator providing knowledge about the type of programming and methods that would enhance David's functioning at home and at school.

This type of interdisciplinary team evaluation allows each evaluator to use his or her own expertise and to capitalize on the knowledge and skill of every other evaluator. It provides an excellent forum for sharing with one another, teaching, and learning while providing superior service for the client. Teaming is particularly important with young children, difficult-to-test clients, and clients who have been evaluated many times. It decreases the number of professionals who must interact directly with the client, reduces the number of questions that the client and family must answer, and provides a set of findings which include all aspects of the client's setting and functioning.

Early Intervention

Local, intermediate, and/or cooperative education agencies in many states are now responsible for providing education programs for handicapped infants and young children. Because of the young age of the children involved (birth to age six) and because of the general philosophy in early-childhood education, parents play a major role in these intervention programs. A considerable body of literature exists which describes parental involvement in early-intervention programs for handicapped children (Lynch, 1978; Caldwell and Stedman, 1977; Moersch and Wilson, 1976; Lambie, Bond, and Weikart, 1974; Karnes, Zehrbach, and Teska, 1972; Gordon and Guinagh, 1971).

One of the primary issues that has surfaced as a result of the closer tie between schools and parents in early intervention is the need to be aware of family dynamics and family issues. This area is one in which social workers, special educators, and all of the other members of the team can work together profitably. The need for collaboration in this area became readily apparent in my own practice as a special educator on an early-intervention team. It was my responsibility to provide home visits to several preschoolers served by the project. The purpose of the weekly home visits was to model teaching activities in the home and to provide support (material and moral) to the family for carrying out the activities. Developing creative teaching ideas, adapting materials, working "hands on" with the child, and breaking the task into learnable pieces were strengths that I brought to the situation; and for the first few visits they proved to be enough. What I did not understand was the effect of an open, friendly, weekly visitor in someone's home.

On the fourth visit to Jack's house, his mother looked especially hassled and asked if I could spend a few minutes alone with her. Two hours later I emerged feeling that I was in over my head. She had just sobbed out her anger about Jack's disability, the shame she felt about these feelings, and the despair of a collapsing marriage. I have been trained to be a good listener and to give support without giving advice, but sometimes that is not enough. In this case, Jack's mother needed to share her pain with someone who could take her through a process which included accepting the "OK-ness" of her own feelings, moving her to share these feelings with her husband, and helping them re-examine their relationship as a couple first and parents of a handicapped child second. The team social worker was the person to do this.

There were several ways in which this could be effectively implemented. I could maintain my role as the home visitor for the child and Jack's mother could come into the center for counseling. Or I could continue home visits with Jack and the social worker could arrange counseling sessions in the home. The third option was for me to teach the social worker some of the training strategies I was using with Jack and have her go into the home. spend a few minutes with Jack, and then work with his mother and later his mother and father together. Jack's parents were given the choice, and they chose the last option. With this sharing of skills, Jack and his family could both be served more effectively.

In several other instances in the early-intervention program, the social worker shared her skills with other staff to provide a better program for the children and families involved.

Several families were living at the poverty level and had no knowledge about how to gain access to the welfare system. The project social worker shared step-by-step information with all of the staff about food stamps, Aid to Dependent Children, Crippled Children's Commission, Medicare, and Medicaid. We were then able to help the families through the bureaucratic maze to the resources they needed. Although we could have assigned the social worker to provide this information to the families, we felt that they had already had many people in and out of their homes. It was important for us to provide service through a single individual who would remain constant, so that the parade of "helping people" would at least be reduced by one.

Simply talking with the early-intervention social worker about cases and families proved to be one of the most important collaborations. When I felt the families I worked with were too dependent on me, or at a standstill or when I felt that there was an undercurrent in the household that I could not identify, her insights and comments were invaluable. At the same time, she learned about task analysis, Piaget, and a host of other "educational" issues and concerns.

Training

The value of the collaboration of social work and special education has become more and more apparent to me. As I train students majoring in special education at the university, I see how their functioning is enriched by interaction with social work faculty members and social work students. I have also seen social work students improve their practice by learning from me and my students. And as I work with parents and teachers of handicapped children I see the importance of modeling cooperation between social work and special education. One example of combined special education–social work training for parents and school personnel is a workshop designed to improve communication between home and school and to present strategies for effective teaching at home and at school. The workshop is described below.

Several years ago Martha Dickerson developed a manual, *Fostering Children with Mental Retardation,* for foster-parent training classes. The manual, with worksheets for the class members, focused on developmental disabilities and positive parenting techniques. It was written simply, with chapters devoted to acceptance, limits, rules, privacy, respect, and routines. The manual was later published and used successfully by several trainers with many foster parents of diverse and often educationally limited backgrounds. Its effectiveness caused Martha to examine other ways in which it could be used. As she and I began talking about its generalizability we quickly moved to thinking of the needs of all parents of handicapped children. The material was equally applicable to them; all of the issues related to parenting which it dealt with had come up frequently in her practice as a social worker and my practice as a special educator. One important issue was not covered—the issue of home-school communication. From our work with parents and school staff we knew that the technique of developing and maintaining communication is a major concern that is seldom attended to.

As Martha and I continued to pool our knowledge, our practice, and our thoughts from both a home and a school perspective, we began to see how we could develop a workshop for parents and school staff by elaborating the existing material. The design contains four major components. The first component separates the parents and the school staff into small groups. The parent group is asked to identify things they do that probably irritate school personnel. At the same time, the school group identifies things they do that irritate parents. This introspective beginning prevents the evening from deteriorating into a gripe session, and the large group share-out clearly demonstrates how similar our foibles and failings really are. The similarity opens communication, and the groups are then reorganized to include parents *and* teachers. The newly formed groups are given real problems from practice to resolve. Each of the problems has many possible resolutions, but all depend on open communication. Following the problem resolution in small groups and the share-out, participants return to the original groupings and develop guidelines for how they want to be treated. In other words, the parents develop guidelines for school staff to use when communicating with parents and school staff develop guidelines for parents when communicating with them. As in the first exercise, the guidelines are always similar.

The second component combines large- and small-group teaching using the chapter of the foster-parent manual mentioned earlier. The parenting material has been expanded to include classroom parallels. Privacy, limits, rules, acceptance, and respect are defined. Illustrations are given by the trainers, and participants have an opportunity to apply the information to their own home or classroom.

The third component focuses on modifying the environment instead of modifying the handicapped child. Using both small- and large-group discussion and exercises, it encourages parents and teachers to think about changing the physical setting, the materials, the approach, and the methods when they are having trouble with a youngster *before* they think about changing the child.

The fourth component is a game which gives participants an opportunity to apply all they have learned about communication, parenting, and teaching. It provides a pulling together and summary of the nine-hour experience as well as a positive ending.

This workshop uses some of the most important tenets of education and social work. The presentation of material is varied and provides many opportunities for active learning. The principle of peer learning and teaching is used to demonstrate that there are no experts but that each participant has important things to contribute. The leaders facilitate and keep the process moving but do not lecture, preach, or teach. By combining the school-family expertise of special education and social work, an excellent training design was developed and has now been taught to trainers of other disciplines.

Sexuality and Disability

In my years as a special education classroom teacher, I learned that sexuality was a major concern for the students, the parents, the staff, and the administration. But, like most of the others around me, I found that this was not an issue I could face directly, with myself or anyone else.

I remember looking around during a free-play period in my primary-level classroom for the trainable mentally retarded to see Carolyn and Robbie playing doctor. They had gotten well past the waiting room and were involved in some very systematic examining. Because I was embarrassed, I missed a beautiful opportunity to teach body parts. Instead, I went over and told them that the doctor had to leave for the hospital and they had to close the office!

The incident stayed with me, as did the haunting feeling that there must have been a better way to handle it. Unfortunately, my track record with the next classroom sexuality issue was no better.

One of the little girls in the class overtly masturbated at nap-time. Being extremely put off by this and a neophyte behaviorist, I did everything wrong. As a result of my behavior-modification program Jane quit masturbating and started pulling out little patches of her hair. Although I was able to redirect her hair pulling, I was not able to confront the issue of masturbation with myself, with her, or with my colleagues.

It was several years later, when I was heading a department of psychology in a large, rural state institution for the mentally retarded, that the issues of sexuality were once again raised. The eager young psychologists with whom I worked took the principles of deinstitutionalization and mainstreaming seriously. Although the setting was impossible, that team did more to implement mainstreaming under the worst of conditions in the early 1970s than many of the more "advanced" settings have done to date.

One aspect of change was the implementation of "resident rap groups" with a psychologist and a social worker facilitating. The plan was that the groups would be made up of residents who were about to be placed in community settings. The assumption was that we would deal with their concerns about purchases, money, banking, transportation, group-home living, cooking, laundry, and so forth. Those topics occupied the first twenty minutes of the first session of each group. The remainder of that session and all that followed focused on sexuality in its broadest definition. The residents wanted desperately to sort out their feelings, roles, rights, and responsibilities as adult men and women. They wanted information about their own bodies, about bodies of the opposite sex, about conception, contraception, and childbirth. They wanted to know more about the expressions of sexuality that they had seen at the institution; for even though its operation was Victorian, they had seen masturbation, intercourse, bestiality, and homosexuality. Those men and women who had been institutionalized for one to twenty-five years challenged me and all of the young, liberal doctoral students to examine our own sexuality. In knowledge we were far ahead, but in our ability to see and accept ourselves as sexual beings and to express our own feelings we were often several chapters behind our clients. It was in those years of searching ourselves and the libraries for ways of teaching sexuality to people with retardation that I began to recognize that I too was a sexual being.

Since that time the importance of sexuality in the teaching and training of all people, including those with mental retardation, has become more and more apparent. As a special educator I have skills in individualization, instructional design, and curriculum development but lack the skills in group dynamics and group facilitation that are a part of social work training. When skills from both fields are combined, all affective education and sexuality education can become more productive. In the past four years I have worked closely with a colleague in social work to design training programs in sexuality for developmentally disabled clients, their parents, the professionals and paraprofessionals who provide services to them, and the university students who are training to work in the field.

This joint training began at the Institute for the Study of Mental Retardation and Related Disabilities in 1976 when the social work component was asked to provide sexuality teaching and training to sixteen mentally retarded clients who attended a special social-adjustment program at the Institute four days per week.

After working with these clients on academic subjects, money management, kitchen skills, and grooming, it became apparent to the project staff that sexuality was a major issue. The clients ranged in age from their late twenties into their forties. Half lived at home and half lived in group homes. Their functioning ranged from low-moderate to educable and many had additional handicaps, but they all had in common personal issues related to their sexuality. They had many myths, much misinformation, and little knowledge about their own bodies and how they worked; less information about the opposite sex; and no knowledge about the rights and responsibilities of being a sexual person.

After many conversations and no little hesitancy on my part, I agreed to recruit a male and a female special education student from the four who were doing M. A. internships with me to pair with a male and a female social work student. We negotiated that part of their special education placement would include running sexuality groups with the social work students for the adult clients, under the joint supervision of my social work colleague and myself. It was a new venture for all of us, and all of us were frightened by the enormity of the task as well as the interdisciplinary teaming. In addition, teaching retarded adults about sexuality was a concept that few people supported. But we all believed that it should be done.

The clients were divided into two groups of eight. One group had members who lived at home; the other group's members lived in group homes. Each group had both men and women and was facilitated by a male-female, special education–social work pair. The groups met weekly for ninety minutes. Sometimes, for the introduction of new topics or an in-depth discussion of male or female hygiene, the groups were organized into single-sex grouping during part of the hour and a half. Group norms were established and rules of confidentiality adhered to. The group members were informed that only the supervisors and a designated project staff member would have the privilege of viewing the sessions, which were monitored over closed-circuit TV in our offices.

The beginning was difficult. Nervous laughter, temper tantrums, and refusal to come to group were all symptomatic of the difficult ground we were covering . The students' and supervisors' anxiety was often equally apparent. The ninety-minute debriefing and supervision meetings which we held after each session often lasted much longer. As the weeks went by, it became evident that the less directive style of the social workers was ineffective. The clients needed some group and individualized directive teaching about the basics of body parts, body differences, and body functions. The special education students taught the social work students a great deal about methods, materials, visual aids, and objective setting. At the same time, the social work students taught the special education students much about building a cohesive group, listening, facilitating instead of lecturing, and the stages common to the group process. The exchange was truly interdisciplinary, for the representatives of one profession learned the skills of the other and how to apply them.

Each of us faced conflicts, one of the biggest being the realization that the clients were being prohibited from putting into practice any of the information they were learning. None had privacy and none had been taught to use public transportation, though almost all were capable. The sexuality program then broadened into mobility training and community awareness. The training was done in pairs or groups of three so that it did not look like "handicapped day" at any store, restaurant, or movie. The objectives were individualized so that each client could work on what he or she needed and wanted to know. One woman worked several weeks developing her skills so that she could go purchase her own box of Kotex, something she had never before owned. At the end of seven months, sixteen clients, four students, and two supervisors knew more about themselves than they had ever known before. The combination of process and content of facilitation and education worked; and the concept "interdisciplinary" had become a reality in practice.

From that initial program, our interdisciplinary practice in sexuality and disability has grown into a university seminar, consultation to schools and agencies, and a special federal project, called "Training and Technical Assistance in Human Fulfillment for Developmentally Disabled Persons," which serves a six-state area. Although social work and special education remain key components of the team, physical therapy, psychology, and instructional technology have major roles. The physical therapist on the team has increased our awareness and knowledge about the human-fulfillment needs of persons with physical disabilities. The psychologist has acted as a facilitator and has enriched and strengthened our practice by tying it to theory. The instructional technologist has helped us develop materials that can take our work far beyond our own geographic limitations. Each of these people has learned from us, and their knowledge and skill have improved our practice.

In this process the boundaries of our disciplinary training have begun to blur. Each of us has learned the other's language, way of thinking, knowledge, and skills. I shall never be a social worker nor claim that I know and can practice everything that a social worker knows and can practice, but I am a better special educator because of what I have learned from social work. Likewise, there are some social workers who are better because of what they have learned from a special educator.

Making It Work

It seems to me that perhaps this is the best definition of "interdisciplinary": through our understanding of each other's skills and knowledge we are able to work as a team and enhance our own practice. But putting our beliefs into practice is seldom easy. What exactly, then, does it take to develop effective collaboration between social workers and special educators? Like all growth-producing relationships, developing the social work–special education team takes commitment to the idea that it can happen, a desire to see that it does, hard work, and a little bit of magic. None of the above-mentioned successes came about effortlessly, nor do I believe that any ground that has been gained can be held without continued effort. In every situation and setting there will be factors that promote team building and those that interfere. It seems that the conflicts that arise and the resistance to collaboration can usually be categorized under one of the following generic problems: (1) lack of personal trust, (2) disciplinary elitism, (3) professional insecurity, or (4) territoriality.

The first, lack of personal trust, is perhaps the most difficult. Before you can work with me or I with you, we must each take the risk of assuming that the other has integrity and is being open and honest in the interaction. Trust cannot be assigned, conferred, or awarded; it must be earned. And like the most sophisticated flight equipment, it must be tried, tested, pushed to its limits, torn down, and reassembled many times before it can be relied on. If real collaboration is to occur, I must trust you. In the example of Wendy's EPPC meeting (see page 164), nothing could have been satisfactorily resolved if the social worker had not earned the trust of both the parents and the teacher. Each side knew that it would not be sold out, and this allowed everyone to risk traveling over new and difficult territory to find the best solution for Wendy.

Disciplinary elitism is a second stumbling block to interdisciplinary practice. Unfortunately, most of us still live in hierarchical personal and professional worlds. A status value tends to be assigned to everything from clothes to office space to people. Some professions have higher status than others; and in the field of developmental disabilities, some handicaps have higher status than others. Professional elitists tend to believe that their disciplinary skills are the most important, and they often deny or denigrate the contributions of others. Traditionally, those who provide treatment or therapy have been more highly regarded than those who provide care or education. Although these walls have begun to crumble, much remains to be done. In the area of developmental disabilities, it is impossible to believe for long that the physician who makes the diagnosis or the social worker who counsels the family is more important than the bus driver who gets the child to school or the teacher who works on toileting and feeding when he or she arrives. Perhaps the best way to deflate one's own professional ego is to spend a day trying to do someone else's job!

Professional insecurity is a third barrier to interdisciplinary practice. Only when we are secure in our own skills can we risk sharing them with others. Professional jargon is a good example of this. Only the most competent and confident professionals can discuss a case in plain language; the insecure hide behind specialized words that only serve to make the obvious obscure. Real interdisciplinary functioning relies on each person's sharing his or her knowledge and skill to enrich the other's practice. The more each person invests, the higher the dividends, and no investment yields a zero payoff for the professionals and the clients.

The final major obstacle to interdisciplinary functioning is territoriality. Although in some instances it may stem from professional insecurity, it is often rooted in different soil. Somehow we have managed to train people in the fine art of protecting their turf as if knowledge and skill were diminishing resources. In the area of developmental disabilities we know far too little to try to limit the knowledge to a few. Our science and our art are primitive, as many of our clients could tell us. There must be openness and expansion rather than protectiveness and narrowing.

Over the next few years the move toward more contact in preservice college and university programs will no doubt increase. Students will begin working together, sharing knowledge, and sharing skills before the professional boundaries have been so tightly drawn that each of the disciplines is entrenched. This early, combined training will certainly improve collaborative efforts. We cannot, however, afford to wait for a generation of professionals who have been trained differently; we must begin practicing in cooperative, interdisciplinary ways now. There are guidelines for developing that relationship. The guidelines are easy to state, but often difficult to practice. They require constant review, renewal, and remembrance; and like the negotiated parameters of any relationship they demand mutual respect and open communication. If written on an office poster, they might read something like the following:

1. I will learn your language and teach you mine.
2. I will ask for your perceptions and feedback, not for praise or affirmation, but to learn more of what you know and to challenge my own timeworn positions.
3. I will share my professional strengths and my weaknesses with you so that we can both grow.
4. I will not withhold "disciplinary secrets" from you, or cling tenaciously to my turf; but I will tell you when I am feeling invaded and expect you to do the same.
5. I will confront you, challenge you, listen to you, and learn from you. I will expect you to do the same with me.

If these guidelines were practiced, I have no doubt that social workers and special educators would become stronger allies and would work more effectively and creatively to provide services to handicapped children and their families.

CHAPTER 9

Issues of Social Policy

Gerald Provencal

THE PREVIOUS CHAPTERS HAVE DESCRIBED a trend in the provision of services to mentally retarded persons which clearly reflects a building recognition of the rights of handicapped populations. This recognition would be tremendously significant even if it were evident merely in improved attitudes, stereotypes, or perceived acceptance by the public at large. There is no question but that there has been a positive change in the understanding of mental retardation held by Americans (President's Committee on Mental Retardation, 1975). It is obvious, however, that the telling criterion for gauging a society's acceptance of any group of citizens is its concrete treatment of them and not its abstract feelings about their plight.

I have selected housing to focus on here because it is the most visual expression of the distance we have traveled (and have yet to travel) in coming to receive the mentally retarded as citizens. Progress in rights recognition, teaching concepts, medicine, and therapies are obviously critical to the welfare of the retarded. There is something very basic about where one lives, however, which in some ways says the most about what a person has been allowed to become. The history of such tolerance in this country is well known and not very attractive. For this reason, I would like to review positive changes made in the range of living options now available. What has prompted the possibilities and how they are likely to develop will be discussed. The future role of the social worker as a participant in the field will be touched on, and implications for the profession will be suggested.

177

Deinstitutionalization

PHILOSOPHICAL PROMPTS

While the humanization of the public's image of mentally retarded persons has been evolving for centuries, the greatest movement has occurred over the past decade. The importation of the normalization principle from Scandinavia dramatically affected our way of dealing with mental deficiency, radically altering the professional's and the family's expectation of the client and of the way in which he or she would be received by society (Wolfensberger, 1972). Expectations for all the players in the drama of retardation were elevated to lofty heights with this "new" principle because it not only called on us to teach the client to behave more like the rest of us but demanded that methods be as normative as possible. Not as normative as acceptable or passable or probable; but as normative as *possible.*

The normalization principle gives no quarter to history or practicality and shows no satisfaction with the improvement of conditions unless a normative standard deferred to by the nonhandicapped is used to measure improvement.

Normalization and its corollary principles wakened the field of human services in this country and Canada from a trance of complacency as it defied us to argue against the logic or rightness of its premises. It challenged us to defend it or to provide an alternate philosophy that was strong enough to defeat it. As difficult as it is to change timeworn practices and ideology, it has become perhaps even more difficult for the professional and the advocacy community to resist adoption of the normalization principle as the foundation upon which to build service systems.

Of the many notable publications dealing with normalization in the past decade, one of the most important proved to be a monograph commissioned by the President's Committee on Mental Retardation in 1969, *Changing Patterns in Residential Services for the Mentally Retarded.* The work eloquently laid out the arguments for reforming reliance upon the public institution as the milieu of choice for retarded persons. While it advanced some new models for housing, its predominant theme was that the large, distant and custodial institution was not a place where the handicapped should be sent to live and die (Blatt, 1969; Dunn, 1969; Dybwad, 1969).

The message was not only well stated, it was also well received. President Nixon revealed an ambitious plan for mental retardation, calling for a one-third reduction in the institutional population of the approximately 200,000 mentally retarded citizens before the turn of the century (President's Committee on Mental Retardation, 1971). This call for the deinstitutionalization of over 66,000 individuals was, it should be reminded, not the result of a lawsuit, legislation, or economic depression. It was the product of a fresh, human-rights-oriented philosophy which portrayed handicapped persons as citizens deserving to live among the rest of us.

LEGAL PROMPTS

Legal remedies to cure the atrocious institutional conditions revealed by Blatt and his colleagues began to be pursued in number soon after the President's deinstitutionalization goal was set (Blatt, 1966). For while normalization offered so much, it simultaneously sharpened awareness of the disparity between conditions as they were and as they could be. The principle prompted a great many things. Along with hope came frustration, anger, and lawsuits.

Parents' associations bolstered their position that their sons and daughters were deserving of full, not "noncitizen," status by drawing parallels with other civil rights movements (Skarnulis, 1974). They took lessons from racial and ethnic minority groups and others who had been discriminated against. In effect they said, "We are not going to wait any longer for institutions to improve in their due time, we want it now."

Of the several lawsuits, there were two early ones which greatly affected deinstitutionalizations. In *Wyatt* v. *Stickney,* 1972, the court order focused on assuring fundamental conditions for treatment. Specifically, the court set standards for humane physical and psychological environments, staff qualifications, and individualized habilitation plans. One of the most pertinent rights elaborated on was the right to the least restrictive conditions for treatment. In *New York State Association for Retarded Children* v. *Rockefeller,*1973, a famous case centering on the Willowbrook institution, Judge Orrin Judd ordered a community-placement plan written and carried out for the members of the Willowbrook class. The plan featured a comprehensive continuum of services and alternatives to the institution, where residents' conditions were found to have deteriorated after admission.

Most proponents of social change would agree that litigation is a time-consuming and expensive route to take when seeking to change public policy. When possible, it seems to be more economical, in most respects, to bring about reform through less antagonistic means. From 1970 on, several pieces of state and national legislation were passed which reflected growing dissatisfaction with the practice of giving retarded citizens little choice but to spend their lives in the "total institution" (Goffman, 1963). Section 504 of the Vocational Rehabilitation Act Amendments of 1973 and Public Law 94-142 of 1975 have already been mentioned as examples of such progressive legislation. The Michigan Mental Health Code, Public Act 258 of 1974, is another good illustration of legislation which intentionally set out to liberate a group of citizens and assure them an acceptable quality of life.

While these and other benchmark instances of litigation and legislation are illustrations of a nation trying to right itself, the struggle is far from over. The practicalities of winning in the courts or in the Capitol have been brought nicely into focus by Lottman, who reminds us that "statements of rights . . . are not self-executing." It seems clear that in many respects, at this stage of deinstitutionalization, the hardest work comes after the trial or after the bill is signed into law. Monitoring the processes which assure that the mandate is carried out is what separates the "paper victories from the hard realities" (Lottman, 1976).

A LOOK AT THE LARGE RESIDENTIAL INSTITUTION

A review of the institutional-population data collected since 1969 reveals several interesting trends (Scheerenberger, 1977; Rosen and Callan, 1972). Figure 1 shows the steady decline in total resident population since the beginning of the 1970s. That institutions for the retarded are not admitting the high percentage of children they once did is evident from the fact that 73 percent of the resident population today is at least twenty-two years old—an increase of 15 percent in just four years. There has been a recent tendency for institutions to house predominantly severe to profoundly retarded individuals, with persons in this range accounting for three of every four residents since 1972.

FIGURE 1. Approximate Average Daily Population in Public Residential Facilities

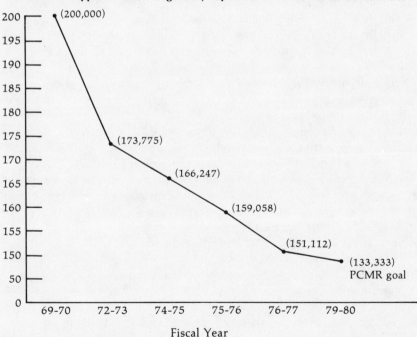

Whether Nixon's one-third reduction goal will be satisfied or not is still in question, as nationally there has been a relative stabilization of the institutionalized population in the past two years.

Considering the strong and frequent attacks to which institutional models have been subjected over the past ten years, it is not surprising that both staff and the surrounding communities are more than curious about their future. With each exposé or lawsuit, and with each step toward more normative residential environments, the institution loses a little more of its original reason for being. The testimony given by the personnel director of a large public institution before a federal judge evaluating progress on his court order to increase staff is not unusual: "I can't maintain attendants in positions because people don't want to work in a place that is on the receiving end of so much lousy publicity. It's as simple as that."

A number of things are being done to improve the image of the institution, the care given to residents, and simultaneously the morale of staff. A few of these are reviewed here.

REGIONAL CENTER CONVERSION

It is becoming increasingly common practice for large institutions to work toward changing the role and stereotype traditionally associated with them. Names are being altered from "State Home" or "Training School" to "Regional Center" or "Developmental Disability Center." The emphasis, at least in title if not in program, is away from the large isolated colony which gave little to the local community and existed as a citadel of secrets and security.

The new trend is toward smaller residential facilities specializing in habilitation[1] of the most seriously handicapped. Rather than being reluctant to share resources with area agencies, the new centers are characterizing their services as "regional" and outreach-oriented, intended to prevent institutional placement or readmission.

STANDARDS SETTING

The establishment of standards for programs given within the institution is another attempt at improving this model's image and product. At least three sets of standards are widely recognized and respected. The Joint Com-

[1]The word "habilitation" is used to differentiate between the work that vocational rehabilitation specialists do with clients and the work pre-vocational specialists do. Vocational rehabilitation concentrates generally on the reacquisition of skills and abilities. Individuals in the client role can be assumed to have once had a skill but because of trauma or some other reason no longer possess it. Habilitation concentrates on helping the client develop a proficiency he or she *never* had. The majority of mentally retarded citizens are working toward skill acquisition, not reacquisition.

mission on Accreditation of Hospitals (JCAH) has developed a very comprehensive evaluation program designed to thoroughly critique every phase of the institution's operation. Weighting of categories and items within categories is used to maintain proper perspective on those functions with greatest significance to resident welfare.

Intermediate Care Facility (ICF) standards bear a strong resemblance to those of JCAH but differ in that they are federal standards and are tied directly to funding. Funding of institutions under Title XIX (Medicaid) is dependent upon the agency's being certified as in compliance with the ICF standards.

The Program Analysis of Service Systems (PASS) evaluation program has been utilized more within the community than in institutional settings, but it has definite application to the latter as well. It is deeply rooted in normalization ideology and is more oriented toward evaluating the system's impact on the client than the structure of its own policies and procedures.

Elements of each of these three evaluation tools have been incorporated into state laws and state plans across the country.

NEW CONSTRUCTION

While the number of new institutions being built is small, tremendous sums of money are being allocated for the remodeling of existing ones (Scheerenberger, 1977). States such as Michigan and California are about to launch new construction and refurbishing programs which will cost well over $100 million in each state. Such expenditures are being championed because they will improve living conditions for mentally retarded residents of old or badly designed facilities. These improvements allow the states to claim almost 50 percent of the remodeled institutions' operating cost as the new improvements will lead toward meeting certification of the institution under the federal government's Title XIX program.

UNDER NEW MANAGEMENT

In an effort to move away from the medical and custodial models of management, institutions have been making serious attempts to increase the administrative skills of key staff. Management training seminars and literature for all levels of institutional personnel have become more prevalent and more comprehensive in recent years. Key principles in leadership, organization, staff motivation, planning evaluation, and the like are being taught to facility directors in state human-service departments, on college campuses, or in more comprehensive and ambitious institutes, such as the Management Training Program taught at the Center for Developmental and Learning Disorders at the University of Alabama. The encouragement and support of these programs reflect a growing understanding that operating a facility with responsibilities as wide and complex as those found in a residential institution is extremely difficult to accomplish properly. The competency required to weave knowledge of program and system management together in order ultimately to benefit clients is considerable. With the institution's walls becoming increasingly transparent, the wisdom of having trained experts on the inside is becoming more and more recognized.

FUTURE PROSPECTS

While the improvements currently being made in the residential institution are no doubt well intended, they probably are too little and too late to save it a place of prominence in a progressive continuum of services. The longstanding problems of overcrowding, understaffing, custodial emphasis, lack of program, and lack of budget are now solvable. The answers are known and the public is ready to pay the price. The fact of the matter is, however, that the possibilities for mentally retarded persons have evolved at a faster rate than the institution's answers. It is true that we are in a position as a society to dramatically remake the institution's residential capability. We could, with the improvements already underway, and coupled with advances in education, psychology, social work, medicine, and related fields, put together excellent large facilities to house the mentally retarded. In fact, with the assistance of architects, some of whom have lately become intrigued with the life space of handicapped populations, I am certain that we could make each facility resplendent in its newness, even pristine.

The situation, however, is one in which today's technology is ready to embrace yesterday's dilemma. This is analogous to a tent and awning company introducing a new canvas for use on the covered wagons of the next westbound pioneers. Even though advertisements speak convincingly about lightness, durability, and choice of colors, we have travelled enough by now to know that there are better ways of getting where we want to go.

It would seem that the large residential institution could best contribute to the field and to its own future by phasing out of concentrated housing and into support of community-based programs. A wealth of professional and paraprofessional resources can be found on every large university campus—e.g., medical and nursing staff; occupational, physical, and recreational therapists, psychologists, social workers, speech and language specialists, educators, vocational rehabilitation counselors, and direct care and training personnel. A gradual conversion of job sites from wards to city blocks would both protect the economic security of faithful employees and bring badly needed help to persons just returning to, or trying to, remain in the larger community.

To argue that the total institution has a valuable long-term role to play for a particular segment of the handicapped population is to deny the existence of other systems which have proven superior for serving individuals at all levels of retardation and with every conceivable secondary disability. It is also to deny the institution an opportunity to creatively deploy its human resources, build on its potential, and evolve prosperously.

Alternatives to the Institution

MODELS THAT WORK

Community living for mentally retarded persons is not new. While the percentages have varied, public and private institutions have never provided housing for more than a small minority of the total retarded population. This minority has generally not been considered suited for community life. The interesting thing about this residual institutional population is that the criterion for being part of it, or being considered unsuitable for placement, has not appeared to change much over the years, but the stratum of people who fit the criterion continues to narrow.

What keeps a severely to profoundly retarded individual who is multiply handicapped within the institution today is what held a person with an IQ of 80 and a seizure disorder from moving off grounds in 1959: the inability of the service system to dispel the following fatal predictions about his future:

"He isn't ready for the community."
"The community isn't ready for him.
"Even if he and the community were ready, there isn't a home he could move to."
"Even if you could find a home, the people wouldn't know how to handle him."
"He can't support himself, and he can't live on charity."

The challenge to overcome these barriers came out of the normalization literature of the 1960s, from a common dissatisfaction with the limits imposed on the mentally retarded, perhaps even from the "new consciousness" predicted in *The Greening of America* (Reich, 1970). Whatever their heritage, programs began to emerge which deemphasized the traditional institutional model. They radically altered the structure of options previously available to mentally retarded persons, and they set out to make the fatal pronouncements obsolete.

In the Omaha region, five counties merged to form the Eastern Nebraska Community Office of Retardation (ENCOR), a coalition of agencies working to provide a continuum of community-based human services which virtually excluded the institution as one of the choices. The continuum was developed to meet the differential needs of all mentally retarded citizens in the area, and it offered housing and follow-along support designed to assure maximal habilitation with minimal restriction on independence. A network of residential services was developed to include small family-type homes for children and adults. The homes took on descriptive names which denoted their purpose: i.e., family-living residences, adult-training residences, adult board-and-room homes, coresident apartments, and supervised independent living arrangements. For individuals exhibiting particularly troublesome behavior (such as self-abuse, aggression, or extreme preoccupation with self-stimulation), problem-behavior-shaping residences were formed. While homes were difficult to staff and support for medically fragile persons, for developmental maximization a small specialized ward within a community hospital was preferred to the large institution located in a rural area removed from the community (Menolascino, 1977).

The problem of obtaining resources once a mentally retarded person returns to the community is considered the major cause for institutional readmission (Scheerenberger, 1977). Recognizing this, the ENCOR program initiated an elaborate network of professional and nonprofessional resources to complement the residential concept utilized by any particular client. By 1974 the agency was proud of a variety of counseling aids available to direct consumers or their families. Speech therapy, recreation, financial assistance, medical attention, or a ride to work could be facilitated or provided by the ENCOR system.

In Michigan, some three years after the founding of ENCOR, the Macomb-Oakland Regional Center (MORC) began its efforts to "Deinstitutionalize the Hard to Place" (Rosen and Provencal, 1972). In contrast to the Nebraska county-initiated project, the MORC effort was launched from an institutional base. The agency was originally intended to offer the metropolitan area north of Detroit a new and better institution. Instead, while the architects worked on the blueprints, a small cadre of professionals hired to design the "on grounds" program structure began working to move residents of existing state facilities back to the MORC catchment area where they had been admitted from originally. Simultaneously, great effort was spent to avoid institutional admission for retarded persons who could benefit more from life in the normative than in the ersatz community.

Like ENCOR, the MORC program made foundational use of proven residential concepts such as the group and foster homes, adding to and subtracting from features of each so as to better accommodate the wide range of individual needs represented by the consumer community.

Mainstays of the MORC are small group homes (four to six residents) and community training homes, a variation of the foster-home concept for one to three residents. In combination, these two institutional alternatives and their variations have provided homes for over eight-hundred persons either leaving the institution or, after formal admission criteria has been satisfied, caught just short of the institution threshold.

As at ENCOR, MORC accentuates follow-along support which prevents readmission: a full range of professional and lay assistance is guaranteed the community-placed resident. Both state agency and generic service providers are used for this purpose.

At the time of this writing, the MORC institutional component is less than one-sixth of the originally planned size. The agency has developed sixty small group homes and over one-hundred and seventy-five community training homes, making admissions to the institution virtually nonexistent.

The two models described have proved to be remarkably sensitive to individual differences and especially effective for persons previously thought to be the poorest candidates for community living. A full 79 percent of all persons residing in MORC's group home and community training home programs function in the severe to profound range of mental retardation.

While these Nebraska and Michigan endeavors are outstanding, there are other exemplary deinstitutionalization operations in the country. The Pennsylvania Office of Mental Retardation has brought together a fine statewide system of community-based services which has received particular attention for making apartment housing available to mentally retarded tenants. Staff of the Eleanor Roosevelt Center in New York, while waiting for the opening of an institution, built an array of community-based residential and support programs which called into question the agency's initial reason for being.

In addition to foundational ideology, the successful programs of deinstitutionalization have several other elements in common. The most important are discussed here.

Client Readiness vs. "He Isn't Ready for the Community." Rather than make the assumption that the institutional resident has to acquire certain skills before community placement, responsibility for readiness is placed on the individual, home, or program receiving the institution's graduate. The absence of readiness criteria puts the pressure on the professionals and the system to create environments which are tailored to meet the particular needs of each individual rather than holding the resident inside until he "learns" his way out.

Community Readiness vs. "The Community Isn't Ready for Him." In previous years, agencies serving the mentally retarded could look forward to news-media interest only through an occasional exposé or human-interest story or coverage of the annual service-club spaghetti dinner. That has changed among the progressive community-based agencies. Very deliberate and continued efforts are directed at all phases of the news media to keep members of the public information industry informed as to what is impacting on mental retardation. Monthly news releases concerning significant events currently affecting the field are routinely sent to newspapers and television and radio stations to make them aware of key issues. While it is difficult to measure the cause and effect of attitude change, recent surveys show increasing understanding and acceptance of mental retardation (*Detroit News, 1978*).

Home Recruitment vs. "Even If He and the Community Were Ready, There Isn't a Home He Could Move To." Whereas it used to be that homes in the community were unavailable for the retarded, this probably was due in large part to the fact that we waited for local citizens to volunteer that they were interested in providing foster care or in running their own group home. Social workers within the institution, if given the responsibility to develop community placements, almost always had the competing responsibilities of case management, crisis intervention, and the like. Today, very aggressive and intelligent recruitment campaigns are aimed at attracting people who could provide good foster homes or group-home variations but are unlikely to come in and volunteer their interest. Specialty staff with singular assignments are becoming expert in the generation of alternatives to the total institution.

Resident Manager Training vs. "Even If You Could Find a Home, the People Wouldn't Know How to Handle Him." In direct contrast to the previous practice of spending much more time and energy in getting the institutional graduate ready for placement than in preparing foster parents or group-home staff for their new resident, today mandatory in-service and continuing educational programs occupy places of importance in many community-based systems (Willowbrook Review Panel, 1976).

Adequate Financial Support vs. "He Can't Support Himself and He Can't Live on Charity." While not all successful placement programs have "the money following the child" from institution to community, the best ones are at least adequately financed. In some agencies—ENCOR, for example—staff operating the homes are considered employees and are paid wages on a par with other organization personnel. In others, such as the Metropolitan Placement Unit in New York City, contracts for the purchase of service are written with providers. With this method, while few people become wealthy, there is a wage to be made which is relatively competitive with the larger area job market. It seems finally to be understood that we cannot spend large sums of money to keep someone in an institution, where he shouldn't be anyway, and claim that lack of dollars justifies his staying there.

Additional Similarities in Community-Based Programs

There are other vital parallels among programs moving effectively away from the total institution.

Case-manager-to-client ratios are adequate to allow relationships to become established and follow-along support to be well coordinated. Ratios of one worker for twenty-five placed clients are typical.

There are identifiable and responsive points of accountability for routine crisis intervention. Case managers actively monitor their caseloads on both visitational and reporting bases. Care providers know whom to contact for what and remain in frequent communication with the case-management agency.

Utilization of generic support services is the preferred choice. Whether seeking the services of a physician or a barber shop, the client has all conceivable needs met locally.

Involvement of consumer, natural parents, and/or guardians is encouraged throughout all planning and program phases. Critiquing of program components is requested and taken seriously.

Productive activity outside the home is the cornerstone of each client's plan of service. All but the acutely ill participate in some age-appropriate program for the major part of the day—i.e., schooling, vocational preparation, or some level of employment.

Relationships with members of the opposite sex, while not universally treated with the same degree of freedom, are at least encouraged. The quandary over what to view as normative under what circumstances also appears to be a common denominator.

Clearly written policies and procedures are given to all providers and are periodically updated. Manuals containing these operational rules are covered in mandatory in-service sessions.

The dignity of the client as a fellow citizen deserving respect is stressed within each home. Care is taken to avoid taking the client or his special needs for granted.

The success of the placement is not seen to be merely the client's responsibility. The providers, case managers, and support personnel view the success of the placement as their particular obligation. Clients do not fail in such systems.

There is avoidance of community outings in conspicuous groups which call attention to the handicaps of all the participants. There is little involvement in the large, segregated circuses or summer picnics sponsored for mentally retarded persons by service clubs.

While staff within the homes usually are eager and enthusiastic, they do not tend to stay long on the job. The tendency to leave to continue education reflects the youth of most staff; leaving to make more money reflects the distance this new industry still has to go to be competitive.

Great pains are taken to make certain that each home is warm and comfortable, as well as an interesting place to live. Interior and exterior decorating is intended to reflect the tastes of residents and be pleasing to them rather than merely to meet criteria of cost-effectiveness and durability.

Community activity programs for adults are shaped and modified to meet the particular needs of clients rather than making it necessary for the clients to meet entrance requirements for enrollment. Emphasis is placed upon tailoring programs to meet clients' needs.

While there are undoubtedly additional elements common to effective deinstitutionalization efforts across the country, the attitude of staff is an interesting one which should be singled out. There often is a zealous camaraderie, a true-believer adherence to the objectives of moving people out of institutions and keeping people out. While the popular titles of annual reports and monographs—e.g., *The Goal is Freedom* and *People Live in Houses*—appear strongly placement-oriented, many workers in the deinstitutionalization projects cited share a feeling about all institutions similar to Rivera's 1972 assessment of the Willowbrook stiuation:

"Change is difficult, but change is necessary. We've got to close that god-damned place down." (See, e.g., President's Committee on Mental Retardation, 1973 and 1975; Baker, 1974.)

NEW DIRECTIONS

Housing and habilitation models will almost certainly continue their evolutionary movement away from the centralized total institution. With each challenge to the old ways of doing things, the rights of retarded persons are more clearly articulated. Opponents of sweeping change are fond of saying that the "state of the art" is such that we are incapable of practically satisfying what courts, legislatures, and normalization advocates are demanding. While we cannot ignore pragmatics, it is good to ask, "Is it a state of art or a state of mind that lulls a society into believing that its prejudicial practices should take as long to change as they took to mature?" The quantum jump forward will not be made without difficulty or even monumental dilemma, but "a right stands on the grounds of justice, indifferent to whether the heavens fall or are more firmly supported after it is implemented" (Glazer, 1978).

From now until the year 2000, I think we can expect to see the following directions in housing opportunities for mentally retarded persons.

OPTIONS FOR ADULTS

In our early attempts at deinstitutionalization of adults, the field frequently made the mistake of moving too many too fast and too poorly (*Newsweek,* 1978; Edgerton, 1967; Comptroller General of the United States, 1977). Cries of "dumping" echoed from professionals and the public at large. Many early proponents of community living for the mentally retarded were repulsed by these wholesale release-without-preparation programs. In reactionary response to the "dumping" of human beings, it was not at all unusual for parents and professionals to prefer having an adult live in an institution, although he was in everyone's judgment unsuited for life there, rather than encounter the publicized drawbacks of mental-health ghettos. It was, and in many places still is, common to see strong opposition to placement which can be traced to those early clumsy attempts at emancipating mentally retarded citizens.

To guarantee against repeating past mistakes in placement, it has been suggested that the field should move more methodically and in a more discriminating manner with regard to whom we choose to deinstitutionalize (Zapf, 1976; Boggs, 1976). At the other end of the spectrum, as has already been intimated, are those who would have the field move with swiftness, viewing the majority of institutional placements as either unconstitutional or needless inhibitors of self-actualization (Broderick opinion, 1977; *Detroit News*, 1978; Dybwad, 1969).

It seems clear that the answer to inadequate community living arrangements is not a retreat to inadequate institutional arrangements but the development of adequacy in the former.

Particularly for mentally retarded adults, the precursors of future housing and habilitation models are in evidence at ENCOR, MORC, and similarly directed agencies across the country. I think that progressive programs in the years ahead will be expansions on the foundations of the Alternative Living Unit (ALU) and the Community Training Home (CTH).

Description of the Community Training Home (CTH) as Developed by Macomb-Oakland Regional Center

Purpose: To provide a normative living environment beyond what the group home offers, within which formal habilitation can take place to augment day programs.

Population Served: Primarily children; however, adaptable to adults. All levels and any combination of handicaps can be accommodated.

Size: One to three clients per home, depending on licensing standards and client needs. Average per home is 1.2.

Staff: Care-givers are licensed foster parents. They are obliged to participate in preservice and continuing training throughout their involvement in the program. All foster parents in the CTH program live in their own homes with the clients. Foster parents are paid by contract for services provided to individual clients rather than by salary.

Location: Private homes, owned or rented by foster parents.

Supervision: Follow-along supervision is provided by a central state agency (MORC). A case manager is assigned to ensure that client-service needs are met. The case-manager-to-client ratio is one to twenty-five.

Accountabilty: A contract is written between the central state agency (MORC) and the foster parents which delineates expectations, responsibilities, and lines of authority concerning room, board, supervision, and in-house programming. Clients' progress is monitored via written report, case-manager visits, and periodic evaluation of the total plan by an interdisciplinary team.

Support Services: The generic service community is preferred when resources are needed to augment day-program and in-home service. The central state agency (MORC) acts as a backup when generic services are not available.

Financing: A combination of local, state, and federal financing.

Strengths: Incorporates the best foster-care features—i.e., normative housing, intimacy, community anonymity. The contractual relationship between the agency and the care-giver eliminates the lack of integrated service that frequently characterizes traditional foster care; the setup is very accommodating of differential client needs.

Weaknesses: Can be too family-oriented for adult clients; it is difficult to recruit enough participants to deal with the large number of individuals able to benefit from such a program.

Description of the Alternative Living Unit (ALU) as Developed by Eastern Nebraska Community Office of Retardation

Purpose: To provide the most normalizing and least restrictive environment that can be devised at any juncture in a mentally retarded person's development.

Population Served: Either children or adults. All levels and any combination of handicaps can be accommodated.

Size: No more than five clients per home. The number depends on agency regulations and client needs.

Staff: Care-givers are referred to as home teachers. They are trained, are considered professional staff of the central agency (ENCOR), and are paid a salary. Home teachers can be live-in or staff rotating across shifts.

Location: Residences rented by the central agency (ENCOR). Homes are single dwellings, apartments, condominiums, etc.

Supervision: Follow-along and supervision are coordinated through case and program managers working from a core residence. The core residence is typically a small group home with diagnostic, prescriptive, management, and administrative authority over the ALU. The core residence may be responsible for several ALU's.

Accountability: First-line administrative control is maintained by the central agency (ENCOR) over core residences, and by the latter over ALU. Case managers with administrative authority are assigned from the core to all ALU's. The individual client's plan of service and evaluation of progress are the responsibility of a core-assigned case manager. Interdisciplinary planning is utilized for this.

Support Services: The generic service community is preferred when resources are needed to augment day programs and in-home service.
The core residence or the central agency (ENCOR) secures or provides
backup support when it is unavailable in the larger community.

Financing: A combination of local, state, and federal financing.

Strengths: Has some of the foster-care strengths but avoids "sympathy"
or "welfare" connotations; it also frees clients from the stigma which
can be associated with group-home residence. Less community resistance than there is to group homes; very adaptable to all levels and
combinations of handicaps. An exceptionally versatile basis upon
which to build an unlimited variety of housing options.

Weaknesses: Can lose some family-like assets as it avoids foster-care
"weaknesses."

Each of these models offers a solid base upon which to build. They are
compatible with liberal philosophy concerning least restriction and normative environments, yet they still offer adequate insulation from hazardous
risk taking. They are increasingly being referred to in litigation and legislation as examples of institutional options which should be promulgated by
the states (U.S. District Court, Eastern District of Michigan, 1978; Willowbrook Review Panel, 1976). Each of the two also lends itself well to advances made within the education and vocational habilitation fields. They
have been used successfully for large and diverse populations and can be
flexible over time. If need be, the ALU or CTH models can be redecorated,
remodeled, redirected, or removed from the resource continuum, depending upon the progress of human science. Neither of the two runs the risk of
being preserved at enormous costs long after its usefulness, nor of being
conspicuous from either a mile or a century away.

FLEXIBILITY/DIVERSITY

Group homes have tended to become synonymous with community
placement. The fact that this is the most widely used institutional alternative outside the natural home does not mean that it is the only or even the
most desirable model at our disposal (Scheerenberger, 1977). Its very size
makes for difficulty in achieving neighborhood anonymity, and the institutional remnants it retains (e.g., standard application of rules, observer traffic) detract from it. In an effort to counter this, future group homes are likely to continue developing toward smaller, more intimate units, eventually
dropping to three or four residents.

What is considered the "ideal" size of group homes has steadily dropped
over the years from somewhere in the teens to no more than six residents.
What holds the figure at six is essentially the same constraint which made
eighteen residents seem a correct figure in 1955: what seems an affordable
possibility. The interesting thing about the cost-effectiveness of housing

numbers of people with special needs is that it appears always to be in a state of flux and "depends on who you talk to." With each new advance in a legislature's human-service consciousness, the number of mentally retarded people a state can afford to support in a single home decreases, and the closer a community comes to providing normative living environments for its handicapped citizens.

Popular cost-effectiveness discussions seem to indicate that we should be able to pay the price required to keep the number of unrelated mentally retarded individuals living in one group home to no more than six. This figure is likely to remain until the next set of financial, empirical, or empathic advances is made.

While the field will undoubtedly continue to take advantage of the positive properties inherent in the group home, future consumers may well perceive our romance with the concept as shortsighted if we do not maintain a search for new, even more normative housing models.

The ALU piloted to excellence at ENCOR represents a versatile hybrid of desirable elements from both group-home and community-training-home choices. The size (two or three residents) effectively neutralizes opposition based on the fear of a neighborhood's being spoiled or the threat of in-home regimentation, since the ALU is physically inconspicuous and perfectly suited to maturing senses of privacy, ownership, and independence. The nature of the ALU invites individualization as it matches the differential needs and resources of both clients and those supervising within the home. Like the community training home, the ALU has the flexibility to include single or married staff and operate from a variety of dwelling types. Extended usage of this alternative to the institution will clearly be a part of future housing continua.

In addition, there are currently several apartment programs operating in Pennsylvania which are predictive of coming trends. At least three types have been identified as major contributors to the arena of choices: the apartment cluster, the single co-residence apartment, and the single maximum-independence apartment (Fritz, Wolfensberger, and Knowlton, 1971). Each of these fosters developing self-reliance with decreasing supervision. They will be used heavily in the future.

OPTIONS FOR CHILDREN AND YOUNG ADULTS

A common complaint of natural parents is that the system of services seldom filters down to the actual place where the problem exists. On one hand, most communities have adequate diagnostic and evaluation centers available to them. Even if a long drive is required, there is someone who can tell the parents basically what the child's situation is and what should be done about it. Likewise, there is usually no difficulty finding someone to make a referral to another agency or professional on the child's behalf. There are any number of points within most systems where truly expert evaluation and recommendation can be obtained (e.g., state institutions, juvenile courts, children's hospitals, child guidance clinics, life consultation centers, university-affiliated facilities, and intermediate schools). As a matter of fact, there frequently are so many junctures which offer this initial step in assistance that agencies continually work hard to avoid overlap and duplication of effort. On the other hand, the search for someone to work directly with the family, with the child, in the home is another matter. There is little competition to provide this hands-on help.

Future programs will accentuate direct assistance to the family outside the clinic so that the child can stay in the home. Several methods for accomplishing this are already in place but need nurturing.

Respite. Sitter services, day-care centers, and preschool programs which accommodate severely handicapped children will necessarily increase in number and sophistication. The availability of these respite-care opportunities will expand through the integration of existing programs and the generation of new programs funded by redirected institutional dollars. Mainstreaming and the community living emphasis have dramatically reduced the number of school-age children being admitted to public residential facilities (Scheerenberger, 1977). The parents and guardians of this group, bolstered by increasingly informed and demanding alliances of families who have always kept their children at home, will push hard for these relief resources.

In a recent survey of 325 parents who have kept their handicapped son or daughter living at home and out of the state system, 90 percent said they had immediate need but nowhere to turn for respite. The remaining 10 percent envisioned the need for respite when older siblings grew up and moved away (Wing Lake Developmental Center, 1978).

Of the many possible solutions for this problem, three are relatively apparent and easy to accomplish. Essentially, the same process used to develop new group homes and maintain their operating costs can be used for respite homes. Such a resource would have no permanent residents, but would be utilized by families who would sign up for particular dates throughout the year (Marin County Association for Retarded Citizens, 1979). The occupancy of the home would, then, be virtually 100 percent, but residents would change throughout the twelve months. Such homes would have to be licensed, with a trained staff, and would have to offer adequate program and health-care resources. A second method of assuring some respite availability would be through the process of having certain group homes licensed for one respite or emergency accommodation in addition to that home's permanent or routine population of residents. For example, a group home which normally houses five residents would, space and past record permitting, be approved to increase capacity to six. The sixth placement would be used for respite by families with handicapped sons and daughters residing at home. A third option would be to make a similar arrangement with foster parents to provide occasional respite to natural families; in exchange for either private payment or some agency-agreed-upon amount the foster parents would keep a ready vacancy open for emergency use.

In-Home Support. In response to parents' need to have someone actually come into the home and work "hands on" with the child, several direct-intervention programs have been developed. Some of these initiatives concentrate on teaching family members to be in better control of their household through the honing of new skills under the tutelage of experts. Good success has been reported in programs where parents and siblings of handicapped persons have been taught to use behavior-management techniques, infant stimulation, and speech and language programs. (e.g., Portage Project, 1979). Such programs call for the expert to leave the office, clinic, or lab to assist the client, and they also require that the parent or sibling listen more intently, since progress at the learning site can be evaluated more critically than in simulated settings.

A parent-trainer program operated from the MORC features the use of institutional or community-based direct-care staff. These staff spend an average of twenty hours per week in the home of a family with a mentally retarded child or adult who, in the opinion of an interdisciplinary team, is better suited to living in his or her own home provided that the parents can develop control of the situation. Emphasis is placed upon teaching parents whatever techniques are required to facilitate their child's habilitation. Such trainers are in the homes at stress periods of the day and involve all members of the family pertinent to the child's plan.

Added intervention resources may well be drawn from expansions of the Foster Grandparent program and similar programs for senior citizens. The former already occupies a highly respected position among the ancillary human service network, with Foster Grandparents giving love and attention to handicapped children in institutions and nursing homes. Placement of Foster Grandparents within group and foster homes is less prevalent but has enjoyed success when it has been tried. Movement to Foster Grandparent placement in the natural home is a logical next step.

Youth-oriented programs such as the Summer Work Experience and Training program (SWEAT) and federally funded projects under the government's ACTION umbrella are likely to be reinvigorated. Both the importance of maintaining the family constellation intact and the use of younger generations with handicapped populations dependent upon special assistance will increase through these efforts.

Full Family Subsidy. One of the most common questions raised by the natural parents of retarded children in the MORC community training home program is, "Why can't I get the same amount of money as a foster parent for taking care of my child? If I could, then he wouldn't need your program."

While it isn't quite so simple as paying all families to take their children home, in the present system of service delivery there clearly is an injustice being perpetrated on both family and child. In our interest to generate the best immediate services possible, we have in some ways neglected the long term. Whether the motivation has been the protection of other family members, shame, ultimate faith in a physician, or social worker, or just an attempt to do the best thing for everyone at the time, parents of mentally retarded children have been placing their sons and daughters outside their home for generations. Professionals in the field have often participated enthusiastically in this practice. (We are very good at working with a parent's guilt after a child's departure.) Indeed, it has been charged that a great many people are institutionalized less for their own benefit than for the comfort of others. (U.S. District Court for the District of Nebraska, 1973).

It has been the practice of our society to make it at least attractive, if not essential, to remove the mentally retarded child from his or her family (Skarnulis, 1974). Consider that until P.L. 94–142 was passed, the only place that parents of a boy with a severe intellectual deficiency could get schooling for their child was the state home. The student had to leave the family to get an education. The parents' dilemma: keep him at home and he loses his schooling; put him in school and he loses his home.

The situation has not been much different with regard to medical treatment or therapy. After elaborate evaluation processes, parents have been sold on the importance of a twenty-four-hour supervised setting where their child can have thirty minutes of physical therapy twice a week, his seizures observed and reviewed by a physician once a week, and friends to rock with in day-rooms throughout the week. If everything goes according to plan, all of this will presumably lead to the child's becoming healthier. And this is important, because he will need his health to cope with the bewildering feelings of abandonment and loneliness caused by the new prescription for health. Like Yossarian, the dubious hero of *Catch-22*, parents in this situation have to be moved by the "spinning reasonableness" of this set of choices, since there is "an elliptical precision about its perfect pairs of parts that [is] graceful and shocking" (Heller, 1955).

There is no longer any reason to encourage breakup of the family constellation merely to free up services for one of the members. While community-based residential programs are gargantuan improvements over total institutions, they still can provide disincentives for keeping the entire family intact if they make a particular service available exclusively to individuals who have moved from their natural homes. To illustrate the point: The money paid to foster parents in the MORC community training home program for providing room, board, supervision, and client training amounts to over $600 per month. Though preliminary plans are being made to alter present exclusionary practices, currently the natural parents of the child, generating over $20 per day to a foster family, receive nothing if their son or daughter remains at home. This is true even if they provide supervision and prescribed training.

While there would be good reason to maintain tight accountability in a program that would run counter to a strong American work ethic by paying families to care for their own children, there is little reason to eliminate natural parents so totally from the habilitation arena. Possible abuses of such a program could be kept at a minimum through strict standards. For example: eligibility criteria, periodic assessment of the program, and case management might all be the statutory responsibility of a designated state agency. Natural parents would be obliged to meet the same requirements as foster parents with regard to mandatory skills training, monthly meetings, activity reporting, and reception of case-management supervision and consultation recommendations.

In a more comprehensive plan for reversing the past practice of moving away from families toward reliance upon institutional systems of service, it has been suggested that a "free-choice principle" be used in the case of persons who are mentally retarded (Cooke, 1969). Basically, this concept would be managed similarly to the Medicare Act of 1965, which allows full-cost reimbursement for approved medical expenses. Though there are predictable procedural difficulties with any ponderous bureaucratic program of the Medicare or Medicaid size, it has given an array of options to individuals who under previous welfare programs were forced to rely almost exclusively upon county hospitals and infirmaries for the poor. A mental-retardation care act which would lead families away from institutional dependence, conceived ten years ago, has not yet materialized. The original Medicare Act, and particularly Title XIX of that act, has, however, opened the doors of the medical community to the mentally retarded.

In an interesting experiment, which is a testament to both the power of advocacy groups and the progressiveness of government, a two-year project is now underway in British Columbia which is designed to put the free-choice principle into full effect. At the relentless urgings of a consumer-advocacy association, the provinaical government agreed to make available to a parent-founded organization the capital which would ordinarily be expended to care for developmentally disabled persons in one region of the province. Along with the budget, the new agency also assumes the responsibility for the welfare of each client. In effect, it has a credit card which can be used to pay the bills incurred in the attempt to meet client needs within the community and within the home whenever this is indicated as desirable.

If, in the wisdom of an interdisciplinary team of professionals, it is decided that the natural family of a client could meet his or her needs at least as well as the next most appropriate out-of-home alternative, given the money and professional supports that would be required by that alternative, there is little reason to eliminate the natural home as the milieu of choice. While this seems an obvious suggestion to make, I know of no national program which evaluates the needs of a retarded child, tabulates the costs of meeting them, and offers this sum to parents who, in everyone's judgment, could do a superior job to the placement agency.

The fact of the matter is that in spite of the advances in human services, families can still bring more specialty resources to bear upon the world of their child if they send the child packing rather than keeping him or her at home. This must change.

A CONTINUUM

For both children and adults who require some residential support, it is helpful to think in terms of a continuum of independence. Housing options along this continuum would range from one in which others make all the decisions to the pole representing total independence. While this range of options is a popular way of conceptualizing service delivery to the mentally retarded, most continua begin with a traditional institution holding down the dependent extreme.

I am firmly convinced that the increasingly positive experiences of handicapped individuals living in normative environments and the trend of civil rights recognition will all but push the total institution off the line of acceptable choices. With each successive advance in habilitation technology and consciousness, the continuum increases its capacity to grow into one where the poorest option is a good one. Whether this is likely to happen in the remaining years of the twentieth century or sometime thereafter will depend primarily upon whether the local commitment is invested more in heritage or ambition.

Impediments to Progress

Although there is good reason to believe that the larger community will become the environment of choice for all mentally retarded citizens, there are impediments to progress. The factors most responsible for stalling deinstitutionalization vary from region to region; however, there is a common issue of prejudice which transcends regional boundaries.

Routing retarded persons only to training schools, accepting their exclusion from public education, preventing them from taking risks, treating them as children, viewing their return to their home towns as an intrusion, feeling that before they can participate in an area's life the area deserves time to prepare—all are examples of a veiled bigotry that has plagued other devalued minority groups. And while attitudes and behaviors are changing in a positive direction, vestiges of the prejudice which views high intellect as a prerequisite to citizenship impede progress.

Although recent years have witnessed a number of victories for important human rights, mentally retarded persons continue to be haunted by the past. What has happened, in effect, is that a parasitic industry has grown up around them; indeed, a veritable way of life has come to be dependent upon traditional methods of dealing with retarded persons, and there is little incentive for it to change. Investors in the long-established routine include a complete cross-section of every community.

For a hundred years, each generation of workers in the field of mental retardation in this country has passed on the same legacy: endorsement of the large residential institution's prominence in the lives of mentally retarded persons and the fabric of local life. Though the names, numbers, focus, and architecture have changed, each new worker in the field is introduced to the legitimacy of the public or private residential institution as appropriate for some members of the population. Even today, when it is being demonstrated that the most seriously handicapped can thrive in normative housing, our tradition of keeping a certain segment of the mentally retarded within institutions prevails over progress.

The tradition is given new life when states spend the lion's share of their budgets on institutional rather than community programs and appropriate huge amounts of capital to rebuild facilities and none to build small normative housing.

The state home and training school has become such a fixture that each new generation of human-service workers can look forward to using it as a place to hone their skills and lean on when time robs them of skills.

The public system of service provision has the pressure of a huge residential-institution lobby, budget, and habit to contend with. It is virtually impossible for a state to support simultaneously a desirable large-scale community-living program for its retarded citizens and a large residential-institution program. To date, conciliation has always favored supporting the latter; it is as comfortable as an old shoe.

Nonprofessional employees within institutional organizations frequently perceive community placement as a threat to their livelihood; in turn the surrounding community shudders at the potential impact of a loss of institutional jobs on its economy. Professional personnel working in large residential facilities perhaps fear unemployment less than their colleagues in direct care, but clearly their locus of practice would change if housing and habilitation were phased from a single to multiple sites. This change is not necessarily welcomed.

Natural parents and family members of individuals residing in institutions also frequently reveal an investment in the traditional way. In spite of all its inadequacies, the state home and training school does represent permanence and predictability. Parents do not have to fear angry property owners or worry about the fate of their loved one when they pass away. The risks of independence inherent in community living are deliberately avoided in on-grounds programs, and there is shelter from misunderstanding, ridicule, and failure. For all that it lacks, the residential institution does represent a tangible point of security and a source of some measure of peace of mind to the families of its residents.

One of the more prevalent traditional obstacles to deinstitutionalization might be called a perception of uniqueness. It is very common to hear those who oppose community placement say that their area is so unlike any other that it couldn't possibly work there. Likewise, the peculiarities of specific residents are pointed to by parents; the unusual politics of institutional support are emphasized by staff; and the inside influence of associations, unions, and local power figures has at one time or another been said to be so unique as to make anything more than a token community-living program impossible to effect. Belief in such uniqueness can deter even the most ardent libertarians.

Since the history of successful deinstitutionalization is an abbreviated one, critics can feel safe in suggesting that movement away from traditional methodology be approached ever so cautiously. Detractors can point to weaknesses in support systems, individual failures of clients, failure of homes, and vagueness in accountability. They can berate past mistakes and mistrust innovation, since doubt seems an inextricable companion of novelty. In truth, it would be easy to identify a hundred reasons why the residential institution is safest for this group or that. In the end, we have to be mindful that the emancipation of any people has always begun with great misgiving, even turmoil. The lack of instant or smooth success should not be considered a reason to return to the old ways but rather a predictable developmental phase in the maturation of a society coming to terms with its promise.

The future of human services is clearly in need of professionals to concentrate on what has been called "boundary work" on the client's behalf, or the intervention between social systems where they interface with one another (Horejsi, 1979). Mentally retarded citizens should not have to develop a comprehensive understanding of the resource maze, which somewhere in a tangled order holds desperately needed answers, before they receive assistance from it. Our constituents should neither be left to carry on a lonely vigil, a solitary fight with the system, nor allowed to be beaten down by its maddeningly slow pace. Our clients do not need our charity, but they do need our help to interject, to expedite to shake the knotted bureaucracy, to champion their march on dignity.

The heritage of social work, at the heart of public policy reform and consciousness raising, makes it well suited for the role. We should lionize our ownership of it.

Epilogue

CHAPTER 9 FOCUSED ON the range of living options that must be developed to ensure the mentally retarded citizen personal comfort and public acceptance. Once the setting for living has been established, attention must focus upon improving the quality of life within the setting. How a person lives and with whom he or she lives are additional constructs that demand attention in order to guarantee a life of fulfillment for any citizen. This is no less true for the mentally retarded adult.

Every adult should have the right to be as productive as possible within his or her range of skill. The community must provide a range of work options that will maximize the contributions the mentally retarded citizen may make to the community. Such contributions will result in increased mutual respect. Recent legislative action and direction to the Department of Vocational Rehabilitation are encouraging signs that many opportunities are forthcoming for the retarded adult.

All adults should have the right to experience their lives with other individuals with whom they are compatible. The community must permit a range of relationship options for retarded adults so that they may experience a social-sexual life. Mentally retarded citizens must be permitted to enter into mutually selected relationships so that they may experience the fulfillment of giving and receiving love.

To summarize, I believe that there are *three* options that must be readily accessible for the retarded citizen: (1) range of living (where); (2) range of work (how); and (3) range of relationship (with whom). Each of these three options must be developed concurrently or none of the other options is feasible. For example, it is ridiculous to say that a "living option" includes independent living in an apartment only to turn around and *assign* two individuals to share the apartment.

Parents and professionals have accepted the charge to address the concerns of housing and work for the retarded citizen. However, there has been reluctance on the part of many to address the issues of relationships and sexuality. This reluctance must dissipate. Parents and professionals must become advocates for the rights of the retarded individual to be a sexually expressive person in a relationship of choice. Such a relationship is the privilege of every citizen, and it is the validation of that person's human experience.

Social workers must become advocates for the mentally retarded individual as he or she attempts to learn appropriate self-expression as a sexual person. They must be available to counsel, guide, teach, and enable their clients who have concerns related to sexuality. They must confront the segments of the community that deny sexuality to the retarded person. To do less is to deny a basic commitment of social work—to enable individuals to achieve their maximum potential.

Throughout this book there are many examples of retarded men and women assuming the responsibility of closing the social gap between themselves and so-called normal men and women. They are trying to be like us! They strive to understand and accept a condition of birth and development over which they had no control. They work to overcome handicapping conditions that are the *result* of retardation. They learn to adapt, conform, compensate, and adjust in order to meet our expectations for them—to be like us.

How hypocritical and hollow for us to encourage them to be like us. We have conspired through the centuries to perpetuate the distance between us. How else do we explain trapping them in institutions? Recently, the brave among us have struggled to overcome our bigotry, intolerance, and ignorance. Some of us, urged on by the retarded men and women themselves, have begun to recognize the loss to ourselves and our community in permitting the alienation between us and them to continue. There have been changes—legislative and judicial. "Normalization" is no longer a theory, but a statement of a way of life.

Normalization affects "us" as well as "them." Normalization means that mentally retarded individuals will live among us—in our cities and towns. They will walk down our streets, attend our schools, and play in our parks. They will teach us how to accept them—how to reach out, adapt, compensate, and adjust to their presence among us. We must learn from them. We must overcome our bigotry and ignorance even as they overcome their retardation. We must accept the challenge to explore the expanding dimensions of our humanity.

APPENDIX

Video Cassette List

Human Fulfillment for
Developmentally Disabled Individuals*

THE FOLLOWING VIDEO CASSETTES are available in black and white on three-quarter-inch U-Matic. They are available for rental from Videotape Rental Library, Michigan Media, 400 Fourth Street, Ann Arbor, Michigan 48109. Each time a video cassette is rented, one copy of that cassette may be made at no charge. Use of the copy is limited to educational and community-awareness purposes for which no fees are charged.

Am I My Brother's Keeper?

This tape examines some of the concerns that family members may have about an adult who is developmentally disabled. Jane Cooper describes her brother, Corky; his disability; and the impact this had upon the family, the neighborhood, and the community. She tells about her parents' efforts to ensure a place in the family for Corky and compares her process of achieving maturity to Corky's more limited experience.

28 minutes

Henry

Confusion exists for young people with developmental disabilities who are making the transition from the natural sheltering of a home environment to a more independent

*Referred to in Chapter 5, page 78.

life-style. Even though Henry has never been institutionalized, living at home has infantilized him just the same. It has also sheltered him from exploratory experiences and information vital to his growth. In this program, Henry discusses his prospects for the future.

25 minutes

I Am a Man

Mark is a multiply impaired young man confronted with the decisions that all young adults must make regarding their future. As he gets ready to move to a more independent living situation, we find him ill-prepared and inexperienced. This program explores the limitations, real and imagined, that are associated with handicapped people.

14 minutes

I Can Only Speak for Myself

Margaret Bever is an advocate for persons with developmental disabilities. Until her husband's death, the two of them struggled with society's view of their rights as disabled people. In this program Margaret reflects on many of the conflicts they faced in order to overcome society's handicaps and live with their own.

28 minutes

Let No Man Put Asunder

Linda and Paul Burns are two adults who have finally been allowed to live their own lives. After spending most of their lives in institutions or foster homes, they have now received the necessary support services to allow them the freedom to make their own decisions. This program examines the type of support services needed by people with developmental disabilities to establish themselves as equal and fulfilled members of the community.

22 minutes

More Alike than Different

This program begins with a letter written by a parent of an institutionalized thirty-three-year-old woman. After discussing her concerns about sexuality and disability, Dr. Matthew Trippe explores some of the underlying factors that prevent persons with disabilities from achieving sexual fulfillment. A case is made for the importance of independence and the assumption of personal responsibility. Sexual rights and responsibilities are viewed as central to the achievement of maximum independence.

25 minutes

Stop-Go-Caution

The "Stop-Go-Caution" technique demonstrates a model of behavior management for parents and care-givers to use with children. The model emphasizes communication, problem definition, and the steps to problem resolution. Although this program is designed to teach management skills for application to the sexual behaviors of people with developmental disabilities, it is a useful technique for everyone.

20 minutes

There's Someone for Everyone

In this program Sol Gordon, a well-known educator and author in the field of sexuality, speaks to the topic of fulfillment for everyone, disabled or not.

55 minutes

What's Dirty in a Word?

In order to feel comfortable in discussing sexuality it is important to be familiar with the words people use to describe sexual activities. This program introduces the viewer to a wide range of sexual jargon and presents techniques that are useful in developing awareness concerning the use of these words.

23 minutes

We Are a Family

Pat and Dick Steinbrunner have cerebral palsy. Along with their two children, they are a family overcoming the obstacles created by the stereotyping of handicapped people. This videotape examines some of the problems that the Steinbrunner parents and family confront.

30 minutes

The Workshop

The workshop format has proved to be successful in positively changing attitudes about human fulfillment and developmentally disabled individuals. This videotape describes a two-day process shared by parents and professionals in an effort to learn about themselves and their attitudes toward sexuality and disability.

28 minutes

Bibliography

ADAMS, M., 1971. *Mental Retardation and Its Social Dimensions.* New York: Columbia University Press.

———, 1967. "First Aid to Parents of Retarded Children." *Social Casework,* vol. 48, pp. 148–153.

———, 1967a. "Siblings of the Retarded: Their Problems and Treatment." *Child Welfare,* vol. 46, pp. 310–316.

ADDAMS, J., 1913. *Democracy and Social Ethics.* London: MacMillan & Co., p. 273.

ADULT FOSTER CARE, 1974. *Provider Training Manual.* Developed by Behavioral Resources, Inc., for the Michigan Dept. of Mental Health and the Michigan Dept. of Social Services, Dept. of Social Services Publication 260, Lansing, Mich. 48926.

AMERICAN ASSOCIATION ON MENTAL DEFICIENCY, 1973. "Rights of the Mentally Handicapped." *Mental Retardation,* vol. 11, no. 5, pp. 56–58.

ATTWELL, A., and CLABBY, A., 1971. *The Retarded Child: Answers to Questions Parents Ask.* Los Angeles: Western Psychological Services.

AYRAULT, E., 1971. *Growing Up Handicapped: A Guide for Parents and Professionals to Helping the Exceptional Child.* New York: Seabury Press.

———, 1971a. *Helping the Handicapped Teenager Mature.* New York: Association Press.

AZRIN, N., and ARMSTRONG, P., 1973. "The 'Mini-Meal': A Method for Teaching Eating Skills to the Profoundly Retarded." *Mental Retardation,* vol. 11, no. 1, pp. 9–13.

AZRIN, N., and FOXX, R., 1971. "A Rapid Method of Toilet-Training the Institutionalized Retarded." *Journal of Applied Behavior Analysis,* vol. 4, no. 2, pp. 89–99.

———, 1974a. *Toilet-Training in Less Than a Day.* New York: Simon & Schuster.

AZRIN, N., GOTTLIEB, L., HUGHART, L., WESOLOWSKI, M., and RAHN, T., 1975. "Eliminating Self-Injurious Behavior by Educative Procedures." *Behavior Research and Therapy*, vol. 13, pp. 101–111.

AZRIN, N., SCHAEFFER, R., and WESOLOWSKI, M., 1976. "A Rapid Method of Teaching Profoundly Retarded Persons to Dress by a Reinforcement-Guidance Method." *Mental Retardation*, vol. 14, no. 6, pp. 29–33.

BAKER, B., SELTZER, G., and SELTZER, M., 1974. *As Close as Possible: Community Residences for Retarded Adults*. Boston: Little, Brown & Co.

BALTHAZAR, E., and STEVENS, H., 1971. *Managing the Mentally Retarded Through Interdisciplinary Action*, vol. 8, no. 3. Madison, Wisc.: Central Wisconsin Colony and Training School Research Dept.

BANDURA, A., 1969. *Principles of Behavior Modification*. New York: Holt, Rinehart, & Winston.

BARNARD, P., DEMERY, M., DICKERSON, M., KAMBOURIS, A., and LYNCH, E., Chairperson, 1977. *You and Me*. Detroit: Wayne County Intermediate School District.

BAROFF, G., 1974. "The Vocational Potential of Mentally Retarded Persons." In *Modification of Behavior of the Mentally Retarded*, edited by R. Hardy and J. Cull. Springfield, Ill.: Charles C Thomas.

BASS, M., 1963. "Marriage, Parenthood, and Prevention of Pregnancy." *American Journal of Mental Deficiency*, vol. 68, no. 3, pp. 318–333.

BAUMEISTER, A. (ed.), 1967. *Mental Retardation: Appraisal, Education, and Rehabilitation*. Chicago: Aldine Publishing Co.

BECK, H., 1969. *Social Services to the Mentally Retarded*. Springfield, Ill.: Charles C Thomas.

BECKER, W., 1971. *Parents Are Teachers: A Child Management Program*. Champaign, Ill.: Research Press.

BEGAB, M., 1963. *The Mentally Retarded Child: A Guide to Services of Social Agencies*. DHEW, Children's Bureau Publication no. 404. Washington, D.C.: U.S. Government Printing Office.

BENASSI, V., and BENASSI, B., 1973. "An Approach to Teaching Behavior-Modification Principles to Parents." *Rehabilitation Literature*, vol. 34, no. 5, pp. 134–137.

BETTELHEIM, B., 1950. *Love Is Not Enough: The Treatment of Emotionally Disturbed Children*. New York: The Free Press.

BIESTEK, F., 1957. *The Casework Relationship*. Chicago: Loyola University Press.

BIRENBAUM, A., and SEIFFER, S., 1976. *Resettling Retarded Adults in a Managed Community*. New York: Praeger Publishers.

BLATT, B., 1969. "Recommendations for Institutional Reform." In *Changing Patterns in Residential Services for the Mentally Retarded*, edited by R. Kugel and W. Wolfensberger for the President's Committee on Mental Retardation. Washington, D.C.: U. S. Government Printing Office.

———, and KAPLAN, F., 1966. *Christmas in Purgatory: A Photographic Essay on Mental Retardation*. Boston: Allyn and Bacon.

BLUMA, S., SCHEARER, M., FROHMAN, A., and HILLIARD, F., 1979. *The Portage Project Checklist*. Portage, Wisconsin: Cooperative Educational Services Agency No. 12.

BOGGS, E., 1976. "Elizabeth Boggs Tells of Her Twenty-seven Years as a N.A.R.C. Member and as a Mother of a Retarded Son." *Mental Retardation News*, vol. 25, no. 10, pp. 4–5.

BRADDOCK, D., 1977. *Opening Closed Doors: the Deinstitutionalizaton of Disabled Individuals*. Reston, Virginia: The Council for Exceptional Children.

Broderick Opinion, Dec. 23, 1977. U. S. District Court for the Eastern District of Pennsylvania, No. 74-1345.

BRODY, E., 1974. *A Social Work Guide for Long-term Care Facilities*. Maryland: National Institute of Mental Health (DHEW).

BUCHAN, L., TEED, S., and PETERSON, C., 1976. "Role Playing and Behavior Modification: A Demonstration with Mentally Retarded Children." *The Clearing House*, vol. 50, no. 2, pp. 77-80.

BYNUM, E., LARKIN, M., and CURTIS, A., 1978. "Who Can Help?" In N. Fallen and J. McGovern, *Young Children with Special Needs*. Columbus, Ohio: Charles E. Merrill Publishing Co.

CALDWELL, B., and STEDMAN, D., 1977. *Infant Education: A Guide for Helping Handicapped Children in the First Three Years*. New York: Walker & Co.

CENTERWALL, W., and CENTERWALL, S., 1961. "Phenylketonuria: The Story of Its Discovery." *Journal of the History of Medicine and Applied Sciences*, vol. 16, pp. 292-296.

CHAFFIN, J., 1974. "Will the Real 'Mainstream' Program Please Stand Up?" *Focus on Exceptional Children*, vol. 6, no. 5, pp. 1-18.

CLARKE, C., 1962. *Genetics for the Clinician*. Oxford, England: Blackwell Scientific Publications.

COHEN, J., 1977. "Litigation and Psycho-Educational Services." In W. Rhodes and D. Sweeney (eds.), *Alternatives to Litigation: The Necessity for Parental Consultation*. Lansing: Michigan Dept. of Education, and Institute for the Study of Mental Retardation and Related Disabilities, pp. 1-23.

_____, 1961. "A Workshop Operation Within the Framework of a State Institution." *American Journal of Mental Deficiency*, vol. 66, pp. 51-56.

_____, 1960. "An Analysis of Vocational Failures of Mental Retardates Placed in the Community After a Period of Institutionalization." *American Journal of Mental Deficiency*, vol. 65, pp. 371-375.

COMPTROLLER GENERAL OF THE UNITED STATES, Report to Congress, Jan. 7, 1977. *Returning the Mentally Disabled to the Community: Government Needs to Do More*, HRD-76-152.

COOKE, R., 1969. "The Free Choice Principle in the Care of the Mentally Retarded." In *Changing Patterns in Residential Services for the Mentally Retarded*, edited by R. Kugel and W. Wolfensberger for the President's Committee on Mental Retardation. Washington, D.C.: U. S. Government Printing Office.

CRAIN, L., and MILLOR, G., 1978. "Forgotten Children: Maltreated Children of Mentally Retarded Parents." *Pediatrics*, vol. 61, no. 1, pp. 130-132.

CRISSEY, M., Aug. 1975. "Mental Retardation: Past, Present, and Future." *American Psychologist*, vol. 30, no. 8, pp. 800-808.

CRUICKSHANK, W., 1955. *Psychology of Exceptional Children and Youth*. Englewood Cliffs, N.J.: Prentice-Hall.

_____, and JOHNSON, G., (eds.), 1975. *Education of Exceptional Children and Youth*. Englewood Cliffs, N. J.: Prentice-Hall.

DARNELL, R., 1972. "Concepts and Patterns of Interaction among Professions Working with the Mentally Retarded: A Position Paper." Ann Arbor, Mich.: Institute for the Study of Mental Retardation and Related Disabilities.

DAVID, H., SMITH, J., and FRIEDMAN, E., 1976. "Family Planning Services for Persons Handicapped by Mental Retardation." *American Journal of Public Health*, vol. 66, no. 11.

DAVIS, D., 1965; 2nd ed., 1972. "Counseling the Mentally Retarded." In J. Gowan, G. Demos, C. Kokaska (eds.), *The Guidance of Exceptional Children: A Book of Readings*. New York: David McKay Co.

DAVIS, S., 1959. *The Mentally Retarded in Society*. New York: Columbia University Press.

DE LA CRUZ, F., and LAVECK, G., (eds.), 1973. *Human Sexuality and the Mentally Retarded*. New York: Brunner/Mazel. Proceedings of a Conference on Human Sexuality and the Mentally Retarded, November 7-10, 1971, Hot Springs, Arkansas. Sponsored by Mental Retardation Programs at the National Institute of Child Health and Human Development, HEW, Public Health Service, and National Institutes of Health, Bethesda, Maryland.

Detroit News, Nov. 3, 1978. "Most Rate Retarded as Good Neighbors."

———, Sept. 28, 1978. "Big Mental Institutions Criticized."

"Development of Social Work Knowledge and Intervention Skills Related to Helping Handicapped Children and Improving Family/School Relationships." Proceedings of the Michigan Dept. of Education, Institute for School of Social Work, February 4-6, 1976. Dept. of Education Consultant, Theodore Chavis, Institute Director.

DICKERSON, M., 1978. *Our Four Boys: Foster-Parenting Retarded Teenagers*. Syracuse, N.Y.: Syracuse University Press.

———, 1977. *Fostering Children with Mental Retardation*. Instructors' Manual, Trainees' Workbook, Foster-Parent Training Program. Ypsilanti, Mich.: Eastern Michigan University.

———, HAMILTON, J., HUBER, R., and SEGAL, R., 1974. "The Invisible Client." Presented at the Annual Meeting of the American Association on Mental Deficiency, Toronto, Canada.

DUGDALE, R. L., 1877. *The Jukes: A Study in Crime, Pauperism, Disease, and Heredity*. New York: G. P. Putnam's Sons.

DUNCAN, A., 1971. "Precision Teaching in Perspective: An Interview with Ogden R. Lindsley." *Teaching Exceptional Children*, vol. 3, no. 1, pp. 3-5.

DUNN, L., 1969. "Small, Special-Purpose Residential Facilities for the Retarded." In *Changing Patterns in Residential Services for the Mentally Retarded*, edited by R. Kugel and W. Wolfensberger for the President's Committee on Mental Retardation. Washington, D.C.: U. S. Government Printing Office.

DYBWAD, G., 1973. "The International Scene: Patterns of Organization and Development in Member Association of the International League of Societies for the Mentally Handicapped." *Mental Retardation*, vol. 11, no. 1, pp. 3-5.

———, 1969. "Action Implications, U.S.A. Today." In *Changing Patterns in Residential Services for the Mentally Retarded*, edited by R. Kugel and W. Wolfensberger for the President's Committee on Mental Retardation. Washington, D.C.: U. S. Government Printing Office.

———, 1964. "Group Approaches in Working with Parents of the Retarded: An Overview." In *Challenges in Mental Retardation*. New York: Columbia University Press.

EDGERTON, R., 1967. *The Cloak of Competence: Stigma in the Lives of the Mentally Retarded.* Berkeley and Los Angeles: University of California Press.

_____, and BERCOVICI, S., 1976. "The Cloak of Competence: Years Later." *American Journal of Mental Deficiency,* vol. 80, no. 5.

ERIKSON, E., 1968. *Identity, Youth and Crisis.* New York: W. W. Norton & Co.

_____, 1963. *Childhood and Society.* New York: W. W. Norton & Co.

FALCK, H., 1977. "Interdisciplinary Education and Implications for Social Work Practice." *Journal of Education for Social Work,* vol. 13, no. 2.

FALLEN, N., with McGOVERN, J., 1978. *Young Children with Special Needs.* Columbus, Ohio: Charles E. Merrill Publishing Co.

FARBER, B., 1968. *Mental Retardation: Its Social Context and Social Consequences.* Boston: Houghton Mifflin Co.

FILS, D., 1977. *The Developmental Disabilities Handbook.* Los Angeles: Western Psychological Services.

FISCHER, M., and KRAJICEK, M., 1974. "Sexual Development of the Moderately Retarded Child: How Can the Pediatrician Be Helpful?" *Clinical Pediatrics,* vol. 13, no. 1, pp. 79–83.

FLYNN, R., and SHA'KED, A., 1977. "Normative Sex Behavior and the Person with a Disability: Assessing the Effectiveness of the Rehabilitation Agencies." *Journal of Rehabilitation,* vol. 43, no. 5, pp. 34–38.

FRAENKEL, W., 1961. *The Mentally Retarded and Their Vocational Rehabilitation: A Resource Handbook.* New York: National Association for Retarded Children.

FRAIBERG, S., 1959. *The Magic Years.* New York: Charles Scribner's Sons.

FRIEDMAN, P., 1976. *The Rights of Mentally Retarded Persons: The Basic ACLU Guide for the Mentally Retarded Persons' Rights.* New York: American Civil Liberties Union.

FRIEDRICH, W., and BORISKIN, J., April 1978. "Primary Prevention of Child Abuse: Focus on the Special Child." *Hospital and Community Psychiatry,* vol. 29, no. 4, pp. 248–251.

FRITZ, M., WOLFENSBERGER, W., and KNOWLTON, M., 1971. *An Apartment-Living Plan to Promote Integration and Normalization of Mentally Retarded Adults.* Downsview, Ontario: Canadian Association for the Mentally Retarded.

GALLAGER, J., 1956. "Rejecting Parents." *Exceptional Children,* vol. 22, no. 7, pp. 273–276, 294–295.

Gallup Poll released by President's Committee on Mental Retardation. Reported in the *Mail Tribune,* Medford, Ore., March 10, 1975.

GARDNER, J., 1967. *A First Report to the President on the Nation's Progress and Remaining Great Needs in the Campaign to Combat Mental Retardation.* MR 67. Washington, D.C.: U. S. Government Printing Office.

GARRETT, B., 1970. "Foster-Family Services for Mentally Retarded Children." *Children,* vol. 17, no. 6, pp. 228–233.

GEISER, R., and MALINOWSKI, S., 1978. "Realities of Foster-Child Care." *American Journal of Nursing,* vol. 78, no. 3, pp. 430–433.

GINZBERG, E., and BRAY, D., 1953. *The Uneducated.* New York: Columbia University Press.

GLAZER, N., 1978. "Should Judges Administer Social Services?" *The Public Interest,* vol. 50, Winter, pp. 64–80.

GODDARD, H. H., 1914. *The Kallikak Family: A Study in the Heredity of Feeble-Mindedness.* New York: The Macmillan Co.

GOFFMAN, E., 1963. *Stigma: Notes on the Management of Spoiled Identity.* Englewood Cliffs, N.J.: Prentice-Hall.

GOLDSTEIN, H. (ed.), 1978. *Readings in Mental Retardation.* Guilford, Conn.: Special Learning Corporation.

GOLLAY, E., FREEDMAN, R., WYNGAARDEN, M., and KURTZ, N., 1978. *Coming Back: The Community Experiences of Deinstitutionalized Mentally Retarded People.* Cambridge, Mass.: Abt Books.

GORDON, I., and GUINAGH, B., July 1974. "A Home Learning Center Approach to Early Stimulation." Gainesville, Fla.: University of Florida, Gainesville Institute for Development of Human Resources.

GORDON, S., 1976. "Sex Education Programs: Guidelines and Materials." *The Exceptional Parent,* vol. 6, no. 1, pp. 27–29.

――――, 1973. *The Sexual Adolescent: Communicating with Teenagers About Sex.* Massachusetts: Duxbury Press.

――――, 1971. *Ten Heavy Facts.* Syracuse, N.Y.: Ed-U-Press.

GORDON, T., 1970. *Parent Effectiveness Training.* New York: Peter H. Wyden, Publisher.

GOWAN, J., DEMOS, G., and KOKASKA, C., (eds.), 1972. *The Guidance of Exceptional Children: A Book of Readings.* 2nd ed. New York: David McKay Co.

GRIFFITHS, M., 1973. *The Young Retarded Child: Medical Aspects of Care.* Baltimore: Williams & Wilkins.

GROSSMAN, H., (ed.), 1977, revised. *Manual on Terminology and Classification in Mental Retardation.* Washington: American Association on Mental Deficiency.

HALL, J., 1974. "Sexual Behavior." In J. Wortis (ed.), *Mental Retardation and Developmental Disabilities: An annual review (6).* New York: Bruner/Mazel.

HAMILTON, J., and SEGAL, R., 1975. *Consultation-Conference on the Gerontological Aspects of Mental Retardation.* (Proceedings of a Conference, Ann Arbor.) Ann Arbor, Mich.: Institute for the Study of Mental Retardation and Related Disabilities.

HARDY, R., and CULL, J., 1974. *Modification of Behavior of the Mentally Retarded.* Springfield, Ill.: Charles C Thomas.

HARRIS, D., and ROBERTS, J., 1972. *Intellectual Maturity of Children: Demographic and Socioeconomic Factors.* DHEW Publication No. (HSM) 72–1059. Washington, D.C.: U. S. Government Printing Office.

HEISLER, V., 1972. *A Handicapped Child in the Family. A Guide for Parents.* New York: Grune & Stratton.

HELLER, J., 1955. *Catch 22.* New York: Simon & Schuster.

HOREJSI, C., 1979. "Developmental Disabilities: Opportunities for Social Workers. *Social Work,* vol. 24, no. 1, pp. 40–43.

HUNGERFORD, R., DEPROSPO, C. J., and ROSENZWEIG, L., 1952. "Education of the Mentally Handicapped Child in Childhood and Adolescence." *American Journal of Mental Deficiency,* vol. 57, pp. 214–228.

HUNTER, M., SCHUCMAN, H., and FRIEDLANDER, G., 1972. *The Retarded Child from Birth to Five: A Multidisciplinary Program for the Child and Family.* Scranton, Pa.: John Day Co.

Hutt, L., and Gibby, R., 1976. *The Mentally Retarded Child: Development, Education, and Treatment.* 3rd ed., Boston: Allyn & Bacon.

Inside/Out, 1973. Instructional Movie Series. Bloomington, Ind.: Agency for Instructional Television, Box A.

Itard J. M. G. (1775–1838), 1962. *The Wild Boy of Aveyron,* translated by George and Muriel Humphrey. New York: Appleton-Century-Crofts.

Jacobs, L., 1977. "The Right of the Mentally Disabled to Marry: A Statutory Evaluation." *Journal of Family Law,* vol. 15, pp. 463–507.

Jastak, J., MacPhee, H. M., and Whiteman , M., 1963. "Mental Retardation, Its Nature and Incidence: A Population Survey of the State of Delaware." Newark, Del.: University of Delaware Press.

Jordan, T., 1976. *The Mentally Retarded.* 4th ed. Columbus, Ohio: Charles E. Merrill Publishing Co.

Kadushin, A., 1972. *The Social Work Interview.* New York & London: Columbia University Press.

Karnes, M., Zehrbach, R., and Teska, J., June 1972. "Involving Families of Handicapped Children." *Theory Into Practice,* vol. 11, no. 3, pp. 150–156. Columbus, Ohio: Ohio State University School of Education.

Katz, E., 1968. *The Retarded Adult in the Community.* Springfield, Ill.: Charles C Thomas.

Kauffman, J., and Payne, J. (eds.), 1975. *Mental Retardation: Introduction and Personal Perspectives.* Columbus, Ohio: Charles E. Merrill Publishing Co.

Kempton, W., 1973. *Guidelines for Planning a Training Course in the Subject of Human Sexuality and the Retarded.* Philadelphia: Planned Parenthood Assoc. of Southeastern Pennsylvania.

_____, Bass, M., and Gordon, S., 1973. *Love, Sex, and Birth Control for the Mentally Retarded: A Guide for Parents.* Philadelphia: Planned Parenthood Assoc. of Southeastern Pennsylvania.

Kindred, M., Cohen, J., Penrod, D., and Shaffer, T. (eds.), 1976. *The Mentally Retarded Citizen and the Law.* New York: The Free Press.

Kirk, S. A., 1972. *Educating Exceptional Children.* Boston: Houghton Mifflin Co.

Kirman, B., and Bicknell, J., 1975. *Mental Handicap.* New York: Churchill Livingstone.

Knowles, M., and Knowles, H., 1959. *Introduction to Group Dynamics.* New York: Association Press.

Koch, R., and Dobson, J. (eds.), 1971. *The Mentally Retarded Child and His Family —A Multidisciplinary Handbook.* New York: Brunner/Mazel.

Konopka, G., 1963. *Social Group Work: A Helping Process.* Englewood Cliffs, N.J.: Prentice-Hall.

Kovenock, E., 1966. *Informal Group Process in Social Work: An Account of A Series of Discussions on Parent Education.* Madison, Wisc.: Division of Child Behavior and Development, Wisconsin Board of Health.

Lambie, D., Bond, J., and Weikart, D., 1974. *Home Teaching with Mothers and Infants.* Ypsilanti, Mich.: High/Scope Educational Research Foundation.

Lazarus, A., 1971. *Behavior Therapy and Beyond.* New York: McGraw-Hill Book Co.

Lee, J., Hegge, T., and Voelker, P., 1959. *A Study of Social Adequacy and of Social*

Failure of Mentally Retarded Youth in Wayne County, Michigan. Report to U.S. Office of Education, Project No. 178 (Jan. 1957 to June 1959). Detroit: Wayne State University.

LELAND, H., and SMITH, D., 1974. *Mental Retardation: Present and Future Perspectives.* Worthington, Ohio: Charles A. Jones Publishing Co.

LEVINSON, A., 1965. *The Mentally Retarded Child.* New York: John Day Co.

LOTTMAN, M., 1976. "Paper Victories and Hard Realities." In *Paper Victories and Hard Realities: The Implementation of the Legal and Constitutional Rights of the Mentally Disabled,* edited by V. Bradley and G. Clarke. Washington, D.C.: The Health Policy Center, Georgetown University.

LOVE, H., 1973. *The Mentally Retarded Child and His Family.* Springfield, Ill.: Charles C Thomas.

LYNCH, E., 1978. "The Home-School Partnership." In *Parents on the Team,* edited by S. Brown and M. Moersch. Ann Arbor, Mich.: University of Michigan Press.

MCGOVERN, K., and BROWNING, P., 1972. *Mental Retardation and the Future.* Eugene, Ore.: University of Oregon Rehabilitation Research and Training Center in Mental Retardation.

MACMILLAN, D., JONES, R., and ALOIA, G., 1974. "The 'Mentally Retarded' Label: A Theoretical Analysis and Review of Research." *American Journal of Mental Deficiency,* vol. 79, no. 3, pp. 241–261.

Macomb-Oakland Regional Center Community Training Home Manual, 1974. Macomb-Oakland Regional Center, 16200 Nineteen Mile Road, Mt. Clemens, Mich.

MADDOCK, J., 1974. "Sex Education for the Exceptional Person: A Rationale." *Exceptional Children,* vol. 40, no. 4, pp. 273–278.

MAGNUSSON, P., 1978. "Housing for Retarded Protested." *Detroit Free Press,* May 17, 1978.

————, and WATSON, S., 1978. "Children Tortured: State Center Covers Up." *Detroit Free Press,* Feb. 19, 1978.

MAMULA, R., and NEWMAN, N., 1973. *Community Placement of the Mentally Retarded: A Handbook for Community Agencies and Social Work Practitioners.* Springfield, Ill.: Charles C Thomas.

MARIN COUNTY ASSOCIATION FOR RETARDED CITIZENS, 1979. "The Respite Story: Interim Care for Exceptional People." Marin County, Calif.: The Association.

MASLACH, C., 1976. "Burned Out." *Human Behavior,* vol. 5, no. 9, pp. 16–22.

MENOLASCINO, F., 1977. *Challenges in Mental Retardation: Progressive Ideology and Services.* New York: Human Sciences.

Mental Health Code, Act 258 of 1974 (as amended to Jan. 1, 1977). Michigan Dept. of Mental Health, Lansing, Mich.

MEYEN, E., 1970. "Sex Education for the Mentally Retarded—Implications for Programming and Teacher Training." *Focus on Exceptional Children,* vol. 1, pp. 1–5.

Michigan Association for Retarded Citizens et al. v. *Donald C. Smith, M.D., et al.,* 1978. U.S. District Court, Eastern District of Michigan, Southern Division, Civil Action No. 870384.

MIDDLEMAN, R., 1968. *The Non-Verbal Method in Working With Groups.* New York: Association Press.

MITTLER, P. (ed.), 1977. *Research to Practice in Mental Retardation*. Vol. 1, *Care and Intervention*. Baltimore: University Park Press.

MOERSCH, M., and WILSON, T., 1976. *Early-Intervention Project for Handicapped Infants and Young Children: Final Report 1973-1976*. Ann Arbor, Mich.: University of Michigan Press.

NEISWORTH, J., and SMITH, R., 1978. *Retardation: Issues, Assessment, and Intervention*. New York: McGraw-Hill Book Co.

NELSON, N., 1964. "The Economics of a Sub-Contract and Manufacturing Workshop." *Journal of Rehabilitation*, vol. 30, no. 4, pp. 18-19.

Newsweek, May 15, 1978. "The New Snake Pits: Disappearing Between the Cracks—A New York Protest Against Poor Care of Ex-Mental Patients."

NICHTERN, S., 1974. *Helping the Retarded Child*. New York: Grosset & Dunlap.

NIRJE, B., 1969. "The Normalization Principle and Its Human Management Implications." In R. Kugel and W. Wolfensberger (eds.), *Changing Patterns in Residential Services for the Mentally Retarded*. Washington, D.C.: President's Committee on Mental Retardation.

NORTHERN, H., 1969. *Social Work with Groups*. New York: Columbia University Press.

O'DONNELL, P., and BRADFIELD, R. (eds.), 1976. *Mainstreaming: Controversy and Consensus*. San Rafael: Academic Therapy Publications.

OFFICE OF MENTAL RETARDATION COORDINATION. *Mental Retardation Source Book*. DHEW Publication No. (05) 73-81. Washington, D.C.: U.S. Government Printing Office.

OHLSEN, M., 1970. *Group Counseling*. New York: Holt, Rinehart & Winston.

OLSHANSKY, S., 1966. "Parent Responses to a Mentally Defective Child." *Mental Retardation*, vol. 4, no. 4, pp. 21-23.

_____, 1962. "Chronic Sorrow: A Response to Having a Mentally Defective Child." *Social Casework*, vol. 43, no. 4, pp. 190-193.

"Opening More Doors for the Nation's Retarded." *U.S. News and World Report*, Aug. 1976.

PAUL, J., NEUFELD, G., and PELOSI, J. (eds.), 1977. *Child Advocacy Within the System*. Syracuse, N.Y.: Syracuse University Press.

PAUL, J., STEDMAN, D., and NEUFELD, G. (eds.), 1977. *Deinstitutionalization: Program and Policy Development*. Syracuse, N.Y.: Syracuse University Press.

PAUL, J., TURNBULL, A., and CRUICKSHANK, W., 1977. *Mainstreaming: A Practical Guide*. Syracuse, N.Y.: Syracuse University Press.

PEELING, K., 1969. *The Unwanted*. New York: Vantage Press.

PERSKE, R., 1973. "About Sexual Development: An Attempt to Be Human with the Mentally Retarded." *Mental Retardation*, vol. 11, no. 1, pp. 6-8.

_____, 1973. *New Directions for Parents of Persons Who Are Retarded*. New York: Abingdon Press.

_____, 1972. "The Dignity of Risk." In W. Wolfensberger (ed.), *The Principle of Normalization in Human Services*. Leonard Crainford, Toronto: National Institute on Mental Retardation.

PHILLIPS, H., 1957. *Essentials of Social Group Work*. New York: Association Press.

PIAGET, J., 1973. *The Child and Reality: Problems of Genetic Psychology*. New York: Grossman Publishers.

Plaintiff's Brief in Opposition to Defendant's Motion for Dismissal. U.S. District Court for the District of Nebraska, CU–72–L–299, p. 35.

PORTAGE PROJECT, 1979. Portage, Wisc.: Community Education Services Agency. No. 12.

PRESIDENT'S COMMITTEE ON MENTAL RETARDATION, 1975. *New Environments for Retarded People*. DHEW Publication No. (OHD) 75-21009. Washington, D.C.: U.S. Government Printing Office.

———, 1973. *The Goal Is Freedom*. DHEW Publication No. (OHD) 74-21001. Washington, D.C.: U.S. Government Printing Office.

———, 1971. *Entering the Era of Human Ecology*. DHEW Publication No. (OS) 72-7. Washington, D.C.: U. S. Government Printing Office.

———, 1970. *The Decisive Decade*. DHEW Publication No. 0-413-182. Washington, D.C.: U. S. Government Printing Office.

———, 1970. *The Six-Hour Retarded Child*. DHEW Publication No. (OHD) 381–543. Washington, D.C.: U.S. Government Printing Office.

———, 1969. *Changing Patterns in Residential Services for the Mentally Retarded*. DHEW Publication No. (OHD) 76–21015. Washington, D.C.: U. S. Government Printing Office.

———, 1966. *People Live in Houses: Profiles of Community Residences for Retarded Children and Adults*. DHEW Publication No. (OHD) 75-21006. Washington, D.C.: U.S. Government Printing Office.

PRESIDENT'S PANEL ON MENTAL RETARDATION, 1962. *A Proposed Program for National Action to Combat Mental Retardation*. Washington, D.C.: U.S. Government Printing Office.

RAECH, H., 1966. "A Parent Discusses Initial Counseling." *Mental Retardation*, vol. 4, no. 2, pp. 25–26.

REDL, F., 1966. *When We Deal With Children*. New York: The Free Press.

——— and WINEMAN, D., 1957. *The Aggressive Child*. New York: The Free Press of Glencoe.

REICH, C. A., 1970. *The Greening of America: How the Youth Revolution Is Trying to Make America Livable*. New York: Random House.

RICHARDSON, E., 1971. *Entering the Era of Human Ecology*. Report of the President's Committee on Mental Retardation. DHEW Publication No. (OS) 72-7. Washington, D.C.: U.S. Government Printing Office.

RIVERA, G., 1972. *Willowbrook: A Report on How It Is and Why It Doesn't Have to Be That Way*. New York: Vintage Books.

ROBINSON, N., and ROBINSON, H., 1976. *The Mentally Retarded Child: A Psychological Approach*. 2nd ed. New York: McGraw-Hill Book Co.

ROOS, P., 1970. "Normalization, Dehumanization, and Conditioning: Conflict or Harmony?" *Mental Retardation*, vol. 8, no. 4, pp. 12–14.

ROSE, S., 1973. *Treating Children in Groups*. San Francisco: Jossey-Bass.

ROSEN, D., and CALLAN, L., 1972. *Trends, Residential Services for the Mentally Retarded: Focus—Community Facility Interaction*. National Association of Superintendents of Public Residential Facilities for the Mentally Retarded, Central Wisconsin Center for the Developmentally Disabled, Madison, Wisc.

ROSEN, D., and PROVENCAL, G., 1972. *Deinstitutionalization of the Hard to Place*. Department of Health, Education, and Welfare Service Grant Awarded to

Macomb-Oakland Regional Center, 16200 Nineteen Mile Road, Mt. Clemens, Mich. 48044.

ROSEN, M., CLARK, G., and KIVITZ, M. (eds.), 1976. *The History of Mental Retardation: Collected Papers.* Baltimore: University Park Press.

SANDGRUND, A., GAINES, R., and GREEN, A., 1974. "Child Abuse and Mental Retardation: A Problem of Cause and Effect." *American Journal of Mental Deficiency,* vol. 79, no. 3, pp. 327–330.

SARASON, S., 1949. *Psychological Problems in Mental Deficiency.* New York: Harper & Row.

_____ and GLADWIN, T., 1958. "Psychological and Cultural Problems in Mental Subnormality: A Review of Research." *American Journal of Mental Deficiency,* vol. 62, no. 6, pp. 1115–1307.

SCANLON, J., 1973. *Intellectual Development of Youths as Measured by a Short Form of Wechsler Intelligence Scale.* DHEW Publication No. (HRA) 74–1610. Washington, D.C.: U.S. Government Printing Office.

SCHEERENBERGER, R., 1977. *Public Residential Services for the Mentally Retarded, 1977.* National Association of Superintendents of Public Residential Facilities for the Mentally Retarded, Central Wisconsin Center for the Developmentally Disabled, Madison, Wisc.

SCHILLER, P., 1973. *Creative Approach to Sex Education and Counseling.* New York: Association Press.

SCHREIBER, M. (ed.), 1970. *Social Work and Mental Retardation.* New York: John Day Co.

_____, 1965. "Some Basic Concepts in Social Group Work and Recreation with the Mentally Retarded." *Rehabilitation Literature,* vol. 26, no. 7, pp. 194–203.

_____, and BARNHARDT, S. (eds.), 1967. *Source Book on Mental Retardation for Schools of Social Work.* Vols. 1, 2. New York: Associated Educational Services Corporation.

SEGAL, R. (ed.), June 2, 1972. *Advocacy for the Legal and Human Rights of the Mentally Retarded.* (Proceedings of the Advocacy Conference, Ann Arbor.) Ann Arbor, Mich.: Institute for the Study of Mental Retardation and Related Disabilities.

Self-Incorporated, 1975. Instructional Movie Series. Bloomington, Ind.: Agency for Instructional Television, Box A.

SKARNULIS, E., 1974. "Noncitizen: Plight of the Mentally Retarded." *Social Work,* vol. 19, no. 1, pp. 56–62.

STREAN, H., 1978. *Clinical Social Work: Theory and Practice.* New York: The Free Press.

STUBBLEFIELD, H., 1975. "Religion, Parents, and Mental Retardation." *Mental Retardation,* vol. 3, no. 4, pp. 8–11.

SWEENEY, D., and WILSON, T. (eds.), 1979. *Double Jeopardy: The Plight of Aging and Aged Developmentally Disabled Persons in Mid-America.* Ann Arbor, Mich.: Institute for the Study of Mental Retardation and Related Disabilities.

THORNE, F., 1972. "Tutorial Counseling with Mental Defectives." In J. Gowan, G. Demos, and C. Kokaska (eds.), *The Guidance of Exceptional Children: A Book of Readings.* New York: David McKay Co.

TIZARD, J., and GIAD, J., 1961. *The Mentally Handicapped and Their Families: A Social Survey.* London: Oxford University Press.

TYMCHUK, A., 1973. *The Mental Retardation Dic-tion-ar-y.* Los Angeles: Western Psychological Services.

U.S. DISTRICT COURT FOR THE DISTRICT OF NEBRASKA, 1973. "Plaintiff's Brief in Opposition to Defendant's Motion for Dismissal." CU-72-4-299, p. 35.

U.S. DISTRICT COURT, EASTERN DISTRICT OF MICHIGAN, Southern Division, 1978. *Michigan Association for Retarded Citizens et al. v. Donald C. Smith, M.D., et al.* Civil Action No. 870384.

VANIER, J., 1971. *Eruption to Hope.* New York: Paulist Press.

WEHMAN, P., and GOODWYN, R., 1978. "Self-Help Skill Development." In *Young Children with Special Needs,* by N. Fallen, with J. McGovern. Columbus, Ohio: Charles E. Merrill Publishing Co.

WEINTRAUB, F., 1972. "Recent Influences of Law Regarding the Identification and Educational Placement of Children." *Focus on the Exceptional Child,* vol. 4, no. 2, pp. 1–11.

WIGGLESWORTH, G., 1969. "Malnutrition and Brain Development." *Developmental Medicine Child Neurology,* vol. 11, no. 6, pp. 792–794.

WILLOWBROOK REVIEW PANEL, 1976. *Community Placement Plan for the Members of the Willowbrook Class in NYSARC and Parisi v. Carey.* New York, N.Y.

WING LAKE DEVELOPMENTAL CENTER, 1978. "Bloomfield Hills School District Respite Care Survey." Birmingham, Mich.: The Center.

WOLFENSBERGER, W. (ed.), 1972. *The Principle of Normalization in Human Services.* Leonard Crainford, Toronto: National Institute on Mental Retardation.

_____, 1972. *Citizen Advocacy for the Handicapped, Impaired, and Disadvantaged: An Overview.* DHEW Publication No. (OS) 72–74. Washington, D.C.: U.S. Government Printing Office.

_____, 1971. "Will There Always Be an Institution? II: The Impact of New Service Models." *Mental Retardation,* vol. 9, no. 6, pp. 14–20.

_____, 1965. "Diagnosis Diagnosed." *British Journal of Mental Subnormality,* vol. 11, no. 21, pp. 62–70.

_____, and KURTZ, R. (eds.), 1969. *Management of the Family of the Mentally Retarded.* Chicago, Ill.: Follett Educational Corporation.

_____, and VANIER, J., 1974. *Growing Together.* Richmond Hill, Ontario, Canada: Daybreak Publications.

_____, and ZAUHA, H. (eds.), 1973. *Citizen Advocacy and Protective Services for the Impaired and Handicapped.* Kinsmen Bldg., York University, Ontario, Canada: National Institute on Mental Retardation.

ZAPF, L., 1976. *Occasional Paper: Illusions of Progress.* Madison, Wisc.: National Association of Superintendents of Public Residential Facilities.

Index

DATE DUE
